MYSTERY SCHOOL

I0132559

Gayle Clayton

Mystery School

Introduction

Let there be light! Such simple words conveyed complex creative forces that confused Gayle more than ever. Light was the great mystery substance. In fiber optics light was bounced and modulated along silicon threads; in advanced super computers it generated the on/off signal; and for certain human beings they were blinded by the light. Gayle lit the candle she used to ritually separate her corporate saleswoman persona and her inner secret self.

The mystery of light was hidden in the obvious – whether it was the simple light switch or the purple glow that emerged at night within her mind. Light arose from the emptiness of potential in seemingly spontaneous emission. Electrons jumped orbital levels spitting out photons in the process. God's finger pointed to Adam in the Sistine Chapel as the spark of life leaped the gap. Gods spilled seed upon the fertile dark waters of Egypt and the primal mound arose. Gayle's mind would not settle into the darkness of a quiet meditative mind. The mind of god, as Stephen Hawking called it, haunted her.

Instead Gayle's questions of the heart echoed emptily. Rising from her working student status in college, Gayle first determined success to be when she didn't have to add up everything in her grocery cart before she got to the register. Her marriage would be happy when money was no longer an issue. Watching television would replace homework in the evenings. Just one more thing and then she'd be happy. However she wasn't.

Ten years after college graduation, an achievement almost marred by the inability to understand Einstein's $E=mc^2$ equation for the conversion between light and matter, Gayle's soul still longed for meaning. In stoic fashion she sacrificed dance, art, and poetry in order to obtain a well-paying job. The dramatic spotlight yielded to engineering methodology. Her own innate drive pushed her to know the truth beyond any superficial understanding. Recently her career had been her priority. Yet, career success did not fill the inner void. Something called her and time passed faster.

The candle flickered and then became an elongated flame stretching toward the ceiling. The light of day no longer protected her from the darkness of her dreams. Invading her daily life at odd times were apparitions, ghosts, and voices. The first time she heard them, she had been lying on the couch. Just as she dropped off, multiple voices whispered behind her right ear. Gayle knew that hearing voices meant she was crazy. She asked the voices not to come back.

The voices upset her more than her telepathic abilities. Gayle could at times read people's minds. The IBM executive's shock when she plucked the competition's bid out of the air made her smile. On Langley Air Force base, she informed the Lt. Colonel that he was about to launch an investigation. In France, the layout of Carcassonne was known to her even though she had never been there before. The knowledge came without invocation. At least they were things that helped her and not scared her as the first visions had.

Gayle's initial psychic experiences were of dream death notifications, airplane crashes, or natural disasters. A New York street psychic upon receiving her five dollar payment advised Gayle that the reason she did not get pleasant visions was that she worked so hard to block all of them. Only the strongest messages could get through. Now, though, while on the road Gayle spent evenings reading palms while people bought her drinks. When she touched them, Gayle knew things from their career goals to their deepest secrets. With alcohol to lower her inhibition, her intuition flourished. Having fun with her abilities was new to her. For most of her life, she buried her abilities in hopes to fit in, but she never did. The renewed push to explore her psychic gifts gave her resolve. She knew what she had to do. She needed help. She needed to find a spiritual teacher. Gayle leaned toward the candle and blew it out.

Chapter 1 – The Call for a Teacher

Harmonic Convergence - 1987

Gayle poured her favorite scotch into the gold-rimmed Name-Your-Poison glasses noting that the wedding gift had lasted longer than the marriage. The amber liquid swirled, rose along the sides, and leveled. Scotch was an acquired taste. Scotch on the rocks allowed her to match drinks with the good ole boys. Throughout the evening all their glasses were refilled, but the slowly melting ice always kept her glass full. Gayle never needed a refill, but kept drinking right along with them. The men thought Gayle could handle her liquor alright.

"To success in a man's world," she toasted herself. Success, though, had its price. Her husband hadn't been able to compete with her salary or paranormal abilities. As Gayle had grown more independent, Dana became needier. In the end her husband drifted away. Dana, like others after him, could not accept her secret life. He would have been shaken if she had shared the dream a few months back.

"Gayle, Gayle, wake up. You have to come with me." Her grandmother shook her shoulder. Gayle ignored her and went back to sleep.

"No, no. You have to help me," her grandmother insisted while shaking Gayle harder.

A moment later the woman took Gayle's hand and they flew south through the dark night. Gayle had always been able to fly in dreams, but this was the first time she remembered having a companion. Minutes later the pair entered a concrete block building from above.

"See. Look there. They have my body on that table. It's cold."

Gayle looked at the stainless steel table, the plastic tubes, the tiled floor and the barren room. She had a feeling about the place.

"Help me," her grandmother implored. Gayle was puzzled as to how. The room was dark and there was no one physically present. Besides, unless she was very much mistaken, they were in a back room of a mortuary. Her grandmother's eyes pleaded with her to do something about her cold body on the table.

Then in the far corner, a golden glow slowly emerged. The light grew brighter and larger. After a few moments, rays of golden light coalesced to form the shape of a tall man. While the shape had no obvious features, the familiarity struck her almost immediately. Her grandmother hadn't been talking to her after all.

"Granddaddy!"

Her grandfather had always been an unconditional loving supporter, but he shook his head at Gayle. He wasn't there for her. His total focus was for his wife.

The denser rays of light took on her grandfather's appearance. With his calm smile he offered his rough farmer's hand to calm his wife. The words they exchanged were for them alone. The scene slowly faded to black.

Gayle suddenly moved backward through some kind of tunnel to her own bed. The digital clock glowed 4:30 AM as she fell back asleep.

The phone rang shortly before the scheduled alarm clock. Gayle answered it automatically. No one ever called her before 8 AM unless it was an emergency.

"Hello?" she managed to get out.

"Pumpkin, this is your daddy."

Gayle knew immediately the purpose of the call. At last her grandmother's long years curled in the fetal position at the nursing home were over.

"I have some bad news for you."

"I already know, Daddy. I already know."

A couple of days later Gayle arrived in South Carolina for the visitation. Dread filled her as her sister pulled up to the funeral home. From their parking spot she noted that the back of the mortuary matched her dream version. This dream event had really happened. She had proof.

Though Gayle tried to share this experience with DJ upon her return, his version of reality would not allow ghostly encounters, visions of future events, dead people, and disembodied voices. At least he didn't make her question reality. Gayle tried to shut out the paranormal, but the experiences were back and couldn't be ignored.

Gayle swirled the scotch again. She had just won the National Account Manager award. Anyone else would be proud of this achievement in her first year, so why did she feel she had missed something? These rare occurrences of self-reflection always proved to be the forerunner of huge changes in her life. She either made decisions or they were made for her. She had learned not to take chances with others running her life.

Why had she been gifted with clairvoyance? For what purpose did knowing the future serve if nothing changed? The newly dead came to say goodbye, although her grandmother was the first to take her to see the body. The prerequisite shaman's lightning strike hadn't been necessary for her to talk to the dead. She remembered the lightning hit that blew out the light bulb in her ceiling fixture. Her mother warned her of that Brinkley boy down the road who had gotten struck by lightning while talking on the phone. Afterward Dannion became psychic or was said to have gotten a sixth sense.

Intuition played its part in Gayle's life. Frequently she asked her assistant for an update on a shipment moments before the client called. Once the military's Joint Chiefs of Staff were caught off-guard when after examining a blueprint on the table she asked where the rest of the building was. The staff underlings all turned to the general awaiting instruction. Gayle knew she had stumbled on to something. Her contribution to the network security was weighed against her need to know. The general granted her immediate clearance. With that, a new blueprint revealed the underground portion of the base.

To her disadvantage, the insights were also creating conflict. Gayle didn't believe in war, covert operations, or hidden agendas. Yet, she designed weapons command communication networks that controlled nuclear arsenals. The secure communications networks were a part of her responsibility. What had happened to her dreams of peace, love, and self-fulfillment?

Gayle sipped the scotch again savoring its smoothness. If she wasn't careful, she would become an alcoholic along with DJ. In part, he said he drank to drown out the visions and voices. For a corporate vice-president to be psychic was simply unacceptable. Their relationship was built on acceptance. They lived independently and by their own rules that often included meeting around the world in exotic places such as Singapore, Bangkok, Copenhagen and Paris on corporate expense accounts. From time to time, the two shared the same dream. However, Gayle desired something more permanent and that was not possible with DJ.

The television playing in the background teased a story on the New Age Harmonic Convergence. The New York morning radio talk show hosts had been full of derision and sarcasm. The Channel 7 news team offered a short informative clip:

> The Harmonic Convergence is a globally synchronized meditation on August 16–17, 1987. According to Jose Argüelles' interpretation of Mayan cosmology, this date marks the end of twenty-two cycles of 52 years each, or 1,144 years in all. The beginning of the nine hell cycles began when Cortez landed in Mexico, April 22, 1519 and ends on August 16-17, 1987.

The announcer opined the Harmonic Convergence ushered a change from warlike energy to peaceful coexistence. Gayle stood transfixed. The occult ritual was exactly the shift she wanted.

She walked to the grassy knoll behind her condo where three tall spreading trees had survived the transition from farm fields to urban development. Gayle sat among them. The warm evening air was full of mosquitoes, but she imagined an impenetrable ball of white light around her. As the last rays of the sun disappeared on the horizon, more stars appeared in the sky. One by one major constellations came in view.

Long ago her navigator dad had taught her elementary school class how to steer by the stars. She had been so proud of him then. The fond memory opened her heart to the heavens. The stars twinkled above. Gayle could hear the displaced deer grunting in the small field across the complex where the river ran. As a child and now, nature had been her refuge.

The Harmonic Convergence supposedly began a 25-year countdown to the end of history in 2012. There would be a new sun emerging at that time. There would be a new age. Technology could only bring more powerful weapons, war, and subjugation. The hard cold facts could not be reconciled with the warm heart of a starry being. Sitting on the damp grass beneath the trees and stars, Gayle's soul cried out to find her spiritual path.

"God/Goddess, Abba, Father/Mother, Creator, please send me a teacher. I can't ignore this any longer."

On Notice

Prayers are never answered on demand or on time. Life seemed to carry on much the same as before the Harmonic Convergence. The travel schedule was a killer. Gayle found herself away from home more than she liked. Just this morning she had cursed the hotel for not providing the miniature bottles of shampoo and conditioner until she realized that she was home.

Arriving in Manhattan early for a meeting, Gayle checked out The Quest Bookshop. The narrow aisles among the tall overfilled bookshelves held hundreds of books on diverse topics. Then just in front of her, a book landed from an upper shelf at her feet. Startled, Gayle noted this bookshelf backed against the wall. No one could have pushed the book through. She picked it up and turned to the book's back cover...

Her most controversial book is one you will never forget. An outspoken thinker, a celebrated actress, a truly independent woman, Shirley MacLaine goes beyond her previous two bestsellers to take us on an intimate yet powerful journey into her personal life and inner self. An intense, clandestine love affair with a prominent politician sparks Shirley MacLaine's quest of self-discovery. From Stockholm to Hawaii to the mountain vastness of Peru, from disbelief to radiant affirmation, she at last discovers the roots of her very existence. . . and the infinite possibilities of life…

Gayle didn't need to read more; she bought the book for reading on the plane. Those weekly flights to Washington, DC for work were taking its toll. Once she loved to fly, but the last flight had convinced her change was imminent. Her premonition was strong that she wasn't supposed to be on that plane. The day before, she told DJ she needed to change her reservation, but that flight was the only one to arrive in time. When the aborted takeoff left a silent plane whose nose reached out over the NJ Turnpike, Gayle knew the world was making a decision for her.

The Dream Journal

Stress increased as work divisions closed, manufacturing restructured and sales forces consolidated. Gayle found her only escape from her growing desperation in dreams. Fortunately her vivid inner life was recorded in a dream journal where odd snippets of her childhood home, friends from grammar school, her dance recitals, and other strange pieces of information lived.

In one dream an elderly black man plowed her family farm. The sun beat down on the long rows of tilled sandy soil. He stopped the mule, tipped up his weather beaten hat, and looked at her.

"Hi, I am Henry Grimes."

Later, Gayle discovered the original survey of the Clayton home place when researching the family history. The handwritten notations to the lay of the land contained another entry. In the corner was the record of the purchase of a slave named Henry Grimes.

Gayle could make no sense of most of the other dreams. Too vivid to be forgotten and too obscure for its meaning to be known, she longed for a teacher who could put the pieces together. Having psychic abilities seemed of little use unless she could use them for some greater purpose.

Gayle relayed the dream of wild pigs running in the side yard of her childhood home to her sister. Laughing, her sister told her that it had really happened. Gayle hadn't mentioned the giant spotlights shining down. She knew better. In the dream, the little girl saw the small flying car land with a strange oriental man at the helm. The line between dream and reality was becoming indistinguishable.

Flipping back a few pages in the journal, one dream account was of her ancestral family. In period clothes, relatives from near and far gathered at a two-story wood frame Colonial home in the tidewaters of Virginia. A black horse-drawn hearse waited patiently under the large oak. Family members gathered on the front porch waiting for General Lee. Her grandfather had often told stories of General Lee and his horse Traveler as visitors to his family's original Virginia home. The dream was her only visit to the actual house as the place had burned long ago.

Gayle wondered why some of the dreams were recurring. There were the dreams of being taken by bus to the wrong school, the boogeyman dream that woke her screaming, the bad mother dreams she shared with her sisters, the communal bathrooms with overflowing toilets, homes that she recognized in dreams but had never been to, sliding through amusement park tunnels at the end of dreams and the UFO alien abduction dreams. A therapist once said that night was when the unresolved anxieties appeared, but why aliens?

After several dreams about alien abduction, Gayle sought the help of a local hypnotherapist. Strieber's book on alien encounters concerned her. Perhaps they were real. The therapist carefully guided her back to the late night journey in the family car. The entire family remembered that trip, but none of them remembered the details quite the same. The only thing they could agree on was that there was three hours of missing time and that there were three new circular spots on their meticulously kept family car.

Gayle wasn't quite sure she was under hypnosis, but she found the process relaxing enough to let the memory flow. She sat in the backseat of the car with her younger sister who had already fallen asleep. Gayle tilted her head to see the sky as she drifted off.

"I think we got off the wrong exit," her father told her mother.

They only made the trip once a year or so. Now late at night, they were lost on a rural two-lane road. Gayle was too drowsy to worry. Even with her eyes closed, she became aware of an annoying bright light in her eyes. The light flashed repeatedly. Finally she woke up enough to see a hovering light following them down the deserted road.

"Daddy, what's that following us?"

Her father looked into the mirror and frowned. Yet, in the time it took to look, the object had moved from directly behind them to a far point on the horizon.

"I've never seen anything move like that," the retired Air Force navigator said.

"What are y'all talking about?" Gayle's sister asked sleepily.

"A UFO."

The object danced in the sky on the far horizon. Its lights blinked in white, then purple, and then green in odd darting patterns that neither a helicopter nor plane could make.

"I'm going to see what this thing is."

The car was slowing down. The object had moved from the left horizon to what seemed to be a midpoint directly in front of them.

"No! No! No!" Gayle screamed to no avail.

Then inexplicably the car stopped and everything was silent. Gayle's family went to sleep almost instantaneously as if some sleeping gas had overcome them. Under hypnosis, Gayle saw three small gray beings come over the rise and approach the car. One gray being now stood outside her car window and waited for her.

The next moment Gayle was strapped onto a cold metal examination table. As an asthmatic child she had been in the hospital often, but this was quite different. Still she was aware of other tables and other people. When the examiners approached her with long metal probes she tried to scream, but no sound came out.

"You're not going to be hurt," a voice from her side said softly. "We can't hurt you."

A strange white-skinned three-fingered hand touched her arm. Warmth flowed where the strange hand made contact. Part of Gayle's fear was alleviated. She felt no pain as a long flexible rod was inserted up her nose. There were further tests and probes, but Gayle's attention was totally fixated on the probe in her head pulsing purple light.

The white being sat quietly beside her the entire time. Others asked her for instructions as their duties were completed. When the probe was removed, Gayle got a glimpse of the strange creature and began sobbing. The sobbing was enough to bring her out of hypnosis. Seeing her disorientation, the therapist handed her tissues.

"Do you remember it?"

Gayle nodded. All she wanted to do was get out of there.

No wonder she had been terrified by the face she had seen on the book *Communion* at the bookstore. The alien face was the same. Whitley Strieber's accounts of dreams paralleled her own. Now she was learning that there might be more to them. Gayle knew the truth now—she was crazy. All she knew how to do was run.

Thanksgiving at Stonehenge

Gayle's plane landed in Newark on the Tuesday before Thanksgiving. She idly glanced over to the adjoining gate where Virgin Atlantic offered flights to London for a ridiculously cheap $199.

Why not? She did a U-turn to purchase a ticket, and then booked a hotel for the first night and a rental car in London. She would drive to Stonehenge. She had always wanted to go.

Onboard for her impromptu trip, she flipped to the inflight magazine feature *In the Steps of King Arthur*. Dreams of Merlin, magic and mystery had reemerged with Moyers' *Power of Myth*. Gayle tore the magazine page out with the map of Arthurian related sites. Her adventure was on.

The rolling pastures and fields left her unprepared for the unexpected stones silhouettes on the hill. No one had told her that Stonehenge was really out in the middle of a cow pasture. The place was deserted when Gayle arrived in the chilly early evening. Even with the almost full moon rising, the feeling was desolate. She considered climbing the fence to walk among the stones, but reconsidered. She was hardly prepared for that. She shook her fist at the moon and asked, "Is there no magic left anywhere?"

Arriving at her night's lodging, the elderly couple greeted her kindly. The elderly man attempted to explain the game of snooker playing on the telly. Gayle politely drank her white tea with them.

The great disappointment at the lack of magic at the stones didn't prevent her from touring them the next day. At the gift shop, Gayle bought a book explaining the site's astrological significance before wandering among the stones. She still longed for Merlin to magically appear and take her away, but wasn't too surprised when he didn't.

With a bit of sadness and disappointment, Gayle headed for Carleon, a place some said to be the location for Camelot. Camelot was first mentioned in a work titled *Lancelot* by Chretien de Troyes around 1180. Gayle had made a destination list for her trip, a rather whimsical one: Stonehenge, Carleon, Land's End, Tintangel, Avalon, and the town of Clayton from which many surmised her surname was derived. She motored down the high hedged narrow unpaved roads amazed that she did not encounter an oncoming car. The left hand driving still brought anxiety that was only heightened by the British roundabouts. She managed, but still got into the wrong side of the car every morning. The driver's side was on the right!

Carleon offered little stimulation for Gayle's imagination so she drove on to Tintangel, the supposed birthplace of Arthur and the resting place of the Round Table. The romantic story of King Uther's love for the married woman of his dreams was mixed with Merlin's magic. Uther, disguised as the Duke of Cornwall, gained entry into the castle and made love to Ygraine, his ally's wife. The future King Arthur was conceived through that union. Cornwall died in battle that night, and the delay of a single night would have made the child legitimate, but the stars had deemed the future king's conception. The lines of karma had been drawn and fate set.

Gayle loved Tintangel. At the high rocky site which projected out into the sea was a cave purported to be used by Merlin. Irregular stone steps led steeply upward to the old stone monastery walls built upon ruins of the Cornwall castle. Tourists walked among them at the flat top of the cliff. The salt breezes in the cool air were invigorating. She twirled around much like Maria had in the *Sound of Music*. Here the

Mists of Avalon came alive for her. This small town on the cliff edge of the island was remote and removed from modern times.

The sun was moving downward and Gayle started up the steep uneven stone steps. She climbed for only a few minutes before her chest tightened. This was no time for an asthma attack. She tried to go up a another step, but panic gripped her. She forced herself to climb a few more steps. The air was too cold and too damp. She couldn't breathe.

Gayle didn't want to admit that her fear of heights had gotten the better of her. She sat down on the stone stairs. She was only about halfway up to the top. Looking back down the path Gayle became dizzy and faint. She knew she had to get back down. Putting her pride aside, she descended by moving her seat down step by step. She couldn't stand up until she was only a few feet from the bottom.

Gayle was never sure where her fear of heights originated. As a toddler she had stumbled and helplessly rolled down the bank toward the Savannah River. The sound of her grandmother's horrified calls alerted her to some unidentified danger. She had been an innocent to the danger.

Elevators always made her stomach queasy, but that fear probably stemmed from the open antique iron cage elevator that led to her childhood dentist's office. The sound of the closing metal gate clanking shut, the sight of the floor dropping away through the open grill, and hearing the large cable grind against its wheel encouraged an impressible child to imagine torturous devices to be close at hand. While she didn't like elevators, heights were unbearable. Even the visit to the top of the NYC World Trade Tower required her to stand back four feet from the windows. The sway of the building terrified her. She was afraid the building would collapse.

Embarrassed by her fear in Tintangel, Gayle cowered at the bottom. If there was magic still at Tintangel, it would have to wait for another lifetime when she was not afraid of heights. She stood for a long time looking at the ocean to the horizon. While this wasn't Land's End, there was nothing but the infinite expanse of sea and sky out to the horizon. Many miles across the waters was America, a fresh start for many who had little future on this island. Rarely does one get a chance to start over. After all, the past is the foundation for the future. Tintangel was an isolated place – one far from the culture of London and what was once Camelot. A lovely queen could get very lonely here. Gayle could relate.

Glastonbury

Weary upon arriving in Glastonbury, Gayle booked a room with a bed and breakfast. This was her base for exploring the last of the Arthurian mysteries. The hostess was delighted to have a single traveler as her only guest and fed her dinner. Her attic room had steeply sloping walls, a bath down the hall as is customary in many European establishments, and a homey guest feel. The impersonal business stays at large chain establishments had kept Gayle from feeling the lay of the land. Here the peace of the plain that had once been the lake bed for the Isle of Avalon wafted mists to her window. The plain below was dominated by the tower on the Tor behind.

The morning's cool air sent Gayle off for a short trip to Cadbury Castle which some considered the former location of the castle of Camelot. She arrived at the classic hill fort surrounded with earthworks throughout the eighteen acre plateau. From there she had a strategic view of the entire countryside as would any army lookout for the approach of invaders. The site was a perfect fit for defense of a king and a castle. She took a few pictures, but found the site devoid of tourist exploitation.

At Glastonbury, however, she explored the many tourist shops and bookstores and walked to Glastonbury Abbey. The myth stated that when King Arthur had been wounded by his son Mordred in battle, he was taken to the Isle of Avalon for the priestesses there to heal him. His wound was mortal though. Some said he was buried at Glastonbury Abby between two stone pylons. Gayle read the sign 'Here is the site of King Arthur's Tomb' marking the supposed grave site of the king and woman with golden locks who many attribute to have been Guinevere. A local guide informed her that Arthur's ghost still haunted the ruins, but Gayle didn't encounter him.

Dark arrives early in Great Britain in the winter time. Gayle lay quietly in her bed in the small attic room wondering why she had made this excursion after all. Looking for magic and mystery had seemed fun, but like her search for a teacher it seemed a lesson in futility.

"So far," she said to the corners of her room. It probably was only 9 PM but she didn't feel like being social with people she would never see again. The room was fairly dark with only a small alcove window that allowed the moonlight to filter in. She wondered about DJ and her relationship with him. Why had she felt so drawn to be with him? Why were they so comfortable with each other?

"Show me!" she cried out silently to whatever remnants of magic that still existed.

A flash of ultraviolet light filled the room momentarily. Then magical movie screens played films on every wall as if in a cyclorama. The first scene showed two black brothers walking across the African plain. Barefoot, dressed in red robes draped like a tunic, she recognized them as members of the Masai tribe. Then in a flash of insight, she realized that the two were DJ and her. As soon as she recognized the relationship, her focus shifted.

Now a desert scene was before her. In a large canyon a Native American woman stood. Gayle sensed her as a matriarch and from the clothing as a Navajo. The White Horse ruins were on one side of the canyon walls. She and DJ had once visited there. The place felt like home. Far below, the old woman called for her crow. The raucous bird came and settled on her shoulder as the Indian wandered back to her hogan hidden in the deep canyon. There the medicine woman found a basket of corn and potatoes had been gifted to her. She took it in where a man lay on a brightly woven blanket awaiting healing. Suddenly Gayle recognized the Native American man she had seen in her visions many times. He was a healer. And he was DJ.

Then Gayle was flying in a scene over lush green jungles with a rushing river that wound through a fertile land. The mountainous land met a turquoise sea where an old Asian couple fished in a hollowed out wooden boat. There were no words between them, but their rhythm in handling spears and nets revealed a long intimate relationship. Now she knew where DJ's love of Asia originated.

Lights flashed and crackled in the room and another film seemed to be playing. There was a couple in the royal courtyard. The woman who appeared to be a servant was madly in love with the knight who had had just arrived. His brilliant blue eyes lit up when he saw her. However, their love was secret. From the tower room, the dark-eyed king observed the illicit love.

Gayle knew now who they were. No wonder she and DJ were so connected. They had shared many lives together before this one.

In none of those lives though had DJ been a heavy drinker. There were too many problems emerging in this life's relationship. She could not rescue DJ. Before she turned out the light she wrote in her dream journal, "You destroyed the image I had of this relationship and I am not sure I can deal with the reality."

Chapter 2 – Dreams Become Reality

The Move

"I'm tired of watching you drink yourself to death," Gayle told DJ as he poured another Jack Daniels. "I'm tired of it all. The weather hasn't been above freezing this entire month. I'm getting a new job, moving south, and leaving you."

She slammed the liquor cabinet door for emphasis. DJ wouldn't meet her eyes. He drank knowing that the shakes would soon subside. He hadn't heard or even suspected that Gayle would ever leave.

"So what brought this all on?" he asked cautiously.

"I was in medical today. Barb had to take me there as I suddenly could not see anything. My physical said that my body has aged to more than 20 years older than I am. Some things have to change."

"What do you mean you couldn't see?"

"I was looking at Barb and her face kept getting distorted. She realized before I did that I was getting a migraine. In medical they made me lie down and they shut the door. Thankfully they left me in darkness and silence."

DJ patiently waited. He knew Gayle's anger would spin itself out and he could make sense of why her headache had something to do with her leaving him.

"Then these beings just appeared. No door opened, no footsteps, no warning. These beings just appeared out of nowhere. They told me I wasn't doing what I needed to be doing. And I had to get on with this now. It was time."

Gayle watched for some sign from DJ that would indicate he believed her but his poker face gave her no clue.

"I think I am crazy and my only hope is to find a spiritual teacher who can explain all this to me."

"Well, there are other changes in the works," he started.

"Yeah, I know," she countered. DJ eyed her warily as the changes he knew had not been announced.

"Yeah, you're going to the Far East to head up the new division there. My division will lose the chip manufacturing and sales force. The move to distribution will eliminate many of our own sales forces. And you will be out of here by July."

"When will I die?" he asked quickly.

"January 11, 2011," she replied without thinking.

"Good, we have some time then. When will you die?" Gayle told him.

After that momentous moment, the wheels turned fast. DJ moved to Bangkok and Gayle transferred to the south. She bought a mini-farm in fulfillment of her childhood dream to own horses.

All those visits to the bookstores across the country gave her another idea–she could run a New Age bookstore. Gayle began to explore options. She idly flipped through the Sunday newspaper. In the middle of the event listings was the notice of New Age guest speaker Gloria Karpinski at the Quest Society's monthly meeting.

When Gayle arrived at the run-down hotel where the meeting was being held, she wasn't quite sure what to think about this group. They certainly weren't characters out of *Rosemary's Baby*, but they seemed overeager. Still the Quest Society's monthly meetings with guest speakers could provide a home base for exploration in the community. Next month in fact there was a psychic fair. The organizer signed her up to read palms. She had read for years for friends and family, but she had never done it professionally.

At the fair Gayle read four people before she had a break. Then a camera crew and newswoman walked in and made a beeline for the empty chair at her table.

"So, tell me, how long have you known you were psychic?"

"For as long as I remember."

"So can you tell me something about me?"

"Sure, you're here on a lark, but have had two ghostly encounters that haunt you to this day." The young on-air personality's mouth fell open, but the camera was still rolling and she recovered quickly.

"Well, you're right. Thanks." The TV team moved on to the next interview.

Watching it later that evening Gayle felt the station had given fair coverage to the New Age event. She had seen other coverage that including poking fun, and picking the most outrageous character there to interview. Local coverage usually meant finding a Bubba to explain the tornado damage to the trailer or a woman with pink curlers still in her hair to wail on cue. Gayle seemingly was going public in a big way.

To her surprise, no one noticed her big coming out party. The dread of others noticing how different she was really had all been a figment of her imagination. No one really cared who she was or what she did.

A few weeks later a local newspaper reporter called her for an interview concerning her recent robbery. She had gotten her name and number off the police report from the robbery reports.

"So, there have been several robberies out here of late," Melinda asked. "Can you tell me what is missing?"

"Evidently they were in my house for a long time. All of my silver, gold, TV's, etc. are gone...and most of my jewelry," Gayle offered, "Except for this piece of amethyst my sister had given me." Gayle fingered the gem hanging beside the locket on the long silver chain. "Something told me to wear this today with my other necklace. I don't usually wear two at the same time."

Melinda looked at her closely. "Are you the psychic interviewed on TV a while back?"

"Well, if it was Channel 7, it is likely I am."

"Well, I need to introduce you to Samuel, a channel I know. You would like him." Melinda took the picture of Gayle as the young business woman in her yellow suit against the backdrop of her horse farm for her newspaper.

A few weeks later, Melinda invited her to the channeling session by the entity Samuel in Atlanta. Gayle was skeptical, but kept an open mind. The group seemed pleasant and being more urban, a lot more receptive to alternative spiritual practices. The woman who channeled Samuel, a former minister's wife, took the stage and smiled broadly to the small crowd before taking a seat. Gayle knew what channeling looked like, but she was unprepared for what she felt.

There was a swishing of energy throughout the room reminding her of a light warm breeze that touched everyone in the room. The woman onstage had her eyes closed and was slumped as if asleep. Other people seemed to be meditating or in some kind of trance. Then, Samuel entered the woman's body that stretched awkwardly as if trying to accommodate a much larger male figure. The eyes opened with a twinkle. Could this be her teacher?

"Good morning, dears." The person's whole appearance seemed changed to a masculine feel. The voice now was affected with a Scottish brogue. There was nothing artificial in it. The skepticism gave way to a warm sharing of energy. There was an energetic exchange when eye contact was made. Dialogue engaged people during the aerie faerie stuff as Samuel called it. Gayle had no issues recognizing this teacher as a male despite his expression through the pretty petite woman onstage. The channeling included some exercises and some practical applications of the offered teachings. Gayle was distressed to learn that Samuel did not offer classes or private teachings. His workshops were a resource, but she needed to keep looking for a teacher.

Then, without warning Gayle was let go from her corporate job. She contemplated her next move. Go back to school? Find a different type of job since she was burned out by sales? Open a new age bookstore in the middle of the Bible Belt? Go off to India in search of a guru? Nothing was clear for her. Her career had so preoccupied her that she had forgotten who she was and what she liked.

The blank canvas she had bought on impulse at the handicraft store leaned against the wall on the fireplace mantle. She felt like a blank slate herself. Gayle placed the small canvas on the easel. What should she start with? Should she sketch it out first or boldly just put paint on canvas? She opened the paints and made her own palette. Then dipping the camel hairs into the colors she began to paint the inside of her mind. Her dog Smoky lay at her feet while she worked. When she finished, the crude abstract hid great meaning. One day she might understand it.

Gayle realized her midlife crisis arrived early in the forms of a lover who was slowly drinking himself to death, a former sales career, migraine headaches on a regular basis, unexplained dreams, and a job physical that revealed a lifestyle aging her prematurely. Change was just another turn in the spiral-another pivot point. A horseback ride would break her somber mood.

Gayle saddled Alibi, her retired racing Thoroughbred. The air was crisp and the dog tagged along at Ali's feet. He had not yet learned the danger of flying horse hooves. The young rescue mustang eyed them longingly, but would not approach. He preferred the center of the pasture where he could see all around him as he once had in the plains.

Alibi stretched out in full gallop in the horse park as they made their way to the wooded trails. At a more deliberate pace, they jumped the fallen logs crossing the path and climbed the hills. The mare tossed her head at the dog that crashed into the trail from his brushy shortcut. The three moved downhill to the small stream. Alibi never failed to jump sideways at the moving waters. Gayle anticipated it though and didn't lose her seat.

Then as they walked home, a drum could be heard in the distance. Gayle untacked Alibi and brushed the horse thoroughly. She put feed in the bucket and rattled it for the little mustang that came running. In doing her chores she paid little attention to the deliberate drumming rhythm in the distance. Now as she and Smoky walked to the house, she noted it again. Holding the door open for the dog, the two then plopped on the leather sectional sofa. Smoky cocked his ear.

"Whatcha think, Smoky Doke? Someone is out there?"

She laughed, but at the same time she knew the next closest house was more than a mile away. Gayle slid the sliding glass doors to the pasture open, but she couldn't hear the drum outside. Puzzled, she turned back to Smoky who still had one ear cocked at something in the den. The dog whined as now the drum was beating louder there. After a while, there was a song, barely audible.

The black dog stared intently at the fireplace where a distortion, resembling heat waves on the highway, formed a shape. Intuitively Gayle joined in singing the repetitive childlike song. When she finished, the drumming stopped and the figure the energy waves had made disappeared. Gayle shrugged and petted Smoky on his head.

The following afternoon Gayle was not quite as surprised when the drumming began. As she and the dog approached the den, the song began. Gayle sang and this time she added dance. Smoky followed dutifully behind her slow circle. Gayle swore she could hear a rattle shaking in time.

Soon this figure began a daily appearance. The dog and Gayle would do a circle dance, Gayle would sing whatever song was presented, and gradually she just accepted that there was an active ghost in the house. When she got more comfortable, the shadowy form developed more into a figure of an elderly Native American male. There was no conversation between them, but he taught her simple songs and dances by example. These gave her peace.

Then as she walked the steps of the dance once day, her inner vision opened. In the dark oval screen of her mind, a shining light revealed a deerskin dress. While she had heard of ribbon shirts for the nearby Cherokee men, she had not seen them wear skins. She noted the details, the cut and the simple lines. Then the dress was worn by a dancer, a woman with long raven hair, who danced in the pasture beneath the stars and the full moon. The woman was filled with power; she had none of the uncertainty or anxiety that plagued Gayle.

The next week an old friend dropped by with deer pelts he had in his garage. He thought she might have a use for them. Though she had not sewn for years, Gayle still knew the basic patterns and she pinned the parts together. Within a few days, she had a makeshift version of her dancing dress.

At the next full moon Gayle felt a bit awkward in the heavy deerskin dress. She hadn't thought to make shoes so she stood barefoot in the pasture. The horses were grazing in the back pasture and Smoky was rolling in what was sure to be manure. It was midnight. She was in the middle of her pasture under a full moon.

Gayle's voice started out squeaky as began the spiral dance she had seen in her vision. The fullness of the moment made her bolder. She laughed with joy, made grand jetés over manure piles, and coaxed the dog into playing. Just as suddenly it was over. She had not been aware of the drum accompanying her, but now only because of its absence did she know they were done.

Gayle slept soundly that night without dreams. If it hadn't been a priority to feed the animals she wouldn't have been up at dawn. Yet she had a routine to follow and expectations to fulfill. In the afternoon Gayle waited expectantly for the ghost teacher to arrive. He did, but without a drum or a song. He smiled. His face was now familiar, but Gayle sensed a shift in energy.

"I won't be seeing you again," he said softly.

"What do you mean?"

"You're going to get a teacher in the physical."

"What do you mean? I like you," Gayle protested. He smiled and his form started to disappear. "Wait! Wait! I don't even know your name."

"Black Elk," he replied and disappeared.

NCAA Final Four Predictions

"Hey, a friend of mine wants to do a fun TV segment on basketball and psychics. You up for that?" Melinda asked over the telephone.

"Sure." Within hours a local TV crew drove up. The team staged some candles behind Gayle, put up some bright lights, and miked her. Gayle meditated a few minutes to raise her energy so she could access the realm where she could see the future.

"Ready," she said. However before they could begin, the light bulb exploded in the cameraman's fill light.

"OK," he said, "I have a spare in the truck." Gayle relaxed as he went out and she talked to the sportscaster.

"Who's playing, Fred?" Fred provided the names of the teams. "I'll just give you my impressions on each team, you can cut to game footage, and we'll see where it goes."

The cameraman indicated that they were ready to start so Gayle began to meditate under the bright lights.

"Ker splash!" The second light bulb exploded.

"This never happens," the cameraman said as he nervously reached for the last spare bulb. His eyes conveyed wariness.

"I know," Gayle offered. "It's the energy level. It happens sometimes in my electronics lab when I walk in after meditation. Everything goes awry. Let me lower my vibration."

The light was on now and the interview began. Gayle flowed with descriptive playing styles and coaching mannerisms as if she was a regular at center court. She dropped the term four corner offense appropriately. The interview went well and she had put it all on the line by saying that Duke would be the champion. She and Fred chatted as the cameraman packed all the gear out. He didn't want to remain there a second longer than he had to.

"Not only will Duke win tonight, but mark my words the championship game won't even be close. Duke by almost 30 points."

Watching the interview that evening, Gayle smiled as the cuts to game footage revealed the accuracy with which she had described each team. At the conclusion of the clip, Fred adlibbed, "And get this, the psychic said the championship game will be won by almost 30 points by Duke."

Gayle wasn't too surprised to see the sports page days later showing Duke as national champion with an unexpected winning spread of 29 points.

The Next Step & Gloria

Gayle was growing more desperate. There was no income coming in and no new direction had magically appeared. This quest for understanding her spiritual connection was costing her dearly. Though the horse farm kept her preoccupied, she formed a small meditation group from the Quest Society. Ken and Larry were soon joined by three more of their friends who shared teachings from another group–Sally, Janet and Stuart. This new group called themselves the Next Step and met once a month. On this evening, it was a quiet gathering. When the meditation ended, Stuart exclaimed, "There's a goat outside looking in the window."

When everyone turned to see, there was nothing there. Stuart was looking a bit foolish until Gayle started laughing.

"Meet Gloria-our escapee from the rodeo held across the street. No one can catch her, but she seems to like hanging out here. She walks on the rock ledge peering into windows until she finds out where I am."

The group laughed. The next meditation was deeper after the group settled down. Yet Gayle found herself looking at the group from above. She wondered where the individuals were. Drawn to locate Ken, she found him in a pyramid with golden light. Next she located Larry who was seated in a shining white house and then Janet was flying as if on Pegasus or a dragon. Sally was in primitive earth energy, one that was not comfortable for Gayle. She saw Stuart in Atlantean colors, those dream colors made of light, and not reflections of it.

Gayle then saw each of them become swirling balls of energy lights that coalesced into a circle moving at light speed counterclockwise. Gayle realized she was to balance them. When she did, geometric patterns, pyramids, a five pointed star, a circle and then a yin/yang sign of black and white formed. As all the lights balanced, a six-pointed star formed, not the Star of David, but two overlapping pyramids. The pyramid then extended itself through space with a white light pouring out of one end and a black light pouring out the other. She and the crystal were one. Gayle tried to explain the insight to the group.

"It was like looking into a universe with six very dim and unique stars who were attempting to ignite the spark to leap out of humanity."

The group gave secretive glances. Finally Larry offered, "You need to meet our teacher Ron. He runs a mystery school."

The purple light in Gayle's head exploded. She nodded.

White Wolf

Though there was little progress in finding a teacher, Gayle still hoped. There remained extraordinary dream adventures. Tonight she was flying home. Gayle stopped short when she arrived. Puzzled, she hovered over the sleeping body in the huge ornate bed. Something was very wrong.

The sleeping body in the bed was hers. However, tall ghostly beings surrounded it and Gayle didn't know how to get around them. Silently they moved the limbs of the doll-like body. One took her right arm, bent it at the elbow and then placed her hand under her mid-back. On the opposite side, another being did the same with her left arm. Their robes made crinkling noises when they moved. Another being took her left leg, flexed into a turned out position and placed the foot behind the knee of the right leg. One being remained focused on her head where Gayle noted that her own face was surrounded by an eerie golden light.

The body position was the Hanged Man in the Tarot deck. The Hanged Man in mythology equated to Odin, the Norse god who hung upside down for nine days to attain wisdom in the form of the runes. When Odin glimpsed the runes, he died. However, the knowledge of them brought him immediately back to life.

"Shoot! Am I dead?" Gayle thought.

Alarmed, she rushed back into the physical body lying so unaware on the bed. Yet, she had no control in the physical world. She could hear rustling noises but wasn't able to open her eyes or speak. She could feel her physical body in exactly the same position seen in the "dream."

The beings still worked on her. She wanted to demand to know what they were doing. They adjusted her body in another way. Gayle began to panic. How could she be alert and aware yet not be in control of her body? Briefly she thought, "This must be what it feels like to be paralyzed."

Not one to like being out of control, especially of her own body, Gayle decided to act. Gayle's focus shifted to move her index finger. Every bit of energy, thought, and desire was placed on forcing a finger to move. After substantial effort, the index finger jerked slightly.

"Shh! She's awake," one of the beings cautioned the others.

Gayle's efforts had alerted them. Had they really spoken or had she heard them telepathically? Gayle struggled to no avail to open her eyes. She wanted to see them from the physical eyes. Clairvoyant vision was okay, but Gayle still held that seeing is believing. She had to make sense of these events and here she was lying paralyzed.

As if on cue, the beings ceased all activities. Gayle sensed that even though they had been interrupted, the shining ones had completed their mission. Her bed vibrated like the vibrating magic beds at cheap hotels.

"Perhaps their ship, hovering over the pasture, caused these phenomena." The beings' movement and the rustling noise began again. Gayle redoubled her effort to move. Any additional movement might break the paralysis. She concentrated on her right hand index finger again.

"Move," she urged. "Stretch. Move."

Gayle had no control over her body. She kept trying to move her finger. Sometime during her intense efforts, the shining ones left. The rustling was gone now, and the vibration diminished. Gayle should have felt relief, but instead she was even more puzzled. A heavy warm weight lay on her leg.

"The dog's jumped up on the bed," Gayle thought. Then she remembered that he was in the barn. This was not her dog.

Gayle focused again on breaking the paralysis. Her inner vision imagined the index finger moving. Pouring her thought and vitality into her finger, she could feel the blood vessels strain from the efforts. Her dogged concentration increased the blood flow and stimulated the nerve endings. Seconds later her finger jerked. With a gasp, the paralysis had broken. Gayle immediately reached out to the weight on her legs.

Her fingers stroked the long hair of an animal's coat. It was soft. His chest rose and fell as her hand rested on its body. Inexplicably, her eyes were suddenly open. There, asleep on her legs and facing the foot board, was a large white dog. She stroked the back of his head gently. He stirred at her touch. His massive head lifted and turned toward her. Gayle suddenly realized this was no dog. An Arctic wolf was lying in her bed. There was no fear. The white wolf was beautiful. His eyes had white light for irises. There was a loving radiance that surrounded them both. She was lost in the light of his eyes.

Gayle's whole being was fascinated with this magnificent wolf. She forgot about the visitors; she forgot about the ship's vibrations; she forgot about the Hanged Man position. Nothing matter but the unconditional love she shared with the wolf.

A flash of light and a tremble alerted her to something leaving outside. She briefly wondered what that was, but was answered with, "Go to sleep." So she did.

Confluence

Gayle made her coffee in the morning and stepped out onto the patio. She whistled for the dog. This simple act triggered a recall of the night's events.

"How come whenever anything strange happens my response is to go to bed, pull the covers over my head, and go to sleep?"

The horses stamped at the barn door. No matter how unreal her world could be, the reality of farm chores always brought her back to earth. Memories of the night's events seeped back into her awareness. That wolf! How could she have ever forgotten that white wolf?

Gayle didn't know where to begin to learn more about her experience. She had never exchanged words with her Native American spirit guide until the day of his departure. Her friends, while enthralled with the story, had no idea of its meaning. They were of no help. She had to find a spiritual teacher.

This Sunday's ad announced the Quest Society was sponsoring a talk by Chief Medicine Bear. Her skin tingled all over. That had always been her sign that she was on the right track. If she hurried, she would make the seminar on time.

Approximately fifty people gathered at the Quest Society's meeting to hear the Chief. Medicine Bear was Cherokee and spoke of the casino on the reservation and the impact on the people. While he felt mostly good that the teachings had been opened to the "wannabees," he also expressed dismay about the false teachings, the lack of cultural awareness needed for true understanding, and how to embrace creation as one. Medicine Bear overran the allotted time leaving no time for questions. The man was already heading for the door.

Gayle followed him out to the parking lot; Medicine Bear was already engaged in a private conversation with another seeker. Gayle stood within earshot waiting for her chance.

"Now I have to go," he stated and turned for his car. Gayle ran to his car that was already backing out. She couldn't be put off. She insistently rapped on his closed car window.

"Please I need your help and I don't know where else to turn," she pleaded as he rolled the window down for the crazed person beating on his car.

"Yes?"

"I had a white wolf come visit me and I don't know what it means." Gayle poured out the short version of the story. The man sized her up before speaking.

"The place you will find the answer is a sacred Cherokee place where the quartz rock stands guardian of the merger of three flowing waters." He started to roll up the car window.

"Wait, please. There are thousands of acres in the Cherokee reservations here. Can't you please help me narrow it down?"

"Near here." Medicine Bear rolled up his window, put his old rusty brown Pontiac in reverse and sped away. Gayle was devastated. She had wanted answers-concrete answers. All she had was a vague clue. This definitely was not her teacher.

For days Gayle poured over reservation maps in western North Carolina. Trips into the mountains revealed she was looking for a needle in a haystack. Real life took priority. She needed to make a living. A New Age bookstore in the Bible Belt wasn't going to fly. The mental resistance of the Bible Belt populace over generations was too much to overcome. Money drained from her bank account even as the hard work of tending the horses, taming a runaway rodeo goat, and working a mini-farm were taking a physical toll. Life decisions had to be made.

Frustrated, Gayle accepted her limitations in finding jobs. She had intended to work for AT&T for her entire career. However with the divestiture of the corporation, change and downsize that was not to be. For most of her corporate career, the Executive Vice President of AT&T would place her in poor performing sectors of the business.

"Fix it or close it down," he would tell her. "Do whatever you need to do."

Now it was her time to fix her own life or close it down. A step in any direction was better than standing still doing nothing. She signed up for a technical graduate degree, but quickly found the fit there did not work out any better than it had the first time she studied engineering. At least she had ruled out one direction. Everything collapsed instead of expanding out into a new horizon.

Reluctantly Gayle put the horse farm up for sale. She found good homes for the animals and lightened her load. Everything was being taken care of, but her. She never wanted to be a burden. The robbery had taken most of her valuables and she had little attachment to anything. Depression settled in with bouts of insomnia and contemplation. Without a teacher, a guide, or some path to follow, Gayle treaded water emotionally and financially. She was at the end of her rope. Her savings reserve was gone. There were no obvious options.

This morning she had found it impossible to get out of bed despite the sun streaming in through the windows. She didn't feel well. Remembering how her mother made her go to school unless she had a fever, she pulled out the thermometer.

"95.7" It beeped to her. No wonder she did not feel well. She was dying. However, she didn't want to die here. She pulled on some jeans and a sweatshirt.

"Where can I go?" She laughed at her own absurdity. If she was going somewhere to die, it really didn't matter. She just wanted to be found in a reasonable time. No dragging off of body parts by wild animals allowed. Before leaving, she ripped the For Sale sign out of the ground and stashed it in her garage. The real estate agent had done nothing to promote a sale other than place a sign there. The contract had ended the day before and the agent was too lazy to come get her sign.

Gayle's trusty black Honda turned for the mountains. She would know when she got there. The air was still very cool, but it felt good to be far away from people. She hadn't seen another car for the last hour or so. There were still rural two lane roads to nowhere in the world. A small Mom and Pop restaurant was on the rise ahead. The only car there was leaving the parking lot. The sign read "Closed until dinner."

"Perfect!" she thought. She pulled the car around to the back of the restaurant so it couldn't be seen. Locking the doors, she pressed the seat release so that she could lay all the way back. Now comfortable, Gayle closed her eyes to await death.

A great emptiness coursed through her mind only to be interrupted by the occasional thought or feeling. Her life had no meaning. Betrayal of beloved ones left her with no familial connections. No great awakening had happened since that long ago night of the Harmonic Convergence under the trees asking for help. Despite Black Elk's promise of a new teacher in the physical, no one had shown up. Gayle was done - ready to toss in the towel.

The sunlight warmed the car interior and made it quite comfortable. Yet, again nothing happened. Gayle laid there for a long time. Then, without warning, it was time to go home. The drive back was uneventful. The sun was very low in the sky and she arrived home just as darkness was settling in. She walked to get the mail. To her surprise, the only thing in the mailbox was a handwritten note saying:

> "I noticed that your for sale sign is gone. If you are interested in selling your home for cash, please call me at 555-4135."

"Miracles do happen," said Gayle to the first star appearing in the night sky. "Starlight, star bright. First star I see tonight. I wish I may, I wish I might, have this wish I make tonight. Let this sale go through."

Within a week Gayle closed on the house, stored all her furniture and books, and made a plan to go to graduate school to get a counseling degree. In meditation, she asked to know the place she was to move.

"Athens," said an inner voice.

"Greece!" she exclaimed. Gayle always loved the scenes from the old Disney movie *The Moonspinners*.

"No," corrected the voice, "Georgia."

Pathfinder

The move to Athens was chaotic much like the town itself. The home of the University of Georgia was also known as the music capital of the South. Bands such as the B52's, REM and Trinket played among the many indie groups. Athen's downtown had the coffee house, the Bluebird Cafe, East-West Bistro, used bookstores, boutiques and music stores. There was a creative vibe here, sort of scaled down-slowed down version of New York with a Southern accent. The college town was perpetually dominated by the 18-24 year old population.

Gayle's application to the MSW program was rejected. Disappointed by the termination of her counseling future, she entertained opening her long awaited New Age store. It could work here. No sooner than she had that thought than the phone rang.

"Hey, Gayle, my spiritual teacher, the one I have been telling you about from New York will be in Asheville. Would you like to go with me to have dinner with him?" asked Larry, her meditation friend from Quest.

"Sure."

Gayle was uncharacteristically quiet during the drive up to Asheville. Being a passenger in a car was a form of an emotional prison. Larry was a talker and rambled on until Gayle realized he had paused long enough to ask a question.

"Do you know you have little people at your house?"

"Uh, no."

"Well, when I drove up to your garage a little guy came around the corner, waved at me, and then ran into the woods."

"Interesting," was all she had to say before Larry continued talking again.

Their arrival at the Black Mountain home revealed a rustic, quaint cottage. The dropping of the autumn leaves revealed a view of the mountain valley. Larry introduced the host and his girlfriend before he disappeared to converse with his long term friends. Gayle sensed she was another one in a line of Larry's girlfriends. Yet, the man she came here to meet was nowhere to be found. This could be her teacher.

The lively conversation in the living room covered Gayle as she wandered the cottage. For years she had drawn house plans like this one. Rounding the corner, she peered into the kitchen doorway where an older man was busily preparing shrimp.

"Do you like scampi?" he asked.

"I love it," she said. He nodded, expertly flipped the shrimp in the pan and continued cooking. That was her introduction to Ron, the spiritual teacher that several of the Next Step meditation group spoke so highly about.

"Mmmm." At the table Gayle closed her eyes savoring the butter and garlic sauce over fresh cooked shrimp. Fresh was seldom found inland from the coast and her grandmother had long ago spoiled her with local coastal catches. The group never even noticed her silence caught up in their own fast conversation. However, when Ron spoke everyone quieted reverentially. Gayle became a bit annoyed. As the dinner party wound down, she could take it no longer.

"So who are you anyway?" she blurted out to Ron.

The table was aghast, but went silent. Ron took the hand of his girlfriend before answering. Gayle couldn't understand what he was trying to convey, but she could feel the intensity. She didn't like the dynamics of the group in their deference to him, but later when Larry asked how she felt about the evening, she replied it was alright.

Upon returning to Athens, Gayle noted a "For Rent" sign in the window of the small rundown storefront a block from the UGA campus. Within a month she was creating a small bookstore. The cook from the Bluebird Cafe took interest in her effort and dropped off their special blueberry biscuits. Gayle didn't know a soul here and the cook became her confidante. The creative energy pervaded the small town big attitude of Athens.

Gayle brought her home furnishings that didn't fit into her small home to the storefront. A friend bought huge leafy ficus plants to fill in the spaces and bring an earth element inside. Gayle had never been overly concerned with esthetics, but with a little help Pathfinder had its own creative vibe.

When a young reporter stopped in with her mandatory hundred questions, Gayle found a friend in Rachel who worked at the newspaper a few doors down the street. Rachel's column mention of Pathfinder Bookstore, named for the car she had once been behind while stuck in traffic on the George Washington Bridge, brought a flurry of customers during her opening. Among them came an invitation to a drum circle and Gayle accepted. There were people like her in the world after all.

Gayle loved the store. She got to talk to kindred spirits, do a few readings, and find a place in the world for the first time in her life. New venders displayed their wares on consignment, she hosted an art opening, and began teaching a few classes in the chakras, pendulum dowsing, and the long ago practice of seeing that she learned from Samuel's seminar. When a young handsome professor wandered into Pathfinder, he suggested applying to the department of religion graduate school.

"Why not?" thought Gayle. This seemed to be a legitimate avenue in exploring her spirituality. Gayle was accepted for the Master's program. With a bit of rearranging Gayle could manage the store and her classes.

When Angela wandered into the store, she suggested that Gayle plan a buying trip to check out the NC gem and mineral show. The drive up was easy and she came into Clayton, a small mountain town. That meant a stop was in order. For years, her family's road trips required a visit to any town sharing their family name.

A tourist sign pointed to a roadside park–Warwoman Dell, an intriguing name. A few miles down a winding mountain road led to the entrance of the wooded roadside park. She remembered Christy had mentioned it at one of the drum circles.

The park was small and seemed far more remote than its roadside location. The wind rustled through the trees while the sound of falling water was in the distance. An old railroad trestle bed loomed high overhead. No one else was there.

When Gayle got out of the car, she noted the huge white quartz boulder standing guard. Christy had said that the wise Cherokee woman on the Trail of Tears had to leave her teachings encoded in the crystal.

The Cherokee on the forced evacuation of their homelands became ill and many died. The rough conditions of the march meant many sacred articles and teachings were left behind. Since crystalline materials can hold electromagnetic fields, Gayle felt the memories and magic of the Cherokee stored within the quartz. She kissed the boulder for luck. And then she remembered.

"The place you will find the answer is a sacred Cherokee place where the quartz rock stands guardian of the merger of three flowing waters," Medicine Bear had said.

Goose pimples formed on her arms as an indicator she was on the right track. She took the path to the right. As she reached a small rise, Gayle noted a lowland covered with ferns and water loving plants. Two small streams merged together under the rustic log she stood on.

"Two waters, not three."

However, the ferns like the earth that opened up for Demeter to enter the underworld in search of Persephone beckoned her closer. Gayle stepped gingerly among the glade. Then from the left, she saw the third small stream hidden by the plant life adding its flow to the gathering waters. Three waters were flowing together in one place.

"Three in one–a trinity," Gayle exclaimed. All the hair on her body stood up as energy rushed through. She was there. Finally she had arrived at the promised place the dream had shown her so long ago. White Wolf had led her here.

Gayle could now hear invisible voices bantering on the cliff above where the water fell to the earth. Her heart opened and the inner senses took in the scene. The Dell was an initiation site for Native Americans-sacred to women. She was home. Now that she had found the site, a teacher would surely appear.

Chapter 3 – Teacher's Choice

World Religions

"Turned the stone and looked beneath...'Peace on Earth' was all it said." Gayle sang as she walked the University of Georgia campus. The quadrangle, comprised of the main library, the Peabody building that housed the religion and philosophy department, the law school and the Demosthenian Hall was a favorite film location for independents. Yet, no one was here this morning. Athens, Georgia was a party town. Opening acts at music venues seldom started before 11 PM. Only a few students chose early morning classes.

She climbed the wide steps to the white columned colonial building that housed the main library. The song *One Tin Soldier* played endlessly in Gayle's head as she perused the books lining the back shelves. Sometimes in just wandering the aisles a book would stand out for her to open. Today, only one oversized edition spoke. Flipping through it, she read "the birth of religion rose to overcome the fear of the death." She pondered that a moment. In some poll, the fear of death was the number one fear of the majority of the population. Religion offered much comfort to many.

Gayle's many ghosts had convinced her that death was a transition and not a definitive end. Still, she brought the book to one of the empty tables to copy the passages and ponder where this was all leading. Larry's call last night was to say that his teacher was starting a new wave of training for his Modern Mystery School.

"What's a mystery school?"

"Well, it is a training school for leaders in the world. In the olden days, the eldest son of a family was sent to a school to learn the science and mysteries so that he would be prepared for future leadership. The ancient mysteries were based on natural cycles."

"So like the Pythagorean School?" Gayle had learned of the sage's school of enlightenment when she had studied geometry in middle school. Geometry came naturally to her much to the dismay of Liz who studied nightly on it. Gayle had simply learned the theorems and intuitively knew how to apply them.

"Exactly, though these mysteries extended into the mysteries of life itself. Ron always says if you complete the training you may become transcendent. If you don't, then the booby prize is enlightenment."

Gayle laughed though she really did know the distinction. Yet the myths themselves were a part of the ancient mysteries. Her academic study of religion said that Eleusis Greece was the center. There the mysteries were revealed as the seed of life in a stalk of grain. The myth said the goddess of vegetation, Demeter, searched for her daughter Persephone who was abducted by Hades.

The cycles of birth, life, death and ultimately rebirth spoken through the seasons and planting cycles seemed endless. Buddhists taught that one could escape the cycle. So in some way Gayle determined that enlightenment was within the cycle and transcendence was the escape. For now, reincarnation was her answer to the fear of death.

"So what do I have to do to join?" Gayle asked Larry.

"You should probably attend one of his workshops or do a private session with him. I'll let you know as soon as I have the Atlanta dates."

The idea of a mystery school intrigued her. Inspiration had been lacking lately. Nothing else had drawn her in quite the same way as $E=mc^2$. There was mystery in the equation relating energy, mass and form. That and infinity were something that she never grasped. It didn't matter that thousands or millions of other people didn't understand it as well.

Gayle studied religion now instead of science to understand the mystery of light and matter. The hologram in *Star Wars* saying "Help me Obi Wan Kanobi" had inspired her to look at reality differently. What was real? What happened after death? Gayle closed the book and left it for re-shelving. She had a new class this afternoon– *An Introduction to Buddhism.*

Gayle sat in the back, a bit intimidated being a middle-aged woman among the young students. She flipped through the textbook idly. The professor opened the door and entered the classroom. He was from Sri Lanka, dressed casually, and was small in stature. However, at second glance she saw a monk in saffron robes. Then suddenly she knew–she had unexpectedly found a real teacher.

The Invitation to Dance

Gayle found it difficult to converse with her Buddhism professor. The other professors were easily available, but Gayle was strangely intimidated by the little Buddhist monk or LBM as she and a friend jokingly called him. However, the professor held credentials from Columbia University, was an author, and had obviously been ordained as a monk at some stage of his life. He posed an enigma to the western mind.

Shanta, as the professor asked to be called, read the textbook during class. Perhaps it was because of his accented English or the lack of student preparation. Shanta seldom deviated from his lecture or engaged students in dialogue. Yet, he greeted and ended each class with his hands placed together in a prayer position, a slight bow and the Sanskrit word *Namasté.*

Out of classroom boredom, Gayle started meditating in Shanta's early morning classes. It felt good to have her eyes closed to focus on the words. When test time came, Gayle found she could simply close her eyes and recall word for word the lecture. While Shanta didn't single her out, she could feel him looking at her even with her eyes closed. He did begin writing notes on the papers she submitted though. And slowly they began to work together to study Buddhism academically and through meditation during class times.

When Ken invited her to Ron's workshop, Gayle agreed to go. Ken offered to pick her up, perhaps sensing her skepticism and her tendency to back out of commitments she didn't want to keep. The workshop was hosted at Deb's home. However, it was Joe's house that Ken drove to.

"There are people here you can meet before the workshop tomorrow."

Joe's subdivision home was filled with people who obviously knew each other pretty well. The conversation was animated and as the new kid on the block, Gayle became uncomfortable with the barrage of questions.

Brenda asked, "I heard you did readings. Wanna give me one?"

Gayle eyed the 50ish woman warily before pronouncing, "You're a dancer!'

"Hard to believe this old woman to be a dancer, isn't it? But you're right."

Brenda's eyes twinkled. Gayle realized she had passed some unknown test. She helped herself to the lasagna on the breakfast bar and tried to stay out of the group's focus. They hardly noticed.

The group reminded her of her New Jersey sales team. They were often rowdy, fun, and drinking. They had shared successes and failures. However, what surprised her was that in this group no one talked about Ron or the workshop topics. They certainly didn't act like a spiritual group, but more of a party group. She was relieved when the doorbell rang.

"That's Ron," she offered.

The room went deadly quiet. Ron was not expected to show up until the following day. However, Gayle was not surprised to see him at the door. He didn't stay long as the workshop was to begin early the next morning. Ron had just opted to walk over as he had needed the exercise after the long drive from North Carolina.

Deb's living room was crowded when Ken and Gayle arrived for the seminar. Backjacks were set up around the room. People were seated on the floor, close together on the sofa, or on the few chairs in the dining room. Gayle took a spot where she had only one person by her side, a massage therapist named Georgie. Gayle seemed to be the only outsider to the group.

Ron was fiddling with the electrical cords to his recording equipment. He sold copies of the tapes of the workshops. He finally set a scarab embroidered pillow down for his seat and began. He opened by directing his remarks to her:

"Well, I wasn't expecting you here today. Since you are a newcomer and uninitiated, I won't be able to discuss some of the mysteries."

Gayle squirmed since now it seemed that the others would be denied part of the teachings they expected. She didn't understand a lot of the jargon that Ron had developed with his group. She found it rather boring. Ken slipped a piece of paper with a question to ask Ron when there was an opening.

The trouble with Ken's request was that it was hard to determine when there was an opening. Ron's speech had unusual cadence. There were odd spaces and the speed of his delivery varied. The man did not shut up. Finally, he announced that there was a break for lunch. Before she could get up, Georgie grabbed her arm.

"I always have had trouble getting out of my body," she offered. "Do you mind giving me a short reading?"

"If you don't mind going outside with our lunch, we can do it."

They sat on the sun-warmed rocks, balancing the sandwiches and pasta salad. Georgie dutifully extended her hand to her, palm up, to be read. When Gayle saw the lines, she was troubled.

"You're going to have a heart attack."

"Nah, I already had one. Three years ago."

"You're not hearing me." Gayle shook the palm to bring Georgie's attention back. "This is right on you; it's not three years ago."

"You're not hearing me. I'm not going to live through another heart attack."

Georgie jerked her palm back eyes flashing in anger. Gayle ended the reading a bit troubled about her message. However, Georgie was in fine humor when the workshop began again.

Gayle was tired of being squashed together with only the back of couch leg to support her back. Ron droned on about spiritual work, some ritual they had done the last time, and kept a steady pace of information flowing. Gayle looked at the group. Many of them were asleep, some lounging and not paying attention, and she wondered why Ron did not change up the situation.

"Let's meditate before taking a break." Ron's voice had penetrated into her awareness and Gayle found him looking at her knowingly. Gayle crossed her legs, sat up straight, and closed her eyes. The others in the group did likewise. Gayle was relieved that there would be only a few minutes of torturous practice before they would break.

Yet something was different this time. She felt a rising above thoughts, a clarity that she had seldom felt. Meditation had never been like this before. She was more alert, more aware, yet it felt like the precipice to something more. If only she had a few more minutes, she would know.

"Ring...," Ron had tapped the small brazen bowl to signal the end of meditation. He asked for comments, but no one offered any. There was a general consensus to break–for snacks, water, bathroom etc. Gayle hung back waiting as Ron rose a bit awkwardly from his floor cushion. The older man was frailer than she had first thought.

"Excuse me," she said as she sidled up to him, "Do you know what an event horizon is?"

He stopped mid-stride and turned to her.

"Yes."

"Well, in that meditation I felt like I was standing at the event horizon. If I went further, I could never come back. This felt like a one way ticket to someplace."

"Interesting." Ron walked over to join Ken. He whispered, "Keep your friend near; she might be a good addition to the group."

Gayle was extremely puzzled. She had paid good money for this workshop and all she got was a rude "interesting." Well, she had another day to endure here. Then, well then, she never had to deal with them again.

Ron talked for another three hours until most of the group's eyes had glazed over. The break for dinner was a journey back to Joe's house. Afterward there was an invite to join the group in the hot tub.

"I didn't bring a suit."

"You don't need one," Sally said.

By the time Gayle had undressed, everyone was already crowded into the small tub on the back deck. She dropped her towel and could feel eyes on her. She knew she had a beautiful body, but she had never been comfortable with public nudity. Or semi-private in this case.

The hot water bubbles accompanied by cold beers made it difficult to follow conversations. Even as a little child she had learned not to listen to the words, but to follow the emotions that accompanied them. There was more truth there anyway. She was distracted by Ron's thigh against hers as someone else crowded into the tub. There was a flush of arousal that she found slightly distressing. Ron was much older and even in his youth would never have been her type. She loved beautiful men–tall, dark and handsome who spoke with a melodious accent. How she ended up with blondes as her partners was a story all by itself. Still Gayle could not move away and just allowed the feeling to be present. When Ron began teaching in the tub, Gayle tuned him out and gazed at the stars far above and wondered how many black holes might be out there.

The hung-over group straggled in haphazardly the next morning into Deb's living room and found seats for the opening meditation. Gayle just daydreamed through them. It didn't seem to matter to Ron whether people paid attention or not. She was tired of these spiritual wannabees. She had classes tomorrow and reading to do. Ron was talking on and on. After a couple of hours, Ken nudged her suggesting it was time to ask a question.

"What advice would you give to someone trying to start a working meditation group?" Gayle jumped in when Ron finally stopped to catch his breath.

"Depends on what kind of group you want it to be."

Suddenly Gayle couldn't hear the words Ron was saying, but she struggled for the content. His presence at the front of the room was now drowned by a blinding golden light. The only thing she could see was his face. Ron's lips were moving, but everything else was in shadow.

Then his eyes met hers. She was drowning in pools of dark brown. The golden light formed a pyramid bridge between them.

"Anything else?"

Gayle managed to shake her head as the room slowly came back into focus. She glanced at the others, but none of them acted as if anything had happened. However, she had found a teacher.

The Book of the Dead

Joe's email arrived the next day. Joe prided himself on being the email and address keeper of Ron's Foundation group. To his credit, he did a good job of providing an information link. He wrote:

"I'm sorry to let you know that our friend Georgie had a massive heart attack upon her return home on Monday. She had baked her son's birthday cake and celebrated with her family earlier that day as she had planned. No details announced for her memorial as of yet."

Gayle was shaken. She had just seen Georgie two days before and given her the news that this heart attack was right on her. It wasn't distrust of what she knew, but the fact that a living breathing person could simple change states that quickly. The phone rang.

"Gayle, did you hear about Georgie? Ron can't find her. I want you to help." Janet was breathless, but certain in her ability. "Tell me what you see." Gayle tuned into her inner space where she went to get answers. To her surprise, she wasn't alone in there.

"Well, first of all she is here with me now. She tells me that she finally figured out how to get out of her body. We are in the golden light of the Egyptian pyramid. There are boats here, but we are not taking one. We are climbing up through the Grand Gallery."

Gayle was astounded at the clarity of the scenes. Others there read the directions of the book of the dead. Gayle talked with Georgie about the next adventure for her being as they climbed the ramp of the Great Pyramid. As they reached the small squarish opening that led to the King's Chamber, Gayle could see the golden light inside. However, she knew that she could not go in. It was not her time. Ron in his dream body stepped forward to help Georgie up into the space. There was no acknowledgment of Gayle from anyone.

"Gayle? Are you still there?" Janet's voice had brought her back to this place. "Nevermind - Ron says he found her." Gayle wasn't surprised when Janet just hung up.

Later she learned that Georgie had been in the emergency room and the doctor had planned to put in a stent. When he left the room to prepare, Georgie made up her mind to leave. The consensus was that there was no reason she could not have lived through this. Georgie had intentionally decided not to.

The Group Dream

Gayle fingered the envelope, scared to open it. The return address was from Fort Lee, NJ and bore the pyramid logo of Ron's group, Foundation. Ken had told her that the invites for Ron's Third Wave of initiate training had been sent out. Rocking on her porch glider, she finally tore the end of the envelope off. Scrawled across the top of her invitation were the words, "I am not sure that you should be a part of this, please call me."

She pondered when she should call and worried over it for a few days. While she enjoyed her graduate school classes, she needed to learn what to do with her talents, not just to academically be able to understand them. She didn't particularly like Ron, but Gayle couldn't forget that moment at the Atlanta workshop where the golden light had filled the room between them. She had been looking for a teacher and this one had shown up. While Shanta satisfied the inner need for quiet and mediation, he remained true to the teachings of Theravadan Buddhism. Gayle wanted to know everything. Ron's arrogance might just be enough for her to learn everything. She would give it a week trial.

"OK, good enough," she thought. "I'll call him."

"Hello?" Ron's voice was brusque and abrupt.

"Hi, you asked me to call you."

"Well, I don't have time for you right now. I'm in my laboratory. Call me back on Sunday."

Gayle was left with a dial tone in her ear. Ron was not making a better impression this time, but she was desperate. Gayle could barely admit that to herself. The sense of urgency permeated her dreams as well. She needed someone to help her use the intuitive gifts. In the meantime, she had academic classes to attend and a bookstore to run.

The intensity of the dream awakened Gayle in the middle of the night. She had been traveling down a well-worn path in an earthen packed tunnel. Her loose fitting robes and sandals were comfortable in the warm air. Two unknown people were walking with her. The sound of voices echoing up from ahead indicated that there were others on this path.

Finally as they rounded a turn the path opened up into a large circular cave-like room with sand on the floor and stars painted on the ceiling. A group of people, none known to her, were sitting around in a circle where Ron sat in the middle and taught. He looked up when she entered.

"Oh, you made it here."

Gayle took a seat as he indicated. When the teaching was done, she made her way outside. As she crested the rise, a huge bird swooped down brushing her head. She reached out her hand and the bird stopped as if it was a command. When Gayle called Ron on Sunday, the conversation was stilted until she mentioned the dream.

"Wait a minute. I'll read it to you." When she finished, Ron only said, "You're in."

Teachers

Gayle now was uncommitted with three totally different spiritual teachers. She had the former Buddhist monk as her academic professor, Samuel as the disembodied channeled teacher and now Ron as the founder of a modern day mystery school. Her simple request for a teacher a few years earlier had now been answered threefold. She would inevitably learn what was meant by "Be careful of what you ask for. You might get it."

The return to college was more of a struggle than she had initially anticipated. The lectures were fascinating and she was delighted with new insights and knowledge. Yet, the tests brought much anxiety. Realizing that the store seldom did business before noon, she changed the hours so that she had all of her mornings free.

The college town made her feel young again. She lost the extra pounds she'd been carrying and took renewed interest in music. Athens was a music town and the University of Georgia a party school. She wasn't eighteen, but she wasn't dead yet either. Customers began dropping in. However, it soon became clear to her that her customers weren't here just to buy, but they were here to talk to her.

Gayle began scheduling psychic arts classes–an idea she had carried with her from some spiritual friends in South Carolina. The religious conservative right in that area had not been suitable, but the vibe of Athens was. College towns were perpetually young – a constant influx of 18-22 year old students discovering the bright independent world. Never mind that some of them drove a new BMW or Lexus.

The Wednesday night energy circle became a favorite of the crowd who afterward left for the new bar around the corner. When she asked Little Andy, called that since his small stature differentiated him from six-footer Big Andy, why he came to the energy circles first he said, "This is the best free high I've ever gotten."

The energy in those circles had many different reactions. For some it was orgasmic, a sexual high without any physical touching; others found transcendent realms of awareness, and obviously some found them to be a great high. In Ron's seminar many people used the available higher energies in different ways. He encouraged the use of them to attain higher levels of awareness.

Gayle experimented with different shapes for the group energy exercises–whether it was a circle, square, triangle and whether she stood among the pattern or within it. She logged the reactions in her notebooks with strange lines and squiggles which encoded the energy without the casual observer knowing the intricacies of the high magic she was performing.

Somewhere Gayle had promised not to do magic in this lifetime. She never explored why; it was a simple promise to be kept. Yet when her two new friends, Jen and Cat, were at her door terrified by psychic attacks, Gayle had no issue with putting things right for them. She surrounded them with her own protective energy. Dark shaped energetic probes poked at her boundary, but were barely worthy of notice. Gayle showed the two how to face fear and not let it reinforce between them. With the visualization of using a mirror to reflect unwanted energy, she gave the couple some basic tools to use. Still, Jen and Cat spent the night in the guest bedroom.

The couple was part of a growing group numbering from twelve to fifty. The circles drew a diverse selection from people in the community, students, energy workers, and wannabes, those who wanted the power without the work. Gayle noted Sue and Michelle loved the high energy work, but usually didn't appreciate the ego work necessary to achieve that space on their own - perhaps because they both were in training for social work counselors. The enigmatic Julie who was so reserved on the outside connected to ecstasy. Computer geek Andy hated the nights she made them dance, but Claire enjoyed them.

Movement was Gayle's first language, her voice of expression. Angela loved those moments when they chanted. She, Michelle, and Chris enjoyed the shamanic journeys and drumming circles. Handsome Mark was a dental mold maker and both ambitious and precocious. Yvonne wasn't sure why she was there, but as long as it was helping people she was glad to serve. BJ was just happy to have found a tribe. Gayle culled the circles from all-time highs of fifty or more attendees down to a select twelve to fifteen.

Part of the training at Pathfinder Bookstore meant learning the discipline of staying with the group. The more talented students could easily soar to the ecstatic states by themselves; however they were encouraged to explore the level where the group identity was located. While teaching, Gayle could sense exactly where each students' identity was and what their thoughts, feelings, and actions were.

On this night, Mark used the group energy to launch himself to a new level. He was going for it. He was irresistibly drawn to the lure of the power without being aware that it was a two-edged sword. The group was always more important than the individual. Gayle let him go.

When the exercise was finished, most of the group got up and left. Yet, Mark lay on the floor on his pillow without making any effort to leave. BJ who often remained behind for a few moments of conversation asked, "What's with him?"

"I'm not sure he made it all the way back."

The two moved to where Mark lay. There was a stony countenance to his face. If he was breathing, then it was so shallow that neither of them could detect it. BJ, a former EMT, asked, "Should I start CPR?"

"No!" Gayle's voice was strong and determined. "He decided to go there. Let me see if he wants to come back."

Gayle never knew how she got to this place of knowing, but she trusted it implicitly. It was how she taught, how she healed, and how she guided her own life. There were very few times she made it to this place, but each time she did she recognized it as the place of all knowing.

She placed her hand on Mark's forehead and then placed the other one on his heart. Then she merged with him. She found that he had crossed that line-the line between life and death that shaman danced between. But Mark was no shaman. He was stuck there. Just as she had done years ago in talking down Deadheads from bad trips and metaphorical trees in alternate realities, she reached for Mark. He was a stubborn one, but she managed to bring him back to his body.

"He's breathing," BJ said unnecessarily.

"Open your eyes, Mark." When he responded, Gayle was further dismayed. These were the eyes of a mad man. There was no sanity. His experience had rendered him incapable to deal with the world where his body rested. While he may have been resurrected, he was now insane.

"We're not done." Gayle informed BJ who put her hands on Mark's ankles drawing him back into this body fully. Gayle would have prayed if she thought that would have helped. However, she knew that Mark had disconnected his ego and personality prematurely. She would need to make that link for him. Within her, she knew how to make that happen. Within seconds, Mark sat up and asked, "What happened?"

BJ and Gayle exchanged grins as Mark gathered his things. Mark never came back to the circle.

The Chair

Gayle settled into graduate school, but still found much anxiety about writing papers. Shanta, now her major professor, often told her to write how she spoke. However Gayle didn't feel comfortable with that. Her AT&T corporate career had given her confidence with speaking and dealing with people in groups. They had spent a lot of money for her to acquire them. Writing was caught up in what her expectations were and her inability to hold the information in her mind holistically. She struggled to hold all the information being downloaded into her brain from all directions.

The eight AM Buddhism class was more than boring this morning. Most of the class was asleep. She meditated into a quiet place, but felt more in a dream than participating in reality.

"Ms. Clayton, perhaps you would like to explain this next section."

Gayle jerked alert and saw Shanta looking directly at her. She was caught, but as she looked around the room Gayle noted that no one was paying attention. Shanta waved her up to the front of the class.

"OK, well, for me it is easier to demonstrate the concept of oneness than it is to read about it."

Gayle's voice was broadcasting loudly in the high ceiling third floor classroom.

"I'll need four volunteers." Gayle didn't wait on them, but called four to the front of the room.

"Can I borrow your chair?" She asked Shanta since his chair was the only one that didn't have a desk attached to it.

"Now," she said bravely, much more bravely than she felt, "We are going to do an old parlor trick of raising the chair up in the air with only our fingertips."

The students frowned, raised eyebrows, and widened their eyes with skepticism. She crooked her finger to Dean, the almost asleep football player sitting in the back of the room.

"You get to be our guinea pig and all you have to do is sit." Then she turned to the four she had selected for her small group.

"Here, just put the tips of your fingers under the seat." The students, now fully awake and more than ready for a shift in the teaching straight from the book, did as instructed.

"On the count of three, lift!"

"One."

"Two."

"Three!" The chair slid, but did not rise into the air as promised. The class laughed as the football player scrambled to not fall out onto the floor.

"Okay, then. That didn't work. Well, it seems that I forgot a step. We're going to try again, but this time I'll let you in on the secret." The students huddled together with Gayle and they put their arms around each other's shoulders. They kept their heads down low and listened to Gayle's whisper.

"We are one!" She put the emphasis on the ONE. "Let's remember to touch each other to connect as we do this."

"OK, again, on the count of three." Gayle announced as the students in silence surrounded the chair. They placed their fingers tips underneath the seat and allowed their bodies to touch as they shouldered in.

"Three!" The chair lifted straight up over a foot in the air despite Dean's weight. Then as the class broke into laughter, the focus was lost and the chair tipped to spill Dean. Her teaching was finished and as she passed Shanta on the way back to her seat, he whispered, "What did you tell them?"

"I told them that there is no separation. We are all one."

Chapter 4 – Introduction to the Dance

Ron's Biography

While Gayle had written the dates of the Third Wave of Ron's intensive training in her Day-Timer calendar, she received no further communication from Ron. A week out from the retreat, she called the number on the sheet for directions. The person on the phone seemed surprised she didn't know how to get to the lodge, but not at the disorganization of the event. His directions were full of landmarks, but not mileage or road signs. She would have to manage somehow. This was certainly not a corporate run event at the Marriott Marquis.

When the date arrived, Gayle headed out on the long drive alone. Driving was her music and reflection time. She put aside everyday concerns to live in her own world singing in the car. Truth was, it was the only place she sung freely.

The Black Mountains rose on the horizon and painted a deep purple accent for the roadway. As she turned off the interstate onto the two lane state road, she noted the rhododendron landscaped yards of the mountain cabins along the stone walled roads. The little resort mountain town was quaint. It had been an uneventful trip despite her worries. The landmarks had been obvious. When she passed through the stone arch to enter the college and retreat acreage, she could feel herself relax. The directions had gotten her this far.

She turned before the lake and made her way uphill on the winding road past the college bookstore and chapel. The yellow house was there on the left just as described. She passed it as directed and made two lefts to find the parking behind the house.

She was the first to arrive. No one had informed her of the time the training was to begin. She certainly hadn't wanted to call Ron to find out. He may have uninvited her or been rude to her again. She wasn't up for that. She was on her own here. When Ron arrived, he was brusque as he brought in supplies and equipment in from his car. He pointed out which room was hers and she rolled her bag down the hall.

The room was disappointing—equipped with two tired twin beds, a well-used end table between them and old style double hung windows. The comforters were faded and of a style that had long passed. There was no air conditioner, but there was a small electric radiator to heat the room when necessary. Calling it rustic would have been charitable.

The bathrooms were communal and an obvious addition to this old lodge. The carpet was well worn, the kitchen dilapidated with no dishwasher, and now she realized they would be doing chores during the week. She hadn't paid the balance of her tuition and at this point she wondered if she was going to stay. She hated the old lodge. Her rationale for the cost of the seminar was a budgeted $100 per day and if it had been a luxury hotel she would have felt it was a bargain.

Gradually people wandered in and they introduced themselves. Most of them were part of regional groups that supported weekend seminars with Ron. Many of the group were from Florida and the Northeast. The new arrivals were mostly women and a few of Ron's advanced group to "hold the energy."

As soon as Gayle could escape the small talk, she crossed the street to where she could hear a small brook tumbling over rocks on its way to the lake. The brush hid her from view from the lodge. She had a bad feeling about all this. Everyone else seemed to know someone. She felt alone.

Upon returning to the lodge, the living room furniture had been re-arranged into a semicircle facing the bay window, the catered dinner was served buffet style, and there was a milling about with an undertone of excitement tinged with anxiety.

After dinner the group assembled in the living room with Ron seated at the far end in the bay window alcove. An unlit candle rested on a plate in the center of the circle where a large greasy stain in the carpet spoke of previous candles of earlier circles. People assembled on the seedy spring-less couch, cushions on the floor or in a wooden rocking chair brought in from the lodge porch. Ron arranged and rearranged the cords on his tape recorder in ritualistic fashion. He adjusted his pillow on the floor for seating. Finally, he was ready to begin.

"I'm going to give you background of how this Bonclarken experiment came into being."

Janet had already informed her that these week-long intensives were called Bonclarken after the old inn where Ron had successfully formed his first group. Gayle had few expectations since the members of his working group had shared little about the training or his secret mystery school.

"I'm not opening the black hole until this evening." The candle remained unlit as Ron launched into his biography.

"About 10 years ago in 1983 or so, there was a compulsion inside of me. One that drove me to change everything: my career, my life, my car. I got a new wife; my wives go when they cannot take any more of me."

The group nervously laughed which broke the standing tension in the room. Ron was a bit surprised, but it shifted his obvious discomfort at the beginning. He was dressed in white cotton yoga style pants with a gray polo style shirt. He adjusted his white socks which had twisted around his feet. Stacked beside him were books and pages of notes where his reading glasses lay.

"Besides sharing such personal events, I will use an alternating pattern-one that ranges between excruciating biography and stuff that has a lot to do with specific teachings."

At this, Bob shifted position to lounge comfortably on the floor. He had worked with Ron from early on and had heard these stories many times.

"The prime reason for this Bonclarken experiment arose from a series of psychic workshops I had done around the country."

Ron had been the president of the Jersey Society of the Paranormal and the speaker at many of the Spiritual Frontiers Fellowship (SFF) conferences. Several of his early group had been handpicked from the SFF workshops in Pennsylvania or in Greensboro, North Carolina.

"The pressure and curiosity to do this increased significantly with a major medical emergency and life crisis at the North Carolina SFF conference hosted by a couple who are members of my working group."

Many glanced at Robert who was a member of this "Third Wave" training group. His wife Maria had been part of the earlier trainings.

"There were functions/ faculties inside of me that I knew were different. I had been a para-psychologist for many years. However, I was at the far end of what psychics did. Was I simply freakish or can what I do be taught? If it was a mild mutation and insignificant or a collective delusion, it would have no real meaning. I regarded these things as important but I wondered if it was part of human evolution? As I began to understand with the results of my first successful group, it had to be a part of humanity. Otherwise for me, a mere amusement would be a waste of time. There were other things I could do: canoe, cook, or when I like you a lot, I will sing for you."

The group laughed again having evidently heard him sing before. Gayle had attended a lot of conferences in her sales career. The rhythmic relationship between a speaker and the audience was quietly observed. Ron's expression was different now. Perhaps he was hitting his stride. The unique cadence of his speech pattern required her to pay closer attention to his words. She barely knew the man so in some small way his introduction was for her.

"Throughout my life, I have had a lot of sickly experiences and major death experiences-many, many shifts and changes throughout my life. In my twenties I was married and had two children. Yet I was compelled to put it all away. I separated from my wife. Some part of me was not being used. I painted, produced some off-Broadway theater, taught mountain climbing and raced cars. None of it was involved enough to satisfy me. Something was driving me."

Gayle related all too well to his story. Her own life paralleled the older man's. Her move to Greenville had set in motion a change of events that she was little prepared for. She was driven to understand infinity, Einstein's equation for energy and mass conversion, but more importantly was to understand her own psychic abilities and how to use them. Something was driving her spiritual quest as well. Ron continued his biography.

"Two catalytic events happened almost simultaneously: an emotional breakup with a deep and intimate companion and a rock climbing accident. Feeling rash and suicidal after this breakup, I got in a position in mountain climbing that I was unable to retreat. I had pushed too far and there was nowhere else to go. I had to let go. I contemplated the results of falling head first onto the boulders below. Things had not been going well. There had been freakish explosions in my chemical lab, I had been involved in car crashes, and now I was going to die from a fall while rock climbing. I let go."

Ron paused dramatically. He knew the power of storytelling and most everyone was holding their breath. While the ending was obvious, Ron's tale had brought them all into that moment. There was a suspension of logic and reasoning. Only Martin, Bob, and other long term members of Ron's working group Foundation seemed unaffected.

"Just before landing and falling on my head, I inexplicably did a somersault and landed feet first. I climbed out of Devils Kitchen in the Catskills on my own. My broken foot never stopped hurting, but it didn't matter. In overcoming the pain, I was opened to those levels of mind. When I returned to Manhattan, I gave up poetry, mystical writing, and painting."

Ron barely paused for breath as he revealed that he had never attended school as a child. He had been very sickly and not expected to live long. However, he had attended handicapped classes in high school. Only when he began college did he have to learn how to make a social life. Ron's list of activities after achieving some semblance of health was pages long. He laughingly admitted he had never worked as a short order cook, but there was still time.

"Then there was a rush of psycho-spiritual energy. I had no interest in anything other than strong predilection for science fiction. In those days, there was no easy access to magic. This was the 1950's before the New Age. There was no buying of crystals on street corners."

Ron talked without taking a break. There were no interruptions-just a steady flow of information. Ron described how culture shapes and controls the attributes of its inhabitants. Many years later he discovered the New Jersey parapsychology group and ultimately became its president. He investigated what later became known as the Amityville Horror out on Long Island. While Ron had urges to do something he couldn't verbalize, it also seemed to elude him. The childhood play with mystical states he had done while lying in bed as a sick boy were not as close or as easily available as before.

"In my late thirties, I made a statement of declaration to the universe to let it began now whether I am ready or not. Within two years, lots of things happened. I could control the energies that drive this work. Those energies were very real; I could control the weather, make wind blow, clouds part. I tell you this not to impress you with what I do, but to help you find coincidences and parallels in your own life."

Ron's monologue continued unabated. He described how traditionally all people are mystical at birth. Then as they grow into their own, they close down by five or six years old. The body then attempts to open the psychic centers again at puberty with the release of sexual hormones. The body as well as the mind is designed to seek a mystical state. Gayle wondered how he stored all this information as Ron seldom looked at his notes until he had thoroughly exhausted a topic. When he finally paused long enough to survey his audience, Ron advised a few.

"I don't mind if you take notes. However, as in the meditation or energy circles when you have to make a choice either to write something down or enter into the experience, choose to participate in the energy."

Gayle took no notes. It had never occurred to her to do so. Yet Marcia, an artist from Atlanta, took copious notes. There was a lot of information to absorb. Plus there was the advantage of Ron's recordings of the teaching that made note-taking seem superfluous.

The seating arrangement was not comfortable, but no one asked for breaks or moved. In fact, Gayle noticed that people were claiming positions. Ron returned to his biography with tales from his late thirties where he entered into a phase when energies that either were culturally or familiarly related to him opened. As he described traits of his party tricks that used energy to shift people's awareness, Gayle wondered how it felt natural to him. Yet in many ways, Ron was describing what she did, but she had always considered her own works to be imagination.

"When these natural abilities are repressed, pressure builds up. The cork for the container is the ego and conditioning," Ron continued. "There is a Greek story of a robber who waylaid travelers who passed by his abode. If the person actually fit into his bed without adjustment, they left the next morning with no knowledge of his intent. However, if a traveler was too tall for the bed, the hosteller cut off the feet so that the bed fit. If a person was too short, the host stretched them until they filled the length of the bed. The host made each of his victims fit his bed by either stretching them, doing nothing and sending them on their way or by cutting off their feet."

Gayle thought the story was a bit morbid as the rest of the group laughed. People did transform information to conform to their expectations just as the Greek hosteller did. She wondered if the group laughed due to Ron's expectation, or to fill the unaccustomed silence or whether they were just exercising a way to divert the monologue into a dialogue. She hoped that the entire week was not like this.

Ron explained that at puberty the physical body erupted when the contained psychic force was released along with the hormones. This type of psychic energy release was the driving energy of a poltergeist. Ron didn't detail his participation in the Amityville Horror investigation. He assumed most of the audience already knew the story and the charge or prestige of it was already gone.

"It was the 1960's and there was a lot of exploration, sharing, and revolution among the actors at a local party. I started talking about bio-energetics at one or two AM. The next thing I know people are reacting in the most peculiar ways. By the way, at that hour I am tired. That's when my intellect cuts out and I can do wild and crazy things. These people were going out of their minds. They would slide down the wall. They would explode in ecstasy and ask for more."

Bob snored softly on the floor. He had been with Ron the longest and he'd probably heard these tales or even been present during some of them. Janet and Larry nodded in fascination in seeming understanding. Meanwhile, Marcia just beamed at the man and kept taking notes. The rest looked a bit skeptical, but Gayle just kept her mind open about the tales. Doing was more important to her. She always enjoyed participating in sports more than watching them.

While Ron talked of his abilities to read minds, his interviews and features in magazines and on TV, Gayle listened with passing interest. So going public had not affected Ron's life in the way she had feared it would affect hers. Of course, he was from NYC while she was from the Deep South's Bible Belt where psychics, vampires, voodoo and ghosts were part of back alley conversations. A psychic's ability was the work of the devil so one must avoid all talk of it.

"...but it wasn't what I was after. I started doing workshops after a pivotal second death experience. After my first year at the southeastern branch of SFF workshops, I was put in a room without air conditioning. In the heat with my heart problems, by the way I have a heart murmur; I spent a restless night without sleep at 90F. Then next morning I considered asking to be taken to the hospital since I was so weak and out of it. Maria came along and asked her husband if she could put me in their air-conditioned bedroom. I rested maybe two hours. A talented gentleman named Joe Tucker encountered me and said, "You're very sick." Joe put his hands over my head and did something and in about 30 seconds to a minute I felt the pain leave me. But then he asked me, 'Do you know who you are?'"

Ron paused dramatically. His story telling style was engaging.

"He said something I have never repeated, 'OK, you get it next. You carry on now.' So even as I was groggy and out of it and most likely totally incoherent as a lecturer during my teaching session, the group was still impressed with what I was emitting as a person. However, I soon realized that I was totally out of control. Even months later, I couldn't pull myself back into psychological shape. Something weird was happening to me."

Gayle was amused that a man who said he could control the weather would describe anything as weird. Others in the group were paying close attention. This was new information to most of the Third Wave.

"In October, I was unable to go to sleep as I had this tearing and rending fight going on within me. Since I often use Scotch to fall asleep, here I was roaming around the apartment naked and with what turned out to be was some explosion within my psyche. I looked at the stained glass window depicting me with the wings of an eagle spread behind me. I looked at it as the rays of the rising sun shone in and collapsed on the floor. I cried 'Finish it. Take me, break me.'"

Ron paused with the emotions momentarily overcoming him. Considering he was giving his entire life history in a few hours, it was understandable. He took a sip of hot water flavored with lemon and honey, adjusted his socks, and pulled himself together to finish his biography.

"While in Switzerland on a business trip my mother died. When I got back, I had a good heart attack and went into recuperation. However, I was a different person. All I knew was I had to do this experiment. I had tried in Vermont, but it didn't work there. Then Barbara suggested that I try the group in Asheville. There was an intuitive, emotional, mental and intellectual knowing about what I was to do. However, I couldn't verbalize it."

Ron started his first group in the same way this new Third Wave was going to. The First Wave of teaching went on for three years or six sessions. There were releases of ego, personal insanity at times, spontaneous mystic eruptions, and lots of drama. Ron indicated there were always six to eight dynamics simultaneously in play. One woman in the First Wave, deciding this process was definitely not for her, left in the middle of the night and stuck him with the taxi bill. Yet Ron moved forward with the experiment.

"I had an intense nonverbal, invisible compulsion with no explanation. This force within my head could change the way you think and experience reality, enlighten you, and break fixed perceptions of reality. There is an absolute, but I doubt if it can be perceived by any individual. My mission was to prepare a group for the 1987 Harmonic Convergence. I had to know how much was teachable. A phenomenon of the process of enlightenment was at best a one to one situation. Certain unusual people found they could communicate it with an energetic transference and later beat into their students. Those who seek the mysteries are driven to know them. Don't give them away."

Gayle paid closer attention even though most had glazed-over eyes. She wasn't sure what enlightenment meant, but she knew it was for her. She felt it had to be experienced and simply telling someone about it didn't work. Besides, Gayle wasn't so sure the person who told her about being enlightened was actually enlightened or simply had an enormous ego.

Ron's own mystical experiences changed the entire motivation of his life. For members of this wave of trainees, he sought fewer with New Age interests or those who sought wild ecstatic dramas to play out. This Third Wave of training was a more grounded group. Gayle looked at the drowsy group in the warm afternoon heat snuggled together to experience something that they had no clue where it would take them. She would not label them brave, but perhaps caught up in the magnetism and charisma of Ron. He enticed them, but left them wanting.

Ron was obviously well read and had an amazing ability to retain information that he fed his groups in a holographic manner. No information was delivered in a linear fashion. One had to assemble a picture from the pieces.

Ron reminded them that they were in the middle of a paradigm shift as a new order approached. Tiellard de Chardin claimed the phenomenon had been isolated to certain few people. The phenomenon of consciousness and enlightenment was not a small part, but an evolutionary end to the process of being human. Ron reminded the group that they were in the middle of something that has far more in front than behind them.

Then as the lecture wore on, Ron dramatically stated that humanity was close to the end of evolution. Instead of enlightenment of a single mind, there would be an enlightenment of a collective group mind. This would be the normal state of affairs–bringing awareness to a group.

"I didn't care if a single individual achieved that state. In some degree the first group did achieve enlightenment. My premise remains that if you get involved deeply within this group, it would eventually happen to you."

Ron could teach something new in NYC and yet when he began to teach it in Tampa someone would tell him 'You've already taught that.' Some had attributed that phenomena as the hundredth monkey phenomena or Rupert Sheldrake's rats running mazes experiment. After a little while, rats in a new location would learn to run the maze much faster after others elsewhere had run it even if there had been no contact previously. They gleaned that information from a different interconnected realm generally perceived as collective consciousness. There was a long pause and Ron finally gave them a break before the evening energy work.

Bonclarken Work Begins

When they returned, the room had darkened and was much cooler. Ron seemed calmer and the general anxiety had dissipated. The moment had arrived. Ron told of people in his consultations springing up out of the woodwork with strange impressions and visions. His clients looked to him as some kind of authority figure. They also had memories of his having done something to them. Every one of those stories he admitted could be examined as nutcases, but they all had the same story. For this commonality, he had invited them to his first group.

Jane interrupted with loud nervous laughter, but the rest of the group sat with a sense of foreboding. The unspoken thought danced among them that they might be sharing a similar story that was not yet known. Gayle wondered who would be the person to undergo some strange release.

"A psychologist in attendance at the first group meeting believed crystals were buried in his head. At another point, middle-aged women suddenly turned into exotic temple dancers. Some people would speak in tongues while others attacked me with imaginary knives. It was all part of what turned out to be a single shared hallucination because as the week went on, almost all of the first group came with a story that was shared. That will come out tomorrow in the official teachings. This is just the prelude."

Ron chuckled to himself. Gayle felt he was stalling–waiting on some invisible sign to move things on or some new topic to emerge. Yet when he spoke on space-time she was totally absorbed. Finally she was getting some insight into Einstein's equations which had puzzled her for decades. Ron explained things she seemingly knew already in ways that brought fresh understanding.

"Psyche doesn't tell time at all. Collective unconsciousness and your hind-brain don't process things linearly. It simply knows; it contains. It is. Everything that has ever happened to you or anything ever seen as real is alive now in this moment. The universe lives in parallel frames. Everything is happening at once."

Ron was speaking faster and louder. His voice alone was charging the group to be more alert and alive. He admitted that what drove those first people to him was the 1987 Harmonic Convergence, but asked this group to forget what they may have heard about it. That was easy for Gayle; she had heard nothing about it other than the newscast that had long ago stimulated a desire to be a part of it in some way.

"The Harmonic Convergence was not a Mayan phenomenon, but a major astrological and astronomical event. These rhythms are causative to humanity and the force behind the first Bonclarken experiment. This group is not about that same story. We will begin soon with opening the energies that precipitate this group."

Ron, being stereotypical Italian, spoke expressively with his arms and body. He imbued passion into his words. In some ways, he mimicked an evangelist.

"You become a slave when your mind is owned. You are victimized by your expectations. You cannot escape, not your karma, but your destiny. However, once you accept your destiny, you can so alter their basic patterns in such a way that those who observe with intellect will comment you have gone far beyond what seemed possible for you. The universe and your development work in great spirals. Your task to go up and manifest whatever energy is up and down that spiral. You cannot overcome your destiny, but you can enlarge it."

The concepts of karma, enlightenment, destiny and freewill had no real meaning within the group yet. Intellectually the words had a meaning, but it was only superficial for most. They had discussed at break that the lecture was felt to have great meaning that they couldn't yet grasp. Yet, they were all fascinated by the enhanced feeling they had in the meeting. There was more than they had ever imagined in this reality. Someone was going to give them the keys if they could just get through this training. There was no magic pill to bring on enlightenment. Even if they didn't know what it was exactly, their souls desired it and had brought them to this gathering.

"There is no time imperative with this group. You will be working with building upon the foundation of the last group's achievements. You will share everything with everyone who is part of my group Foundation. It is bigger than me; it has become a living entity."

Ron barely paused to catch his breath before launching again. He seemed in a hurry to relieve himself of this burden.

"You are beginning a journey to uncovering repressed material to release energies for your use. This may be far duller and less exciting. There is only about half of the original group left. Many left because there was no more acting out, people screaming, talking in tongues, etc. What I am trying to do with a group is to enhance evolution. Human beings have the capacity to know magic-first for the body in the case of a shaman. We're going to do something-the activation of energy in which your body and your emotions are entangled. These will produce very dramatic events. Some people have started fires, disappeared, had car radios turn on by themselves, or channeled information. This is a training stage where energy repressed will be accessed. Eventually this will be done for all of humanity, but we don't have that kind of time. I'm taking you through a process that often requires lifetimes. You are following a path of creative energy with enough charge that you as individuals can't block. I will stop the hysteria if it happens. I want you to understand the mechanics that keep you civilized. Those energies can come under your control."

The group did not react to any of these pronouncements. Gayle wondered if she was the only one who questioned what she had gotten herself into. The group itself did not share fears or desires. A few introduced themselves on the porch during breaks, but they seemingly did not have much in common except for their encounter with Ron.

"I am a mystic-my reality is not bound by what my physical senses dictate to me. I set priorities as to which I experience–physical, emotional, intellectual. I am going to give you odd directions as we begin the rituals. Join into the experience. To understand what is compelling you and under the parameters developed here, I will control some of the releases. We're going to walk a tightrope–don't be destroyed by what is liberated. One third of you will never be the same, another third can be, and the last third must let down their very successful mechanisms. They have the most to lose by letting go. This is not about rolling around on the floor and having hysterics."

For the first time in years, Gayle craved a cigarette. Smoking was a coping mechanism that had given her time to digest foreign information before having to form a response.

"This is the warning on the cigarette pack in partial fulfillment of my obligation to whoever empowered me. A lot of the material we work with is a common ingredient in clinical schizophrenia. Schizophrenics do contain biochemical elements that promote schizophrenia. There is a spectrum of schizophrenia-from unfortunates that are institutionalized, to psychotics, and then neurotics. Are you ready for this? By the mid of week, half will hate me, and the others will think it might be a good idea to."

Ron talked non-stop. The group laughed nervously with identification of his stories. He described how the ego and persona is successful because it blocks a person from psychic input by placing limits to the input to narrow categories. It was part of Ron's plan to selectively break down those barriers.

"I hope I have been reasonably clever about picking you. No schizophrenia or insanity. Don't believe anything I or anyone else is telling you. Janet and Larry advised me on some of you people. There is possibility of breaking and becoming less, but also more than you were. I have been and continue to be wrong about a lot of things. I can be wrong here too, but I am good on my feet. I can quickly correct myself. A little energy work, a break, and then we will open officially."

There was a quick bathroom break, a raid on the kitchen, and small talk among themselves. Some approached Ron who was still seated to ask him a question in private. Sandi brought him a cup of hot water with lemon and honey for his voice. Ron rapped sharply three times on his meditation bowl to bring everyone back together.

"This particular concept we're about to undertake developed late in Bonclarken. My energetic motor has been cranking up this last week. It is my job to play games with you-to play games with your head. I tread a particular line. As far as I know, I will never lie to you. If you know how to ask me a proper question, I will give you an answer as to the energy appropriate to what is going on."

His tone had become more serious; his voice was slower and he calculated the group's reaction before continuing.

"I will carry out my task. Those who stay with this; you will become my peers. I will do things and they may cause you pain, but they will lead you to enlightenment. In bruising egos and uncovering repressed emotions, my goal is psycho-spiritual fusion and growth as priority over individual ego and pride. I have gone home and cried over how much pain I have caused. After all, my own ego wants to be loved and liked. I don't want it more, however, than I want to teach you. I will try to heal these things wherever I can. If I attack you, then you are ready for it. Others will need nurturing."

Gayle wondered if she had been introduced to some weird cult. She remembered the wanted rapist she once had unknowingly talked with over drinks in Oklahoma City. He too had the ability to fascinate her and obviously others. She had not sensed the danger signs regarding that man. Gayle seldom made the same mistakes twice. Wariness would be a part of this work.

"The advantage this group has is that I already know the experiment really does work. Twice. It worked differently, but twice it succeeded. There have been group enlightenments and mystical experiences. I have had saintly experiences. What has happened is that we have collectively explored dimensional material-not alternate realities, but enhanced dimensional experiences. This work is real; there are many people none of whom will ever get to this realm, who would rather watch vicariously what is shared on the screen like in the movie Flatliners. What I am talking about doesn't go away when you go home. It is liberation of blocked energy. Three since last August have described very accurately of what it feels to live in the past and the future. They are not losing their ability to function, but finding enhanced function in their lives. My group Foundation has access to genuine mystical experience which is not contemplating your naval, but enhancing your reality and your experience of it. Experience the gods or the architects. We have opened a reality that extends into fundamental reality- nothingness, being and presence-and gone beyond the level of intellect and mind."

Ron, noticing that the room had gotten dark, put his notes aside. The group waited expectantly.

The Opening Circle

"Alright, we're getting closer now for the opening circle. Patsy, prodigal daughter returned, light our candle ritualistically. This means to be quite serious and focused. This is one of the first teachings. Those of you with certain amount of awareness will notice that Patsy is waiting since the candle flame is not yet steady. She waits in great awareness until she is sure it was lit. Know when you must be here. Snore and nod when I am lecturing, however when there is energy, you must be here."

Gayle had listened to the gossip on the porch. Several of his original group members had left due to disagreements in style and behavior. The details were not provided, but she knew that Barbara, Jill and Patsy had left due to fundamental differences.

"Humanity has always wanted to be more than it was. At every stage of awareness, as passed down to us, it is clear; the bulk of humanity has lived as intelligent animals, except for those strange few. When you drink, kill, torture, or eat too much chocolate, make an effort to find a state of who and what you are. There is a search for not being what you normally are. The search begins when you want to be more than an animal. You may inhabit an animal body."

"Be willing to be a warrior; be like Castaneda to fight a losing battle. To be alive is to be a losing battle. Your death can occur within three seconds. You are constantly in the presence of death. Real warriors know the only way to survive the fight is to be willing to die. If you are a warrior, if you are in the search for transcendence you will know that an animal is born only to die. You cannot avoid death. You cannot win–the instant you are born, the instant you begin to die. This process is about to begin– recognize we are riding a rocket that doesn't have any future. It rises, peaks, and falls. If you cling to it, you are destroyed. If you can learn it all on the way up and someplace on the way up before it crashes back to earth, you realize you can transfer to something else."

Ron was pushing ego buttons everywhere. Gayle had done enough work through her sales training courses to recognize the procedure. He hadn't reached her yet.

"Just before death, they become something more. They are only mortal in the body. A warrior knows the harder it fights against death the more death will come looking for him. These forces have been identified. If they were come to be known, then it would ruin the chance for them to achieve what they seek. Open doors to forces that lead to knowing more than what is right to be known. Some call it the Eagle who seeks this energy and eats it."

Ron made many references to the seminal Castaneda works which had long gone out of the popular culture though they still remained in memory as significant catalysts. Many of the psychedelic movements were attributed to Castaneda's work. Ron seemed willing to push the group into a highly aware alert state. Gayle remembered the library book that stated that the fear of death was one of the founding principles of religious beliefs.

"The warrior wishes to die for a reason. The price is that the warrior has achieved something meaningful. What they want to do is overcome the barrier, that is, the battle between the unknown and the unknowable. They want to know as to overcome the mundane fate of being born, living and then dying. The warrior wants to know. If they know before they go, it would not have been a meaningless life. They gamble with it freely and go into the unknown."

"What I am about to do is formally and ritually state what is my intention and focus with us. When I do this I do it for myself as well. The warrior is ready to plunge into the unknown. At the end of this week only one of us will still be alive."

Gayle straightened her spine when she heard that. She already had met Death before. Her physical will to survive was stronger now. Even when depressed and at death's door, she waited for survival. If only one was going to survive, it was going to be her. Looking about the room she noted that no one else was reacting. Ah, he had finally reached her button.

"Now, if you want to know how it works, you are ready to take just about any step necessary. You might as well learn something for the price of your life. The metaphor I use is a black hole–something nameless opening up, devouring them and negating all they have been. My ritual opening is to create a black hole. I invite you to offer yourself to whatever it does. The energy will be real. It will ultimately lead you throughout your life. The person you are must die to become something more. This is your own transformation. Patsy, turn off lights, but leave the kitchen light on. Time to turn the tape off."

The First Ritual

Ron asked them to clear the room of all personal items and to move the chairs against the wall. Then he linked arms with those closest to him and indicated that everyone should do so to form a circle in the center of the room. Gayle hated all these feel good, touchy feely practices. The group formed a loose circle and listened to Ron's patter.

"When we link like this we are forming a braid of awareness. Wherever we touch the energy passes through the boundary of the body and to the next person. If we don't let go, and its proper ritual etiquette not to let go without permission, then the energy travels around the circle like this."

There was no reaction from the group so Ron informed them he would make it stronger. Ron's suggestion that they feel it coming in from the left and going out the right was powerful. Marcia who stood next to her reported that Gayle's right hand was hot. Gayle knew that she had the hot hands of a healer, but she still didn't trust that the process was real.

"So if I add energy like this," Ron moved his arms to the persons' waists next to him indicating that everyone should do likewise.

"See if this feels different."

Marcia's face was becoming red and beads of sweat were breaking out on her forehead. Jane broke circle to wipe her face and to remove her sweatshirt to stand in her t-shirt. There began a rhythmical swaying back and forth in the circle. For the first time, Gayle felt the energy coming back to her in her left hand.

"The left hand is for receiving while the right is for sending in many healing practices. We'll stay connected for a bit and be silent."

The group continued to sway even as their arms began to ache and they were physically exhausted. Yet Ron did not end the circle. After several minutes, Ron broke the silence.

"Stay with this for a few moments. Work to transcend your fatigue. The crack in the jar is where the light gets in."

Gayle felt the floor open beneath her like a trapdoor. There was a rapid sinking sensation followed by her head expanding into a mass of cloud-like energy. Momentarily she could not sense anything. There was a pool of dark that she seemingly had fallen into. There was nothing. Absolute nothing. No thought, no feeling, no sight. There was awareness, but of what Gayle had no idea. And finally after feeling underwater and about to drown, Gayle rose to the top and gasped for a breath. She took huge breaths of air and felt as if she had narrowly missed drowning. Her intuition knew this was what happened when Ron opened the black hole. Others in the group were also opening their eyes and looking about.

When Gayle glanced at Ron, he had what appeared as a golden halo encompassing his head. A few still had their eyes closed. A couple had slid to their knees as the group now swayed unevenly and no longer in harmony. When the ritual ended, Patty a friend of Janet's from Florida asked Gayle what she thought about it.

"Let me sleep on it." Patty seemed disappointed with the answer, but Gayle couldn't yet formulate an answer.

In her room Gayle pulled the covers back on the twin bed and opened the window in the stuffy little room. But Gayle could not sleep. Dreams and images kept her tossing and turning. In the middle of the night, she got up to draw a three-dimensional box in her notebook crafting equilateral triangles on each side. Below that was a circle with arrows pointing outward in all directions.

Chapter 5 – The Call of the Eagle

A Walk to the Edge

On Monday morning, Ron presented the agenda for the week. Evenings were reserved for the most intense energy work. He also enumerated a number of arts and skills being transferred to this group in four sessions what took six originally. Then Ron planned to blend this Third Wave group with Foundation, the advanced working group. Perhaps some of this wave could attend their meeting so that the groups would blend more rapidly.

Gayle expended a lot of energy to pay attention constantly during the concentrated lectures. Ron's agenda for the week's work would begin with the body using very old techniques such as how to do a power walk and the spiral work. Then he would use techniques for bringing energy into the circle. The job of the initiate was to coordinate perception to control and use innate energies. For the emotional work, there would be a technique called brain-mapping as well as a labyrinth walk. On Wednesday afternoon, Ron planned to make masks.

"A thousand years ago no one changed the expression on their faces. Masks were made to resemble the god since only gods felt emotions. Human beings did not. Humans could feel them inside, but had no expression of their emotions. We're going to make masks of our personalities. We will do some work with crystals. There is no final exam, at least not on paper. We definitely are going to enlarge your capacity."

At the morning break Nancy, a young slender woman from Florida, invited her for a walk. They took the uphill path away from the house. Gayle was out of shape, but they soon found a comfortable gait.

The path wound upward past the stream. The pair stopped momentarily to watch a leaf spin, circle in an eddy, and then float away.

"My perception is different since I've been here," Nancy offered. "It's like I can be one of the water particles and yet observe my path from here."

"For me, it's like a passage of time, you know, like when you take a timed exposure of the water." Gayle felt comfortable with Nancy. There was no need for inane small talk or attempts to fill up the long silence. Nature was their communication.

When they reached the fenced tennis court, they stood for a moment. Nancy idly swung the chain-linked fence door back and forth. Gayle went to the far side where the hillside dropped away sharply to reveal one of the Black Mountain's majesty. The mountains here were known as the Seven Sisters. Gayle could feel the updrafts that lifted the hawks far above the peaks. They circled in a ritualistic dance. Gayle could feel them. The moment she longed to join them, she lifted her arms and flew. She soared high above the peak and glided down to the valley. She let the breeze lift her back to the spiraling warm air. The village below looked quaint and small far below. The shoppers on the sidewalks had no meaning to her. She was free.

"The eagle!" Nancy shouted. And abruptly Gayle returned to her human consciousness and form.

Opening the Door to the Mysteries

There was a lot of sitting during the day as Ron talked. The man had a knack for speaking. Gayle had learned public speaking by doing daily lectures, but she was no match for this man's facility with words. She had not realized how lazy her mind had gotten over the years. The verbiage was college vocabulary and the concepts were at doctorate level. He had a way of dancing all around a subject, but never quite defining it.

On the next break, Gayle strolled by herself down the quaint college town's streets. She found a small park that held an adventure course. It was all the rage for corporations to send their sales teams out to experience the true meaning of team work by a ropes course, building exercises, or stream crossings. They had never meant much to her. She had a sales team that worked well together. Yet, here she had a new entry into the meaning of group work.

The materials that Ron presented were great exercises, but Gayle wasn't really interested in the words. It was the energy circle, transmissions and dream works that fascinated her. She wasn't sure what was happening to her was happening to others so she kept her mouth shut. No one was really sharing in this one-way directive workshop. Gayle seemed to be the only one here without a friend or acquaintance to hang out with. She was used to being alone for much of her life. Here was no different.

When she got back to the lodge, Janet came to collect the money Gayle owed for the balance of the course. Gayle intentionally had not paid in advance as she was not sure she would stay for the week. Her father was having heart surgery and that concerned her. However, when she mentioned that to Ron, he replied, "He will be fine. And you are not leaving."

His assurance about her father comforted her while the follow-up statement unnerved her. While Gayle appeared self-confident to others only she was aware of how much was a mask. "Fake it until you make it" had become a working motto for her. About the only time she could ever remember feeling secure was as a child around her paternal grandfather, a toddler being rocked by her mother, or as an adult traveling with DJ. Here there were no phones, no televisions, and no radios. There was nothing to distract them from the work at hand which seemed to be a direct confrontation of self. She resigned herself to staying.

Her body ached from sitting in the same position for hours. The standing circle also lasted to the brink of exhaustion. Still, when it was time she found a spot on the floor for the next sessions of lecture. Whatever it took for her to learn she would endure.

"Every time someone hears a truth and understands it, it can never be taught the same way again. You must constantly take the same material and return it into the common pile for other people to eat. One person's shit is another person's fertilizer."

The other primary business of this group was to try to teach transcendence – to go beyond the normal state. Ron believed individuals could transcend the state of being human. If they failed, the booby prize was to become enlightened. That he guaranteed. Ron explained how physical miracles overcame the natural laws of physics was easily done.

"It's simple once you understand. You can focus your identity into the physical layer. Or you can focus on the emotional and intellectual realms to be a genius. For some of you, if the focus goes higher, you may become an avatar or master or spiritual being. I will expose you to a spectrum of these things and you will gravitate to your natural level of being. It's hard to stick to a place as you learn."

The key words to Ron's introduction to the real work of the group were: melding into the other group, transcending personal ego, and producing a collective awareness that has been exposed to the spectrum of consciousness for human beings and others. The first group evidently was only interested in the excitement and drama of the tensions within the group. Ron promised to expose this group to the highest level ever recorded and beyond that. From there, he stated there would be a choice where reality lies.

From time to time Ron lapsed into a unique vocabulary that he established in his weekend workshops and Gayle didn't understand. She didn't get the inside jokes, didn't know the people, and was more interested in the material than the stories. To tell the truth, she was just too intellectually burned out to even care. He talked of this black hole and the use of the void to uncover the use of chaos and then to use it to lose all illusion. Then Ron broke his rhythm with stating how surprised the group would be at how much fear was held. Gayle's greatest fear was that she was going to be bored to death most of the time.

Ron's lecture rambled into the introduction to the mystery school material which he had intuited some years before. From the pile of books at his side, he pulled a book titled *Holy Blood, Holy Grail* that he claimed contained this same information that had been intuited by him. He then showed a book called *Genisis* whose cover thoroughly intrigued Gayle. On the front were two cherubim with wings formed into an arch to frame a woman sitting on the famed Ark of the Covenant. She recognized it from somewhere. She didn't know where, but since she owned a bookstore she would find it.

"So to finish out the menu for this week...you are your own tool and your own raw material – you are both. You are both body and mind. We're going to explore the different body types: endomorph, ectomorph, and mesomorph, Gurdjieff's classification of first, second, third, and fourth way people, and then point, spiral, and pattern."

The sound of the crow was a loud interjection into the room. Gayle turned and noted the raucous bird prancing on the porch in front of the open door. His head bobbed up and down. Gayle had always loved crows. She had a fond early childhood memory of sitting in the car parked outside of the liquor store where a huge plastic crow advertising Old Crow stood in the window. She had stood in the plowed fields of her grandfather's farm and imitated their caws. Crows were intelligent birds.

"You are nothing more than a wave." Ron's words drew her back from her reverie. "One last word of warning about the way I deliberately talk. Generally I will present three, four or five different things out of sequence. It is confusing because I won't tie it all together until the end. This overcomes the notion that once you understand it in a linear fashion you know it, because you don't. The mysteries must be grokked, known by gnosis – a nonverbal and internal awareness. You cannot know this stuff intellectually."

Gayle listened with interest as Ron described others' memories of having a UFO abduction experience where they were lying on a cold examination table while crystals were inserted into the middle of their forehead. Her memory flashed back to Whitley Strieber's *Communion* accounts and to her own hypnotic recall of being abducted. There were others like her.

As Ron described accounts of visions of white or squarish almost maze-like rooms, or a room with pillars or huge building seen from a distance, Gayle remembered the recurring dream of the oddly numbered rooms along the corridor and fear of being found out that she was there again. Patty had reported something similar in meditation earlier.

Ron recounted his initial mythic vision with his first group. According to Ron, myth is not fantasy or imagination; its importance is greater than the culture's ability to explain it. There are two fundamental myths–both containing human attributes for spirituality and immortality. Human seekers are looking for awareness or consciousness and generally neither had religious overtones.

Ron stood suddenly to stand with his arm moving through a small arc to find the right angle.

"The right angle is one that follows the natural angles of the formation of quartz crystals. When I find it, the energy gives me goose bumps."

Gayle felt her blood begin to tingle. Goose pimples formed on her arm. Her mind snapped to attention. She couldn't have moved if she had tried. She was fixated until Ron broke the angle and sat down again to check his notes.

"Brain-mapping just erupted in me. Certain residues would be felt in my head. Some of them began to form describable shapes. These have an historical past. I began to have an experience outside of my normal meditation space. I used to be able to imitate any kind of energy structure and take people with me to them."

Ron's whole being charged with energy. He stood straighter, his wrinkles relaxed, and his eyes lit up. He looked much younger than his late fifties chronological age. In his first experience with a working circle, Ron related that the whole circle begin to rise and separate from the internal body. It went up until it turned at a sharp right angle. This was impossible for him to explain.

"How could it rise up and turn at an angle? It was very eerie. Another circle, after enough brain-mapping, instead of seeing the bodies of the people I knew, I saw robes, undyed homespun, male feet in sandals, dusty and dirty. I was in a body and looking at all their feet. I was an invader. I lifted the focused intention of what this circle was." Ron's memory caused him to almost be shy momentarily. He dropped his head with a wry smile of amusement.

"They were to energize something over there–a rock-to make it easier to do something with, to build. I got out because I suddenly got a message and an understanding that they were talking to me there. I was taken aback with that. I was discovered within that group and so then made my way back. Only a short time had passed-maybe two minutes. They had asked me something like what's going on? Since I didn't know how to respond, I got out. Sort of like oh, excuse me, I didn't realize this was a private party. Time was moving at a different rate. This stuff began to unfold through a peculiar pattern of angles I could sense through my psyche."

Gayle wondered if she heard that right. The man was in someone else's body in a different space-time. No one else blinked an eye. Ron then continued with his agenda explaining that the work included experimenting with Castaneda's splitting into parts conventional reality. Moving the assemblage point occurred when bringing the split aspects back together. A nagual reassembled in a slightly different way. Ron's take was that reality was a dance and that initiates could restructure reality or move into another one.

"We'll play with assemblage points. You will find that parents, cultural and personal expectations hold them all together. You affect that place and it loosens up that structure. I was once inside a very large room with no in or no out. In this space or room were entities hanging in space-spindles of energy assembled in space. It had a feeling of an old fashioned gentleman's club. Here I pop up out of nowhere and heads turn. There I had visions of myself being in another place and playing with crystals. I had a knack for crystals."

Gayle remembered pretending in grammar school that she had special abilities to move objects since she came from another planet and was evidently dropped off here. Her childish fantasies led her to a place where she could observe this reality from a higher perspective while still participating in it. Later, as an artist's model she could stand motionless for long periods of time while she visited this alternative reality. She could relate to Ron's experiences; she never knew other people could do this.

"...I was busy doing things in a cave of some sort. This other personality I would go into allows me to continue making dragons, magical kingdoms, collecting energies and sending them out, almost every time I was doing the same boring tasks. Then I was in some weird room–some rock and dirt in the walls I was conducting a workshop with some funny crystals, fragments, lumps, and not clearly defined. On a tray of some kind, the crystals stood and I would adjust them. There were holes in the ceiling to let specific light hit the crystals. In Manhattan when I described this an actor in the room stated he knew where that was. He said that it was a fort or military base of some kind in northeast Georgia. He said that everywhere there was red clay."

After the lunch break, Ron did less lecture as he knew the human body's energy went into digestion and not intellect. People had difficulty focusing so he did some basic physical sensing exercises. Gayle was partnered with Jane and she allowed herself to sense her aura and assemblage point. When Ron came by, he adjusted her hand and Gayle felt an increased sensitivity within her own being.

"Find an identity that is not a reflection of others' expectations..."

There was a discussion going, but while Gayle could hear Ron talking she could make no sense of the words. This lasted for several minutes. When she glanced at Ron, he just smiled at her. Meanwhile, Marcia reported hearing clicking noises that were distracting as it came nearer and then moved away. Others joined in sharing that they too heard the strange clicking. Ron almost looked embarrassed.

"It's my signature sound. I have an artificial heart valve. When I am in my teaching space, it is detectable."

"Kind of like a bell on a cat's collar to warn prey of its approach?" Janet offered.

The group laughed, but Gayle still had wariness about this training and Ron's intentions. However, this was the first time she had found anyone who could explain the paranormal events in her life should he decide to.

The group stood in a circle and Ron asked for observations on the feelings about its balance. He had people suggest how to rearrange the components intuitively. Gayle observed how some used ego and intellect to adjust the composition of the circle. Yet, this finding balance was key to one of Ron's basic concepts to use the group to balance out individual strengths and weakness.

"I'm the conductor of this orchestra," Ron offered. "The whole is greater than the sum of the parts."

Gayle observed Ron throughout the lectures punching psychological buttons in everyone. She could feel when he connected with someone in addition to seeing their facial reactions. Now while standing arms around shoulders, there was a sense of unity. Ron continued his lecture in the standing circle.

"The nature of a crystal is holographic. The I-Ching is holographic and innately connected to the universe. Intellect is the most valuable tool humanity has created. Tools are specialized. You will remember it. Meanwhile Robert has assumptions about what I am doing, Will intellectually grinds through this, Marcia writes down everything I say and Gayle is reasonably concerned that this grind and this boredom are going to be worth the payoff."

Gayle didn't react to the comment. It didn't really affect her. Yet she was physically relieved to be able to break the circle to sit in their spaces. She wasn't a touchy-feely person. For some reason Ron encouraged people to let down their personal boundaries. When he quoted Ben Franklin's admonishment to "Fart proudly" as a result of all the beans they were served at meals, Gayle was appalled.

Ron's afternoon lecture droned on about body types and personality correlations. Ron used the example of a car salesman in learning to recognize body type and know the most efficient selling technique to successfully sell them a new vehicle. For the rounded, pleasure-driven endomorph, the way to sell would be to describe the comfortable ride; for the ectomorph, describe the engineering. Gayle tried to pay attention.

"William Sheldon was an American psychologist who observed and categorized a variety of human bodies. He defined the ectomorph as having small shoulders, a delicate lightly muscled body. The features are square and the face triangular. The lower jaw receded. The hair is fine, grows quickly and is often unruly. The mesomorph is the athletic hard body. For women, it is the hourglass shape while in men it is the rectangle shape. This is a muscular body usually with excellent posture. The features are well defined such as the cheekbones. The hair is heavy and the tanned skin is thick. The endomorph has a soft body and a round physique. Weight loss is difficult and the muscles are often undeveloped. The waist is high. The head is often large and the face broad. Gayle is an endomorph for example."

Gayle was horrified everyone was looking at her. OK, he had found one of her buttons. She was relieved when their gazes returned to Ron. She breathed a bit easier.

The teachings were new, but it was the manner that Ron presented them that intrigued Gayle. Many were basic principles she had known intuitively for some time, but it was the first time someone had given words to her knowing. The thoughts were put in some kind of construct that for some reason Ron seemed to be keeping from her. The hours of lecture since there was no dialogue were particularly tiring. She wasn't exactly bored, but she was far more interested in the energy work than the intellect.

The man continued describing the three types of people, and then used those characteristics to push the psychological buttons in different people. This set of comments had not yet reached her buttons. She had done an enormous amount of self-work when she transitioned from southern engineer to national sales manager in New York. Gayle was an enigma and stranger to Ron. Perhaps she should not have come after all.

She listened to the lecture on sacred geometry with wry amusement. Geometry, angles, triangles, and theorems - Gayle had learned to build conclusions on known facts. In fact, on some level Gayle knew she had once been a teacher in the Pythagorean School in some past life if such a thing existed.

"I'm not that gung ho on human beings; I'm gung ho on consciousness."

Gayle started paying attention again when Ron looked at her.

The Law of Three

Ron explained simple concepts in complicated ways. Yet, each lecture was building on the foundation he deemed necessary for this work. Gayle thought that there would be coursework or a well thought out presentation, but many times Ron switched subjects due to someone's question or comment. Today he had launched into geometry and dimensionality since Patty had spoken of her personal dichotomy to be a mother and a career person.

The first enclosed shape is the triangle which when translated into a three dimensional perspective became the pyramid. The pyramid was able to bring one and two dimensional energies into physical being. Ron emphasized that the fundamental rhythm appears to be three.

"If you master the three-ness, you can transcend that level. Good versus evil are in duality and you cannot escape them until you have a third. The third is an observer capable of seeing both extremes. The only place to be stable is to be at the point of balance. Just like a teeter-totter, it's not just a place of balance that is neutral, but it is a third place completely."

Gayle listened to nature of paradox with interest. She had always considered good and evil to be irreconcilable. The simplicity of her world had always been black or white with no shades of gray. Never had she considered that her judgment created the duality or the anxiety she felt when she could not categorize something. Ron was saying the value of relationships was to create duality. There could be no hot without cold, pleasure without pain, life without death and so on. Ron's lecture continued with the judgments people placed on either extreme.

"Morality depends on the circumstances; ethics do not. Pain/pleasure, life/death...you will learn the middle and that there is a trinity. You can escape duality from the center. When you understand the third thing, you are propelled into another level. When you can understand all three-the duality and the balance point and contain them within yourself at all times, there is no longer a triangular relationship. The flat triangle turns into a tetrahedron. You can resolve this by moving upward or downward. You are creating a new perspective. You are at a level that contains a transcended view of human perspective."

"But that extends to more than just human perspective..." Barbara suggested.

"Of course," Ron answered, "The transformation of the earth is done when the race transforms itself."

Splitting the Beam

Gayle wasn't sure if Ron's stories were for their enlightenment or for his enjoyment in recanting them. Certainly most of the group was fascinated by his adventures. He recounted the vision he had while he was teaching about healing.

"An image flashed into my mind as I stood at the lectern. Just as I taught about being in another person, this was me now standing in an entirely different realm. In front of me was a rounded crystal rock–sort of like it had been broken off a bowl. In a flash, maybe in two or three seconds, I remembered that I had looked for that crystal for years. This was rock crystal–rock crystal that I had put my own psyche into long ago. Around me, people in a semicircle were providing energy. I breathed this energy, focused it into my own brain, and connected to this crystal. In the next moment, I would then smash the crystal in half . The crystal would then become a tool, because like my brain, it was divided. All work is done by duality."

Gayle was intrigued by the relationship of light and crystals. Long ago when the first Star Wars film premiered with its holographic image of Princess Leia requesting help from Obi-Wan Kenobi, she and her husband spent many hours planning to make a hologram. The process required splitting a light beam so that part of it fell on the object and part on the recording medium. The two lights waves intersected and interfered with each other and then the interference pattern was encoded on film. When a light identical to the original illuminated the holographic pattern, the light field generated an image identical to the original scene. It was, however, a virtual image. Any portion of the hologram contained the information to recreate the whole. Nowadays, a form of holograms is on every credit card in her wallet.

Ron's lecture reverted to the teachings on duality. Duality, reality, visible/invisible and everything was a holographic whole. Every piece of a hologram contained the whole. Ron taught that men and woman are basically the same, but the difference between them created a charge of sexual energy that drives the universe.

"Get it right and it is sex magic. I was there to split this crystal and take half with me as an extension of my own brain. I was going to fit the broken fragment into the center of that Egyptian ankh necklace that I wore constantly for years."

Gayle remembered last evening's late night teaching on the ankh. Egyptologists called it the symbol of eternal life, but others called it the crux ansata or handled cross. The symbol was a cross with a circle at the top. Ron had described how this symbolized the union of male and female. The ability to procreate is a gift from the creator. At the end of the ritual Ron had whispered that she had a whole universe inside of her.

"There are certain implications: my group's uncovered myth revealed that crystals are inherently an extension of the human brain or the earth's equivalent brain. Quartz is the nervous system of the planet. The Chinese speak of the dragon or the power lines of the planet. Not all mountains are the spine of the dragon, but only those with quartz. A story in a North Carolina journal interviewed an Indian hunter. They visited a landslide off the face of the mountain that was made of quartz. There had once been a quartz bridge between the faces of the mountain. The people had shaped stone, but it was Plutatta, an old wise woman who had created the bridge."

Ron made no effort to link his change of topics or relate his concepts. Overall the net effect simply overpowered the intellect's ability to process the information. The group seldom discussed the lectures other than their inability to follow them. There were pieces that resonated, but any camaraderie came from the chores they did together or walks throughout the campus. Maybe they never expected to see each other again or the focus was simply on the teachings. People came and went, but the truth was eternal.

Releasing the Mythic Story

Ron talked of specialty crystals designed to let light in, but not out. Gayle knew exactly how that was done. She had been a supervisor of creating fiber optic cables by layering specific chemicals that would either reflect or refract light. The work with lasers, light, and transmission had paid her well over the years.

"You're talking about lasers and fiber optic cables, aren't you?" asked Dick rhetorically. Ron nodded.

"The angle of the crystal allows light to emerge or to contain as in a storage battery for a laser pistol or it could explode as in a photon explosion. There are ways to put stuff into crystals until the energy can be released."

Barb began a low moaning. She slowly slid down off her perch on the couch. Her hands began clawing at her third eye. She was in crisis of some kind. As her moans transformed into increasingly louder wails, Nancy also began wailing with eyes rolled back. She began thrashing on the floor. Jane took a quick look at both of them and began wailing in sympathy.

Ron quit lecturing and moved to Barbara who cowered at his close presence. With a wave of his hand over her face, Barbara began sobbing in fear or pain. Ron's focus remained fixed on her while the rest of the group simply sat in shocked silence. One could not tell from observation what exactly was transpiring.

Meanwhile Janet had moved to her friend Nancy's side and began dancing in strange movements to allow the energy to move through them both and release Nancy's own memory. Jane anxiously looked around to see if anyone was going to pay attention to her. She soon shut up when she realized she was ignored.

Then just as suddenly as it began it was all over. After a short break, Ron went back to lecturing on crystals and how energy was stored in them. His realization was that if you had nothing but a brain, you could still control an entire robotic body. From his memory as an Atlantean priest, Ron described a special movie screen made of light storage crystals that he learned to trigger with his eyes. This was a special process involving taking something internally and then projecting it with light emitting from this screen. You could draw pictures on these things and that world would open up.

Gayle's gut wrenched. The movie screen projectors in Avalon sounded all too similar to Ron's description. Could she be the one projecting those films from the depths of her consciousness? Did the light from her eyes create the realities she saw of the past lives with DJ?

"Dreams create reality. We don't always get things when we are ready for it–for example, nuclear power. We obtained it before our culture was wise enough to use it. Our scientists learned to store information in transistors, a mechanical kind of crystals. Crystals can have information embedded in their makeup: mechanically and psychically. Someone else can pick it up and extract it."

The Crystal Skull

Listening to Ron was like having the encyclopedia of the paranormal being read. He had an opportunity to sit with a crystal skull that belonged to Anna Mitchell. The skull was discovered in Central America, one of the emigrational directions of the Atlanteans. Gayle wondered how he acquired so many experiences. She would like to meditate with a crystal skull.

"Remember the feathered serpent? It has the nature of the highly evolved being, both serpent and bird, and is some shamanistic image. Assume there is a relationship between Egypt and Central America. The symbols are so similar–pharaoh and a sphinx, a total realized human being. Birds represent the spirit, remember? Both cultures built flat-topped pyramids with some distinctions; Egyptians sheathed the sides so they were no longer stepped."

Ron's brief digressions never took him so far off target so that he couldn't get back. He described how the Mitchell crystal skull had been found on a slope by the current owner's father. The native Indians did not know that it was there, but exclaimed at Mitchell's discovery that he had found one of the skulls. The crystal skull had extreme psychic potential. The skull was highly polished, human anatomically correct, but no one knew what they were used for. When Ron questioned the woman if she remembered any hints, Mitchell replied it was used in some form of ritual healing. Remembering back over sixty years, she recalled she had been told that when a wise old man was close to death, the people would have found a young boy and put the skulls between their heads. The crystal skull then would transfer that stored information into the boy's mind.

Gayle shook her head to try to clear all the thoughts and questions running through it. The man kept making connections in her brain that she simply couldn't put together at this time. Some memories were arising but it was like having someone's name on the tip of her tongue. It was just beyond reach.

"If you make a point in the center of what was Atlantis you will find us sitting in it. Right here in North Carolina was once the capital of one of the highest civilizations ever known. The people came across Egypt and Africa and then the migration circled down into Central American. Back to Egypt, it was an offshoot of other civilizations. The oldest temple, the temple of Dendera, was extremely complex and filled with information. The architecture of Egypt began to get simpler as time passed and was an indication that people were forgetting. The culture had totally degenerated by the time of the Ptolemaic kings and Cleopatra. Only a few maintained some of the old knowledge. When they left Atlantis, they went to Egypt."

They took a short break and then sat to meditate. There was no instruction and Gayle just sat and hoped to endure the time. She didn't expect the golden light to return and nothing much had ever happened again in other meditations with other teachers.

When the meditation bell rang for the sitting to commence, Gayle just drifted off. She found in her inner vision that she was across the street in the rhododendrons where she had explored the other day. She followed the stream down for a ways until she became aware she was not alone. There was a face in the underbrush. Something was watching her. She allowed her focus to move closer. The face was a bear. She looked again. Now it was a hawk. She looked again. It was a man. She looked again and it was gone.

"Bringgggggg...." the meditation bell's sound reverberated throughout the room. Ron was looking at her intently. "Does anyone want to share their experience?"

"I just felt so relaxed," Jane offered while nodding at everyone as to obtain their approval.

"Nothing for me," Marcia said and shrugged.

"Just quiet and dark until my cartoon characters soon began dancing through," said Dick.

Ron began staring at Gayle until the silence itself became uncomfortable. Finally she spoke up.

"I felt like I had crossed the street. And a face there kept changing into different things the more I looked at it." Ron smiled enigmatically.

"You were not dreaming. You were there. And not alone. However, you soon became fascinated and fixated on the changing face while I was off doing other things."

Gayle was puzzled. She was really there? This wasn't just her imagination? No one else in the group had anything to offer, so Ron went into his lecture mode.

"In Mesoamerica, the word Atl means water and homeland. Now it also means throwing stick- that which gives power to reach distances. Power–atl. There is a dominant animal every 2000 years or so, both astrological and cultural adaption. We are in the Age of the Fish. The symbol Jesus used was the Fish. Approximately 10,000 years ago it was the great Cave Bear. The European word for the Great Bear is Atli."

At Pathfinder, her friend Pat had run Gayle's astrological chart and explained the basic concepts to her. The precession of the equinoxes changed the signs and locations of the constellations as well as introducing the Ages. Due to the gradual shifting of Earth's axis of rotation, resembling a gyrating top, the poles trace cones in a cycle that takes approximately 26,000 years to complete. In that Great Year, each of the signs of the zodiac rules for over 2000 years. The Age of the Fish or Pisces would bring about universal trends on transcendence, spirituality, contact with other worlds, and mark a transition point where new directions emerge. The birthstone for Pisces was the amethyst, a quartz crystal with trace impurities which gave it the purple color.

"The Cherokee are unique in their search and use of quartz crystals. Caves of clay that grow crystals are a natural part of their lands. I once met a woman in an ashram who moved to their area. She found a humongous crystal, probably 18" tall in the dirt. Led by an Indian to the area, she said that the crystal called to her. She reported a strange compulsion. First, she believed this crystal was conscious. Then, she wanted to get some of it into her body. Ultimately she ended up feeding the bottom of the crystal with her menstrual blood."

Ron shrugged in the way he did when he was amused with his own cleverness. Gayle could recognize that there was more meaning there than explained, but had no clue. It seemed futile to ask questions as Ron managed to answer them without revealing the mysteries themselves.

"Crystals are filled with water that makes them hazy. When kept in the open, the water leaves. The crystal would suck up the blood. That is exactly what the Cherokee women told me later. The brave goes through the light to open the potential to become shaman. He finds a crystal and then must kill the bear. He puts the crystal under the slaughtered bear's liver. In essence he is extracting the energy from the power animal and stores into the crystal. This requires both spiritual power and charisma. Information is a palpable feeling–like anger, love."

Gayle's head was swimming yet she was not repulsed by this story. The bear had always been a symbol of healing power. In her shamanic journeys with Christy she had never encountered the bear. It had always been a bird such as the hawk and eagle. Yet, she had never heard of placing the crystal within the animal in any of her studies of Native American culture.

"There are extraordinary coincidences in the Atlantean diaspora. Atlantis submerged beneath the waves, people migrated to a number of places and something happened ten thousand years ago. Remember Julian Jaynes' concept of a bicameral mind? Intelligent beings were forced to become aware."

Ron appeared to be throwing random bits of information into the group. Gayle had not read Jaynes' book, but she knew it was recommended reading for Foundation. The primary myth underlying Ron's teaching appeared to be of an esoteric nature of sexual enlightenment, or crystals, or Atlanteans. There must be something that tied all this together, but Gayle couldn't figure it out. Wasn't that what teachers were for? To explain things?

"Why are men white and woman red? What a powerful combination that is. Why is a barber pole red and white? What is a barber pole but a maypole wrapped with bandages? An enormous amount of material is encoded. You just need the cornerstone. For me, some archetypal part came to consciousness and let me discover what I already knew."

Ron discussed the primary Atlantean myth of his Foundation group. There was a great god, in fact several of them. Atlas was the primordial Titan who supported the celestial sphere. He was also identified with the Atlas Mountains in northwest Africa. The Atlas Mountains were where the mystical teacher Gurdjieff uncovered his source of information. The Atlantic Ocean was named as the Sea of Atlas. Gayle was getting lost in the names. Others in the group had tuned out as well.

Atlas was the son of Lapetus, the Titan of mortal life and the Oceanid Asia. He was the son of a giant race and a patroness of the waters. After siding with the Titans against the Olympiads, Zeus condemned Atlas to stand at the western edge of the earth and keep the sky from reaching her in their primordial embrace. This same story was the basis of Egyptian mythology as well in that a separation was created between Earth and Sky. On the other hand, Plato says that the first king of Atlantis was named Atlas, but was the son of Poseidon and the mortal woman Cleito.

The Lord of the Oceans was Neptune or Poseidon whose symbol of his power was a horse. His symbol was the trident. Ron explained that there was no such thing as a singular meaning. There were always multi-layered meanings. He considered puns to be the highest form of expression. Words disappeared into power. Words shaped and changed reality.

"Poseidon dwelt beneath the ocean as a fish-like god. The sons of Poseidon did not live beneath the ocean. They could breed with human beings. The sons of gods found the daughters of men exceedingly fair."

Gayle knew that passage from the Bible since it had always troubled her. What gods? What daughters? How did this relate to the creation story of Adam and Eve? Of course she had learned that there were actually two creation stories in Genesis which was confusing enough. In one version the pair was made as equals from the dust of the earth. In another, Eve was formed from Adam's rib. Then in Judaism she learned of Lilith who was Adam's first partner who refused to lie beneath him. There was no need to ask a question since Ron just ignored her.

Ron introduced the concept of Pangaea that theorized that the continents were all once part of one huge land mass. By examining the bulge of West Africa and the indentation of the Caribbean, he suggested they matched perfectly. There was once a single land mass that came apart. The continents were pieces of a continental jigsaw puzzle spread out over the oceans. When reassembled, the line of the Atlas Mountains was contiguous with the Appalachian Mountains. It was once a single mountain chain.

Gayle jumped ahead to surmise that he was going to describe the legend of Atlantis which supposedly sunk in a night and a day. Years ago her mother had been fascinated by those stories. Gayle was surprised to find that the topic had arisen again after decades.

Ron explained how the inhabitants of Atl had a specialized culture-they were not gods, but the direct descendants of gods. Their particular tasks were to teach the natives esoteric skills and to perform some modifications to the native species. Evidently there was maintenance to be done to the underground vessels where cell tissue was grown. Memories from his group included being inside a domed building, or inside a deep well where as one descended one found places where experiments with human tissue growth were done. This tissue was not grown in the tanks, but involved growing human flesh.

Then the topic switched suddenly to the Temple of Solomon where according to Rosicrucian teachings and the Knights Templar, it was designed and manufactured by Hiram, descendent of Tubal Cain also known as the ibis-headed teacher Thoth of Egypt. Thoth was the spiritual father of Hermes, Merlin, and of course the more modern Dr. Frankenstein. Ron's theory was that there exists within humanity the myth of creating a superior human being out of bits and pieces of dead flesh. Frankenstein was an android, not a robot, but made of flesh and animated by some dark evil practice.

"The memory of items being inserted in the forehead also surfaces in other traditions. Tibetan Buddhist monks would take a bone needle whose tip was shaped into a point and at the third eye, reach inside and tickle the underlying area to produce an enhanced consciousness. Genetic experimentation has always been a part of humanity's past. Stimulation of consciousness could be done by producing strange sounds, or manipulating your body in strange ways or in temple dances. Gurdjieff taught little dances and specific positions for the body. All he knew was learned by finding a little temple in the Ural Mountains whose whole mission was to keep alive a body of knowledge. There Gurdjieff saw a tree with jewels on it. The branches of the tree could be moved into angles. People simulating these positions had their consciousness altered immediately."

Gayle's brain seemed to give up when Ron began talking of initiations that some secret societies required. She was revolted when Ron talked of initiates having to kiss the anus of cat. Other than testing one's ability to follow directives, she saw no purpose of this. The intrigue of Robert Anton Wilson's *The Illuminatus Trilogy* had fascinated her with bits and pieces of esoteric knowledge linked to a barely coherent story of sexual intrigue. She was grateful for a break.

Chapter 6 – Meditations and Energy

Meditation and Energy Circle Instruction

Ron's meditation every morning established a stable reliable pattern for the group. There was no talking or food allowed before first meditation sitting. Gayle almost always arrived first in the living room and sat directly across from Ron's seat in the circle. While the car wreck many years ago directed her to sit where she did not have to turn her head constantly, Gayle's place was also as far away from Ron as possible.

She sat in silence, eyes closed, and felt the energy of every person as they joined the circle and found a comfortable position. Then as an overwhelming energy filled the room, she opened her eyes enough to see that it was Ron. He was quite different in the mornings. His movements were slow and aware. His voice was deeper and slower. She much preferred the meditation teacher over the glib lecturer.

Ron spoke very little in giving instructions for meditation. Much of the style developed in the discussions that followed afterward. He had always had the ability to bring people into his own space to share the experience. Over time, he had established a meditation style that correlated to the mental states. He equated his named stages in the same way that Eskimos had various words for different types of snow. While the average person used one word for snow, for those who were more acquainted with the subtler distinctions in the types of snows there were descriptive words for each type. While Ron described many degrees of meditation, he used many different disciplines to invoke a particular awareness. He said that meditation was a change of a state of mind.

"Some meditate to find a place that feels very good because you have stopped thinking. Or the muscle tension lets go and endorphins release. Others meditate because it changes the awareness of space in the head. If you close your eyes and defocus or you feel a purple space inside your head that is either filled with your own processing or churning with voices and or a visible blackness with flashes of color, you continue since meditation attempts to get one to a state where these activities cease and you are aware of an empty presence. The visual sense is graininess that is either silvery gray or silvery blue. When you are aware of your breathing, you simply link to your body process. You can be aware of a change just as when you are hungry and you eat and give your body more vigor."

Ron's voice was soothing and somewhat hypnotic. He led the group into perceiving distinctions between tension and presence of energy. He described a kinesthetic feeling of more or less sense of life presence. His progress led them through in stages although some zoomed by. Gayle felt her awareness first as a small ball inside of herself, then expanding to envelope the body and the room itself.

"The classical progression is to achieve awareness without content while you spread into this wordless sensing of space. Another factor will be energy which is sort of like tuning a radio. Your awareness shifts from physical awareness, still there, but less contact. You can become aware of becoming aware. You may feel the rising by leaving the physical/sensual input and going to simple processing of mental circuit. You may become aware of a spot of light that may change size or a sound/hum/vibration or a floating or lifting sensation or a non-auditory voice or shifting colors."

Gayle considered most of this boring. In fact, she knew she could just go to that place without paying attention to the minute stages Ron referred to. At the same time, she had a choice of either being bored silly or by paying attention and seeking to understand his point to the process. Her resistance to participation in busy work was overcome by her fear of complete boredom. Ron was still talking during the meditation.

"...breaking ordinary process. You may become aware of being aware. My advice is to make that space as empty and clear as possible. You can use a Yogi approach by focusing on the light of a candle, or the tip of your nose, or a sound such as this guttural ringing sound. You can focus on an odor or a pattern like a mantra or name. Or an image of a godlike being. If you have difficulty with that, you can do Zen that is to not focus; instead you ignore everything without trying to exclude it. Your mind notices, but you do not attach to it."

Gayle began to hope this was going to end soon. Her back hurt. She looked at the rest of group from under her eyelashes. Some seemed to be sleeping; some seemed to be in bliss; and others appeared to be faking it just like she was. Ron continued on.

"Circle energy in this room by allowing the energy to pass through the people on either side of you. Focus on your breathing. You can breathe in different patterns: circular, triangle and square breathing. One last thing before we finish, there is a variance on Zen and yogic breathing. When the mind is filled with stuff, don't fight it, watch it, and back away from it. No matter how busy it is, noticing it will separate you from the busyness. There is a place where you can retreat to. By leaving a trail behind you, you keep moving into a calmer and emptier space. Then you shift."

Ron let them meditate in silence for fifteen to twenty minutes. When he rang the bell, people were grateful to shift positions, stretch, and think. Yet, he made it clear this was only a small break to give additional instructions.

"There is a dynamic after overcoming the initial stages of emptying the mind. You are trying to pull a lot of energy in without thinking. If you are calm or on the verge of sleep, you stop thinking. It is a paradox of being awake without the activity. You listen to the sound of this bell as it ripples out into the room. The sound dominates so much you cannot process words. Imagine a visual component such as a shimmering sound going out into the room and echoing back. Listen to the note. It pulls you from where you were drifting. It will hold you in a central place. It is artificial, but it brings focus. Trying to be tremendously awake and alert without thought or words. Let's try this first."

They meditated again for over twenty minutes. Their own fatigue, lack of caffeine, and hunger stimulated Ron to let them break for breakfast. A few ran to the showers while others mixed and mingled while coffee brewed and cereals came out on the counter. The little kitchen was crowded.

Despite the coolness of the morning, Gayle slipped out the door onto the front porch. In doing so, she surprised Ron who evidently had the same desire for a few minutes alone. Gayle went to the opposite side of the porch and settled in a rocker. The two didn't speak. Gayle was beginning to accept this as normal between them. Even though others seemed to easily converse with Ron, he tended to blow her pointed questions off. Gayle wasn't sure how to overcome this, but for now she was content to just sit in silence. She pondered why she had the same relationship with Shanta.

When the group reconvened in the little living room, Gayle found her place had been taken. She moved to the wall where she leaned with Robert against an extra table there. She liked the quiet older man. Ron's intellect had kicked in and after fiddling for several minutes with his recorder and microphone cords, he began.

"What I want to cover this morning is a complex concept intertwining your understanding of your own growth in progress as well as the race. This concept is popularized in the idea of chaos theory combined with holography. Holography implies a real organic system that is replicated throughout the universe. Chaos theory is a way of understanding chaotic physical conditions. The falling of water from a faucet can be smooth or turbulent, called chaotic. I'll speak of it later as well as the difference between self, other and fear, darkness light and chaos. We will learn to process energies. Barbara processed something physical last night. Portions of your mind tell you what is real or not, evil, dark, strange or chaotic. You must treat what you are encountering differently. If you can overcome fear, nothing is evil. Chaos is a great source of panic and a great tool for an initiate."

Ron hit the ground running with his lecture and was gaining speed. Gayle wasn't sure whether he was working in vain in an attempt to catch the new group up with the more advanced Foundation or whether he was afraid that to sit in silence would change the experiment. The material unfolded. Initiation and the various ways it could be accomplished only served one purpose– to introduce a new perspective or awareness. To date in Ron's own accounts, his use of ritual was short, quick and effective. He never allowed the intellect time to set up expectations.

Ron stated that ritual was used to transcend a triad, a unit of human reality. He reminded this diverse group that they had arrived with cultural conditioning such as the distinctions noted in the South, Deep South, far, near, rest of the world, etc. One truly transcends through an initiation when defined as overseen by someone or some force that oversees the process. Gayle guessed that Ron was the overseer.

All initiation was based on overcoming a fear. For example, the human body had one basic fear–fear of death. Whether that death comes about by being sealed in a cave, given a cup of poison, forced into swimming underwater paths while intoxicated or being subjected to a fire furnace, it was a set up where strong healthy persons survived if they didn't give in to fear. Those who set these rites assumed people would pass. It usually was not a set up to fail them. Emotion and mental initiation required abandoning the fear-fear of insanity, disfigurement, surgery, and being dysfunctional.

The eventual goal of all initiation was to reach holographic thinking. As an observer, Ron watched all this process, materialize and interact. Fear was the key to limitation. Initiation was the catalyst to move from one reality to another. Basically, the enlightened individual operated in a rhythm of life.

The Triad System

Ron's teaching system often required a new vocabulary and the abandonment of ideas or systems that were static or known. He suggested leaving the ideas of chakras behind in order to mesh with a more universal system. While Gayle had learned of the Hindu system defining energy centers and pathways of the body through the Theosophical material she had studied, she found Ron's take to give her deeper perspective.

"The chakra system at the most fundamental level is involved with awareness at the base of the spine between the excretory and reproduction system. Like when stepping on a nail, you get a body reaction of a contraction at the perineum area. That is the first chakra. Not at the coccyx. The second chakra encompasses the reproductive system while the third organizes the products of reproduction. This is the first triad where there is motion. From basic physics, motion implies the ability to do work. Flesh is the raw ingredient."

"You exist emotionally at the second triad. You reproduce yourself, and then you organize. Verbalness is its display. You learn to communicate sexually. Emotional expression can be beauty as well. While Ken spoke earlier today in the language of science, the beauty and charm came through anyway. Examine the mathematics for symmetry and beauty. If you have verbal communication, you are multiplying the essence of the person who speaks. Instead of naked kids running around the farm, you have a team. These can be used to enhance that triad."

As Ron expounded on the three-ness of his organization of the universe, the group settled into familiar note taking styles or lounging listening positions.

"The third triad begins with awareness of subtle energies that have nothing to do with intellect or emotions. This can be considered equivalent between the third and fourth chakras. The eighth chakra is initiation. Here is created more of the initial fundamental unit in an awareness above feeling and intellect."

Ron barely paused to catch his breath. On some level he seemed oblivious to his audience and yet on a deeper level, he seemed to be intimately in tune with each one. His topics stimulated different people at different times. It reminded Gayle of the old variety act on the Ed Sullivan show of a man spinning plates on sticks who ran down the line from one to another to keep them all in play.

"At the beginning of the first triad, one says "I." At the second triad and fourth chakra, one says "We." Empathy requires at a minimum of two. Emotion must be shared. At the third triad, there must be more than two."

Ron's obscure facts wove threads into a fabric of mystery to drape around their shoulders. The group had no idea what it meant, but knew it was important. Ron explained how the aborigines count by one, two, and many. Initiation creates more. It is the second part of duplicating the self.

"What could there be without content and fleshy body, but requires that much before it is organized in the third triad?"

"Consciousness?" Dick asked.

"No, it is the fundamental ground." Ron was a bit taken aback by someone attempting to answer his rhetorical questions. It was hard to tell when Ron was pausing to catch his breath or was waiting for a question or even an answer. His speech pattern was like a carrier wave. There was the shift in tone and cadence, the rhythm, the silence, pauses, that lent more meaning behind the words themselves.

"The society and culture is first and second triad. You got it, Dick, but you haven't gotten it into the correct category–an archetype that is made up of qualitative essence that doesn't exist in emotion and flesh. It flavors the fleshy body with characteristics. It loses its identity as it descends. Archetype is a Greek word. Psychologist Carl Jung used it, but not in the way I used it."

"The progression of humanity is of an ever-increasing substance. It rises from individual quanta of energy and combines to form an atom, particle and so on until it forms organs, a body, society, culture, and an archetype. You may say an archetype has no body, but neither does emotion or thought. There is no body on the second triad, but we know it is real. This is the threshold between matter and spirit. Not just a couple; the smallest unit is two. The smallest unit of the third triad is enough to form a group where only by symbol can you count the number. The group leads to the archetypal unit, the building blocks which create a single living entity."

"I'm now sensing the first chakra where I couldn't before," Jane interjected.

"Fortunately the sensations of the first chakra are easily sensed when you accept your body. The second chakra is for making something–not a sex act. The second chakra is the mode of creating from raw material. Feel the sense of the rightness of that statement. Sexual tantra is a form of sexual activity that has little or no use of genitals. Tantra produces much energy above the pubic bone and below the belly button. A warm radiant energy that streams out all over the body."

Gayle realized that her level of awareness had dropped. Ron had given them several techniques to generate chi in the body. She remembered what he called the sacral pump, but she knew it better as the Kegel exercises. Dr. Arnold Kegel had developed pelvic floor exercises that involved repeatedly contracting and relaxing the muscles that controlled the flow of urine. The exercise was pleasurable and like the millions of women who used the pedal sewing machines in the clothing factories to achieve orgasm, it could be done without anyone noticing. Ron gave her a slight nod when she reached a state of increased alertness.

"Very few people ever get to use the third chakra. When you are successful in pulling together a group of people and create the sensation of pleasure, the center is in the solar plexus. Everyone is functioning together. As you rise up the spectrum within a triad, the sensations become subtler and subtler. When the goddess met the men at the close of the 1987 ritual, I invoked pure third chakra energy and put it into the men of the group. Bob felt the infusion of something he was in much need of-an identity from a high masculine source. Maleness includes organization. Remember in standing circle to generate pure solar plexus energy."

Ron had no compunction at using his students as teaching illustrations. He built on their stories and experiences. He went on to explain the significance of the number twelve as it was related to three. Twelve was a very special number and in theory the ideal number to produce an archetypal presence. Twelve was also the proper number of covens, quorums, and disciples.

"The concept is that one of the parallel precipices of this Bonclarken experiment is to introduce this group to the third triad. One speaks of a mystic who begins to function as one who requires a less physical and more of an energetic interaction with the world. An avatar or a master is someone whose consciousness is active in the third triad. It is possible for a human being to change their consciousness so they are primarily an archetypal identity, but it requires more than one body to operate."

"Poseidon's twelve!" Nancy spoke up in the group for the first time.

"Poseidon and Cleito had five sets of male twins-a twelve." Ron beamed broadly. "All mythic beings are archetypes. Although the lines blur because writers seldom know the principles. The archetypal level existed and is not a creation of the human mind. I'm describing what I know about it. Numbers are the same thing. It is that kind of patterning."

Early numerical systems involved tally marks on bones and artifacts for counting. There was no placeholder value on the marks, only a one to one correlation. The ancient Sumerians had used a base 60 system while the Egyptians were seemingly the first to use a base 10 system. Gayle loved mathematics as they gave clear, direct answers. There were no shades of gray in mathematics, unlike philosophy and mystery schools.

"There are a couple of things you should be able to produce–our purpose is to form the body of an archetype. Who will it belong to? To that which Bob has labeled the signature energy of the group. Break down the barriers of your bodies so that you could feel that everybody was an extension of yourself. Yet you should not feel like you are being invaded. That is the condition or mental patterning of the simplest kind of archetypal being. I inhabit many bodies. This is the primary existence of this group. Such bodies have been built twice before and then merged together. Culture is a group of bodies. Society is a blend of attitudes."

Ron then ran down a time line dating back 26,000 years. The half mark was the Atlantean or Sumerian civilization. One third down was the Chinese and Indian cultures. Down from that one encountered Greece. Ron jumped to his feet to the easel equipped with notepad. He flipped back to illustrations he had already used having saved them for just such times. He found a crudely drawn earth with approximate times pointing to the various civilizations.

"All over the globe–contributing to a global awareness-there is a migration of consciousness. We are a wave. At the material level, at the cultural, archetypal contains all the levels below that, but is bounded by collective non-specific spiritual, mystical or religions. Reality is as clearly defined and as operable as the world of music, food, automobiles. I know, because I have been there. There is a fourth triad, and presumably a fifth. Hold on to that."

In his enthusiasm Ron had forgotten his audience who were no longer capable of following what he was presenting. When he remembered, he summarized before promising them a break. The mention of a break was enough to summon enough group energy for him to finish.

"The first Bonclarken group is functional in the third triad level. I can vouch for collective and some individuals who became enlightened. There is a rhythm on the globe of the same pattern. The only concrete realities are frozen in a cross-section of time and space. All reality is a current, blending and passing through itself. My own level perception is that everything happens at once. There is no beginning and no end, but it is a spiral moving in all directions in spacial and temporal directions."

Patty and China

This was going to be a long break. People had been sitting too long, cramped up in uncomfortable chairs or on the floor. Their heads were full and their eyes glazed over. As Gayle headed down the bleak hallway to her room, Patty called out to her.

"Hey, got a minute? I want to show you something."

Gayle walked into the room and she never saw what it was that Patty was holding in her hand. All she could see was the Great Wall in China. Finally when there was a break in the conversation, Gayle got brave enough to ask her.

"Are you going to China?" Patty looked startled but quickly regained composure to share her plans.

"I'm not sure. Rich and I are looking to adopt a child. We've just started considering adopting a girl from China."

"Well, don't worry. You will go to China." Gayle left the room before Patty could ask any more questions.

Point, Spiral, Pattern

The afternoon lecture built on the morning's topics. The holographic presentation wove back and forth along similar concepts on many topics. Now he was building on the fundamental rhythm of all life-point, spiral, and pattern.

The teachings followed the common precept of telling the audience what he was going to talk about, talk about it, and then tell them what he talked about. When she saw it written out on the easel it seemed pretty simple. However, she now knew that Ron would explore the subtleties of the topic and expose her to new perspectives. The simple could be very complex.

"A point comes into being as only and identity. The "I AM" is a point. Castaneda called it the rolling force or if ready a point to transcend the Eagle. No sooner do you claim an identity than a force arises to oppose or destroy it. Eventually you consume yourself because there is no other food. When death is there, relax and enjoy it."

Ron seemed to have a preoccupation with death. His version of the modern mystery school also contained near-death ritual experiences such as the black hole that brought one to clarity. There were times the group was anxious and nervous and times they faced something new and were temporarily transcendent.

"When you are food for the Eagle you are in the grip of something that is going to consume you. The Eagle may leave the mud of the earth and reach the heavens. If you are an old magician, you hold on against the inevitable. If you are a new magician, you court the Eagle. You whistle and ask the Eagle if he is hungry. In modern times, it is called looking for a teacher."

The refrain of looking for a teacher reminded Gayle of her long search for a spiritual mentor. She had no clue what working with one would be like. Perhaps it was best; had she known it would mean having her questions ignored, she would not have come. Ron answered other people's questions, but he sidestepped all of hers. Gayle thought he took a bit too much joy in doing so. Still, she wanted to understand what her abilities were and what their purpose was. She would hang in there a bit longer.

Ron explained how everything comes into existence by beginning as a conscious point. Then the universe supplies the energy of sexuality, duality and dynamism. As Don Juan explained the eagle is not really an eagle, but a huge hovering energy waiting above. It was always a helix or a spiral. All process in the universe was a helix. Nothing moves in a straight line except light which is not in this dimension. When the helix encounters the point, it multiplies the point to where it appears as death by losing personal identity or its uniqueness. The fundamental flaw in ego which isolates a person produces uniqueness. Ego is a paradox.

"A statement of fact is a thing. A concept is partially processed. It evolved in such a way to change reality. Paradox is a change in a concept combination which appears to be impossible or contradictory. Every time you find paradox you have find a step on a ladder to higher perception. If you have relationship, if you let go it comes back to you. You must grasp the paradox and you have gained awareness. The paradox involving ego is that it forces separation as you develop an independent awareness. You must realize you are identical to every other point of awareness. Even identical twins are distinguishable. You are unique just like everyone else. Paradox is the clue to the next level upward. That is the road to enlightenment."

Sandi haltingly asked a question. She and Ron disagreed as to where her current level of awareness was. Ron was a stickler in the precise use of words. After he finally reworded her question and formulated his answer, Ron moved on. While Ron's behavior seemed rather harsh, Gayle noted that after her struggle he did manage to answer her question.

"The wheel of karma is that all things keep repeating. To break the wheel you find new ways to arrange the same material. For example when someone says your lover is going to leave you, then there is no longer a single way to deal with the situation. There are options. There are multiple choices. You don't react the same way as before. You delve further and further into higher ways of functioning."

The chaotic presentation kept people on their toes and overwhelmed them with things that were different and the same. Even Martin who frequently fell asleep during the exercises was awake this afternoon. Marcia continued writing everything down while Jane smiled and laughed at every joke. Patty wrapped up in her blue woven Mexican blanket.

"The helix impacts on you and makes many out of what was one. The most common stimulus is that you fall in love. You have to reorganize. If you are lucky, you never fit it back the way it was. The next stage is to make a pattern of what appears to be chaos. The pattern ingested is a new point. In three-ness there is a double process. Collect yourself and explode. These are nodes that are a functioning of life."

"You are only a point the first time you come to consciousness. You are separate from your parents. There is no final point for most people except the fear of the death. If you reach a high enough level, you recognize your multiplicities and you transcend it. You become point and spiral and the energy. The final stage is the recognizance of rigpa which is the recognition of emptiness, substance and the observer all at the same time. The recognition of substance is pattern. Point is emptiness. And the observer is the helix. I found identity, pattern and energy within myself. Dzogchen, a specialized branch of Buddhism, has defined this."

The metaphor worked at different levels and could be applied at many realms of reality as Ron expounded. In linear fashion, one went point, spiral and pattern all the time. Understanding the relationship with the triad, it created a larger identity, a multiple identity, and crystallization into a new major form. A triad was often a lifetime of work. On a societal level this new being was a spectrum of hunters, farmers, and finally a town, a cultural unit. Ultimately it became a city. The whole is made up of dynamic parts. Gayle's inner world was now expanding with Ron's concept. She never knew that the inner could become the outer as in the Mobius strip she used to make out of construction paper.

"If you live long enough, you will finish a triad of growth. The whole is greater than the sum of the parts."

Ron let the words sink in while the concepts would take much longer to digest. The group energy in the room dropped rapidly.

"Possessions are multiplication of your personality. You integrate and finish a triad. You cannot go from one triad without a guru, or energy, or death experience. You cannot make that transition; yet it does happen. It transcends the normal function of the human being. Find someone above and ask them to eat you and you are taken into the next level. The teacher takes you from where you are to where they are. Initiation is going from one triad to another. As an archetypal third triad of this group I will show the dynamics of how to complete a level and move to the next level."

Ron said that the environment had to become exponentially larger. If cows were more fertile, there must be more land. This physical enlargement was first triad. The concepts of the next triad were not as real. A model citizen may give lip service to higher emotional concepts, but they don't grasp it. Some people had more difficulty with nonphysical concepts such as emotions. The Omega Institute for Holistic Studies' catalog in Ron's opinion was filled with second triad courses–courses filled with feeling, compassion, and love. They went by titles such as "Open your Heart," "Find the Divine" and "Follow Your Dreams." Ron maintained that enlightenment meant seeing multiple meanings at the same level. Transcendence was to shift a level totally.

"If initiates go to a third level by nature and take the time to look back at first and second, there is a marked difference in being. If they don't, it is so boring. Those below see those who rise above as great figures. When you are caught on a stick or in duality and if you can perceive the opposite, the law of threes is what governs enlightenment. Paradox is the stick. If you are good, you can't be evil. You resolve the paradox by seeing both ends are really the same. When you understand, you leave it from it center."

"You can't solve the problem at the level you perceive it as Einstein said," Martin said. Ron nodded in agreement.

"Or those who heal must be able to kill," Andre offered. "It's all in the application of the energy."

"Where does the energy for the transcendence come from? The action of the helix, I am being anthropomorphic. You see a rhythmical motion. Fundamental dynamism in the universe, we abstract it enough to be able to use it. We call it libido. Without sexuality, we are a marble in a shoot. With sexuality you can pull in more energy than you had before. You can do "work." You can access it also through chi, the oriental term for this energy."

Tuesday Evening

The evening topic began with a question Ron had been asked at dinner. Evidently many wondered if he had anticipated what would happen to Barbara and Nancy when he spoke of crystal implantation. His answer involved his evaluation of people in terms of their latent or primal potential. Ron felt the person must operate in a realm of energies that had little connection to primal earth. While there were other people who were closely aligned to the planet, the issues of people who were not earth oriented were significantly capable of spiritual opening. His candidates must be capable of being a successful human being and also a spiritual mystical being.

Gayle didn't understand that all. She was a Capricorn with five planets in earth signs. Everyone took their body from this planet. She had yet to encounter any silicon based life forms or inorganic beings as Carlos Castaneda claimed to have done. Maybe there were other life forms and now that she thought about it, what were ghosts and light beings made of? Nothing was taken for granted here.

"Maybe you think too much, Gayle," Patty whispered to her. "You don't have to understand everything here. Just accept it and move on."

"That's the problem. I could never accept on faith." Gayle knew it would be easier to do so, but something burned inside of her that demanded to know and understand it all.

"We are going to do the energy circle a bit different tonight," Ron stated.

"Different-ly," Sandi corrected his grammar. She was a school teacher in New York.

"Differently," Ron said. "Tonight we are going to create the cosmic fire. Castaneda does a similar thing with the fire from within."

Years ago Gayle had read *A Treatise on Cosmic Fire* by Alice Bailey. She remembered there were three ways to create that fire: using internal friction, utilizing solar fire of the mind, or accessing the fire of the spirit. While she was proud of her recall, her recollection gave her no clue on how to do that.

"These fires are primordial and are governed by the laws of thermodynamics-specifically the conversion of energy. Matter can never be created or destroyed, but it can change forms. That is what Einstein's famous equation is about. Let's begin with a standing circle."

The group joined hands to form a loose circle. Ron coached them to move in closer so that their arms went around the shoulders of the person next to them and their hips were touching.

"Now let's do what Castaneda calls the power walk. We are going to make and break contact with the earth by walking in place." The group began to walk in place with exaggerated movements. "Make and break contact. Feel the movement and friction between you and the ground. Visualize the earth sending up energy to each foot as it meets the ground."

The group obediently did this and at the same time began to feel heat rise in their bodies. Sweatshirts were removed and shoes kicked off and out of the circle.

"The internal fire is of solar origin. It is active, radiative fire and evolutionary. Feel the friction between the bodies and use it to keep building a fire in the center of the circle," Ron coached as he stepped into the center of the circle. "Oh, yes, I can feel you, but I need more."

The group continued this power walk building a flame within their own body and then radiating it to the center. Gayle remembered having been in this type of fire that purifies in her first meditations with Ron. She already knew she would not burn. Ron was finally getting the reaction he had been seeking.

"Just a few minutes more. Build it within yourself and hold it until you are about to explode with it before you release it into the circle."

The group was sweating, moaning, and breathing heavily as they became both physically and psychically warm. Ron stretched his arms skyward as if contacting some force above them. When he did so, the energy of the group exploded in a rush of light as the goddess Kundalini did her work to clear their chakras of any restrictions and open the pathway to the divine.

Chapter 7 – The Paranormal

Exploring Mysteries

The next morning's meditation involved similar coaching to begin to merge as a single entity meditating, but the group just seemed too tired to get the proper form in place. They struggled, but finally Ron opted to intervene.

"For now, I am just going to make this happen for you. You're going to have to learn to do it on your own soon, but for now we need to move on."

The meditation immediately changed. Gayle felt the clear space open in her mind with relief. Her own thoughts had preoccupied her mind this morning. She didn't understand how Ron was teaching in dreams. Her nights contained conversations, visions, and ghostly interactions. Their meeting room looked different and there were different people in them. Now she was grateful to leave those thoughts alone and just be.

After breakfast, Ron's demeanor and clothes had changed. He was wearing his same white yoga pants but had put on a steel gray shirt. More calm and centered now, he opened into a short history of Sufism.

Ron's teachings on Sufism claimed the Sufi purpose of being on the planet was to integrate the energies of the earth with these higher vibratory energies. A Sufi functions on the earth plane. The origins of their order stated they are the oldest spiritual organization. Joseph's Technicolor coat was a hallmark of their blending the wools acquired from various places in their travels. The Sufis wanted to be patchwork of all of humanity. The Sufi truth cannot be verbalized, but must be told in story.

The Sufi according to Ron sought a living vitality, not a staid ritual. The origins of life in Sufism originated over 200,000 years ago and included the idea that they arrived as a collective from another place. They entered into the bodies that the planet had created and subsequently lost the capacity to move on. Like Ron himself who may have derived part of his own myth from the Sufi, he claimed the Sufi served here while attempting to elevate the clay of the planet so that it may break free and carry them away again.

"We are preparing these bodies to bear a god who may break free. The Sufi invented belly dancing for men to loosen and strengthen the pelvis so a man might be able to give birth to a child who might become godlike enough to escape the planet. It was a metaphor of course that seemingly got forgotten. The Sufi spread the concept of romantic or courtly love brought back to Europe by the Crusaders who visited the Muslim countries. The troubadours had a mythic female entity. She may be represented by a living woman, a universal feminine force capable of being a mother to a god. There is a myth–once we were all godlike. The offspring degenerated."

As the group again became intellectually saturated Ron switched to a topic that always brought energy into the group–human sexuality. He introduced the concept of the *Hieros Gamos* as the sacred marriage or union used in many traditions such as the Rosicrucian, the Knights Templar, and the Celts who spoke of it as the ultimate union of dual primal forces. Mercury was white and in another state became red. Ron discussed alchemy that signaled primal sexual energies independent of the fleshy human body. By uniting elemental forces such as menstrual blood and semen mixed within a Bain Marie and then cooked in the presence of the helix, something magical occurred. Amino acids in primal soup turned into something biological by a bolt of lightning.

Experimentation showed the richest concentration formed a living chain so dilute that it seemed unlikely to happen. Ammonia could be a building block. Earth would have been self-contained had not strands of RNA and DNA arrived extra-terrestrially from a comet. Those strands comprising the double helix entered the atmosphere from elsewhere.

Gayle remembered the tales of King Arthur and Morgan le Fay who innocently performed the rites of king-making as the god and goddess. They had no clue that they were actually brother and sister. Yet in many royal lines, particularly the Egyptian ones, marriage between siblings or parent and child was the only way to preserve the bloodline. There had been no taboo there. By chance, she happened upon the fragment of a comet found in Antarctica on display at the University of Georgia. The origin was said to be from Mars. Its significance was that it contained evidence of rudimentary life forms. Ron's stories seemed to bring lines of knowledge together for her in new ways.

"Sacred marriages between two highly advanced human beings added something to their offspring that may be an energy principle and not a flesh and blood baby. Many esoteric traditions speak of an extra-terrestrial origin of life on this planet."

Gayle must have dozed off during part of the ancient Egyptian mythology. She hadn't been sleeping well since she arrived. On the other hand her mind was boggled by the connections Ron could make. It had been far too many years since studying classic mythology for her to grasp the subtlety of the teachings. She was thankful for having watched *The Power of Myth* series on television. Changing her position, she tried to pay closer attention to the lecture.

"Ancient Egypt was an anomaly. Evidently the people there understood how to make beer, use glass making, dig wells, capture hydraulic power, breed livestock and plant crops. There was an explosion of civilizing forces that converted a nomadic tribal people into an advanced civilization. Then 2000 years after this peak civilization, entire tribes went amok. It was as if someone had taught the teenagers how to use the controls without the wisdom as to when and how. It has taken many years to rediscover this knowledge."

Ron described the shape of the Hathor depiction at the Temple of Dendera as a cow headed goddess with two horns to be symbolic of the uterus with fallopian tubes. In other words, this was a goddess of fertility. The Knossos Goddess symbolized her rulership over life and death through the symbol of the double headed ax whose magical shape was placed on six foot poles in her palace. The double headed ax is called a labys because it resembles the labia. The labia are the lips of the vagina that gives birth to initiates.

Gayle as well as the others in the group realized they were seeing familiar objects in an entirely new light. The myths they learned in childhood were the basis for a much larger, but at that time, incomprehensible truth.

"It's like answering the question of how babies were created. The answer given is changed according to the level of understanding of the person asking," Patty offered to Gayle when she complained she just couldn't put it all together. The complexity of the answer grew with time. Ron's teachings on myth, symbols and sexuality were the graduate level answers.

"Bonclarken was to enlighten people and to release them from their bond or block. They have a chance to do what they were designed and trained to do at the Harmonic Convergence. Whether they were an ex-priest, nurse, or soldiers who left in fear, we could bring them back to awareness when the whole business was in need of them. The ritual on August 16, 1987 was a reenactment of a ritual done long before. I channeled higher energy through a wooden staff into a bowl of water. If they could drink the water, they changed. I got rid of the ankh afterward. I had lived just for that moment. I did the ritual again last summer from a different persona, not as an Egyptian priest who was a first descendent of the Atlanteans, but from a different place."

While the importance of these rituals on him and the group had evidently made its mark, this group seemed relatively unattached. A select few had taken part in one of the events, but had little to offer on its effect. Only Sandi commented that it had profoundly changed Ron. He was no longer the person she had first met.

"At one point early on I was so afraid of him that I literally tried to climb the walls to get away." Ron smiled at Sandi in reply.

"Initiates possessing the kind of energy that drew us to the Harmonic Convergence must have it released. To be competent they cannot be driven by an unknown source. You do not need to be physically free of the drive to be a higher consciousness. What is motivating you is your drive, and not your free will. Be conscious and choose. Make the reflex behavior of the body to be in the direction of the desire of your higher consciousness."

"I thought you wanted to kill me," Barbara said. "This Barbara is affected."

"You are seeing the difference of being a subconscious channel of information that you cannot hold yourself versus direct access. You are a fine channeling medium. When I am channeling, I go to a portion of my inner self and simply remember what I need to know. It is all there, just open the book. It's not another being, it's me."

Ron explained the events that caused such extreme personal reactions for Nancy and Barbara were a part of their personal drives. He drained the energy from Barbara and Jane as there was no more drama needed.

"I am opening you to awareness of compelling forces that you are currently unaware of. You never see them because you can't see the forest for the trees."

"When I experienced this crystal you seemed to hold," Barbara offered, "incredible ecstasy filled me. When I started sobbing it was a release of something I could not even put in words. The crystal is taken for granted. Then whack, it opened it all up and brought it all back. I felt the third eye open and this explosion happened in my head."

"If you make it so easy for everyone to understand, then you have called it and it no longer can expand its meaning." Ron smiled, assessed the group, and moved on.

Psychic Phenomena

Ron told of visiting his friends Barb and Les who kept hearing sounds of someone walking on the second floor deck. They kept thinking it was some small animal out there with small hooves. In their own bedroom, Barb saw a bird. Her husband asked why did the bird fly in through the closed window and out the door. Ron was sleeping in the other room.

"If you are opened and as repressed energy comes out there will be dramatic effects such as psychokinetic manifestation. Light bulbs burst or a myth connection may appear to be enacted. Charlotte kept hearing rapping on the window. It was a cardinal who kept leaving feathers on the doorstep. All kinds of manifestations can occur."

Now Gayle was beginning to understand why the bulbs burst during her own television interview. The pieces were starting to form pattern. These kernels were why she was here. She was following a trail as they were tossed before her. She hoped she was not Gretel in the forest home of the wicked witch.

"As you begin to open, there is the same kind of potential to be released. These events are usually benevolent, casual, and an apparent violation of natural law. They provide some kind of meaning to the spectators. Yet it is the same release of energy. Stay awake. It can happen to you."

Walking the Labyrinth

Ron knew that by Wednesday afternoons, groups deserved a break from the teachings. Per his rhythm he designed different kinds of activities for that time slot. While a few went to town to check out the bookstore and the souvenir shops, Ron went outside to draw a pattern in chalk upon the pavement. After seeing that the pattern was complete, Ron energized the lines by walking through them to the center. When he backtracked his way out, he told them that the labyrinth resembled the patterns of the brain.

"Historically, labyrinths served to trap malevolent spirits or created a pathway to god. Modern ones are more of a pilgrimage toward enlightenment. Walking them is an exercise in contemplation. Among the turns, directions are lost and the focus turns from the outside world to the inside world. Who would like to walk it first?"

"I would," Gayle said.

"Great," Ron responded.

He asked everyone to hold focus as she stepped into the maze. Every step became a conscious making and breaking of contact with the earth. Stepping within the lines she was unaware of the outside word. The inner journey began. The chalk lines seemed to grow upward in the charged atmosphere. The perceived low walls guided her on a one-way journey. A simple task that even a drunk could complete.

When she reached the center, Gayle breathed in the energy streaming in from above. Her uplifted arms formed a chalice to be filled. While she wanted to remain there forever, a calling made her pivot and find her way back.

While the path remained the same, her vision of the labyrinth had changed. The light was no longer as pure. Suddenly she could hear the birds chatter and voices from the hill below. Everything was denser and slower. The exit loomed ahead and Gayle anticipated it. Eager to move on, at the last tight turn Gayle lost her center. She stood poised on one leg with the other leaning out of the maze in some jester's form of an arabesque. Her hands automatically went out like a tight wire walker to keep her from falling. She felt Ron's gaze intensify. This was the test. She could not fall outside the lines. In ballet class long ago, her teacher had made them struggle to find their balance and center while standing on one leg. Now her body took over from its memory where her intellect had failed her. The struggle was internal, a battle of emotion, intellect, and physical form. The group said nothing, but held focus. The body then snapped into the position that allowed her to return to standing. Gayle smiled not knowing what battle she had won. A few steps later and she exited the labyrinth.

"I thought that corner would have gotten you," Ron said. "You also have such difficulty returning to the world of form. Who's next?" One by one each of them walked the maze with different results. Some did it easily. Others had similar experiences to Gayle's.

"There were dimensional shifts in there," Barbara told her after Ron had left.

"I felt them," said Nancy.

"I thought it was easy," Jane added before the group dispersed until dinner.

Final Night

Every night the group had stood in circle learning to balance their strengths and weaknesses to form a cohesive whole. These energy circles left the group standing, arms around shoulders, until the muscles excruciatingly ached. When they were properly fatigued Ron trained them to detect subtle shifts and directions of energy. They were being sensitized. He taught them how to use the movements of the body to generate more chi and to bring them to higher consciousness. They stood until they reached their limits.

The lectures were long discourses on a variety of topics interwoven to unseen pattern. Ron wove the Christian, Templar and Freemason mysteries of Rennes-Le-Chateau with tales of royal lineages, Egyptian and Atlantean origin myths, and obscure rituals of secret societies. They had spent the entire day and evening listening and sorting information. A few tried to no avail to ask the appropriate question to unravel the secret.

After dinner Ron made his homemade hot fudge sauce for ice cream. Sandi had put on his favorite music from the 1940's for accompaniment. He had informed them earlier if the ritual was done right there would be a celebration. As Ron finished the sauce, he had the group form the circle in the now familiar living room. For a change he did not have his recorder out.

"Each of you needs to prepare yourself for this ritual tonight. Whatever form of purification you need to do, do that. When you return, Janet will anoint each of you as you enter the room."

Gayle went to wash her face and hands while others changed clothes or did the rite that suited them. When she entered, Janet greeted her with some sort of essential oil. In silence, she placed a drop of oil on her forehead, nodded and directed her to the gathering circle.

Even though they had been doing circles each night, this one felt different. The tension in the room was palpable. When Ron turned, she was surprised to see him wearing a large oversize ankh pendant around his neck. He was dressed in all white and seemed much younger and virile than earlier in the week. Perhaps the energy was good for him as well.

When Jane came in as the latecomer to complete the group, they began to build energy. When most of the group seemed to have closed their eyes, Ron pulled a crystal out of his pocket. Gayle watched him warily as he approached each person. No one had any reaction. Whatever charge there had been had been released. When he reached Gayle, Ron offered her the crystal. She refused by shaking her head. His eyes twinkled and Gayle knew that he had learned something about her through the transaction. Ron moved back to the circle's center and asked them to push their access to energy to the limit.

On this final night at that precise moment when they felt they could not contain their own chi any longer, Ron brought forth the most desirous and incredulous energy that collected into some ecstatic whole. He stood in the center of the circle as the focus of the release of all the energy of the individuals of the circle. A wispy structure formed in the air above the group.

"It is finished," Ron pronounced. "For the first time, a group has formed a perfect double terminated crystal."

Tonight it was hot fudge sundaes, and wine or beer for those who chose to indulge. It was after midnight when Gayle fell into bed exhausted. Throughout the night there was little rest. Long buried issues still arose in the dreams for resolution. New people would be in the circles at night who weren't in attendance there. Gayle appreciated the fact that many of her ego issues were addressed in the dream time. It was far less painful that way. She fell asleep even as the party was continuing in the living room.

Winding Up

The group had reached saturation on many levels. The week fortunately was drawing to a close. A lot of the dramatic tension that had begun the week had been converted into some small glimmers of insight and the possibility of enlightenment. The meditations had shifted into falling in place within moments on this last morning. Gayle had observed something that felt like speed-bumps in empty space–her own paradox to resolve. Ron tried to explain the concept of group mind with the example of schools of fish two miles wide and eight miles long in the Gulf of Mexico all turning left at the same moment. He suggested that something at the speed of light could make them move like that– some quality of mind.

Ron cautioned them that even the most agreeable expansive attitude of friends and family would try to shape the individuals back into the pattern they held the last time they had seen them. He sent the group to pack up and said that if there was time after the house was put back into order, he would do one last teaching.

Touching the Hem

Throughout the week Ron had touched upon the Christian teachings as he expanded the parables and teachings and challenged some of the modern limitations put upon Jesus. He also discussed how the gospels reported events from different perspectives and filters. He used the example of the woman who touched the hem of Jesus' robe for healing. Jesus felt her and cried out, "Who touched me?" The variation became obvious as he read them.

"A large crowd followed and pressed around Him. And a woman was there who had been subject to bleeding for twelve years. She had suffered a great deal under the care of many doctors and had spent all she had, yet instead of getting better she grew worse. When she heard about Jesus, she came up behind Him in the crowd and touched his cloak, because she thought, 'If I just touch His clothes, I will be healed.' Immediately her bleeding stopped and she felt in her body that she was freed from her suffering. At once Jesus realized that power had gone out from Him. He turned around in the crowd and asked, 'Who touched my clothes?' 'You see the people crowding against you,' His disciples answered, 'and yet you can ask, "Who touched me?"' But Jesus kept looking around to see who had done it. Then the woman, knowing what had happened to her, came and knelt at His feet, and trembling with fear, told Him the whole truth. He said to her, 'Daughter, your faith has healed you. Go in peace and be freed from your suffering.'" (MAR 5:25-34).

"As Jesus was on His way, the crowds almost crushed Him. And there was a woman there who had been subject to bleeding for twelve years, but no one could heal her. She came up behind Him and touched the edge of His cloak, and immediately her bleeding stopped. 'Who touched Me?' Jesus asked. When they all denied it, Peter said, 'Master, the people are crowding and pressing against you.' But Jesus said, 'Someone touched Me; I know that power has gone out from Me.' The woman, seeing that she could not go unnoticed, came trembling and fell at His feet. In the presence of all the people, she told why she had touched Him and how she had been instantly healed. Then He said to her, 'Daughter, your faith has healed you. Go in peace.'" (LUK 8:43-47).

"Just then a woman who had been subject to bleeding for twelve years came up behind Him and touched the edge of His cloak. She said to herself, 'If I only touch His cloak, I will be healed.' Jesus turned and saw her, 'Take heart, daughter,' He said, 'your faith has healed you.' And the woman was healed from that moment." (MAT 9:20-22).

Perhaps the teaching had been to remind them that each of them experienced the week differently. Ron kissed the cheek of the person on the left of him and then turned to the right to do the same.

"Pass it on."

The group did until it met on Andre who was kissed on each cheek simultaneously. Ron laughed and reminded him to send it back. A quick kiss in both directions was sent around the circle. There was camaraderie in what they had jointly experienced. Ron beamed at being kissed simultaneously on both cheeks. He was done.

Gayle stood in the small crowd near Ron as they unloaded the leftovers for their parting lunch. The group jostled for position in the small kitchen. Ron suddenly reached over and touched the hem of Gayle's skirt. She felt it. The energy surged from him to her. Despite everyone else leaning over or against her, she felt his touch as different. Her mind began swimming. Was Ron Jesus returned? Was this why he knew so much? Why her? Why did she feel the touch? Others just made a plate of food and sat down to eat. Gayle was silent until the exodus began.

Luggage was piled on the porch and people began saying goodbye. Gayle hated goodbyes. She handled those who expected her to hug them goodbye. None of them seemed aware of her experience or the effect it had on her. She found the precise moment when she could slip down the hall and exit out the back without being seen. As she lugged her suitcase into the hatchback and slammed the trunk down to lock, she turned to find Ron standing there alone.

"I get to Atlanta quite often..." Gayle's shocked face must have given him an unspoken answer. She didn't respond to his unwelcome overture.

Die Before You Die

At home nothing felt quite the same as before she left. The furnishings of the little house were familiar, but no longer held any attachment. Nothing belonged to her. These were just things. Unfortunately her interest in academics was also lessened. She wanted experience versus knowledge. Everything was unsettled.

Gayle found that the bookstore retail aspect was chaining her down. She made more money teaching than in sales of New Age books, crystals, and jewelry. She shared some of the Bonclarken experiences and techniques with her evening classes. Those she still enjoyed.

Gayle attended the next channeling event with Samuel entitled "Letting Your Self Die." The subject matter echoed Ron's mystery school slogan of "die before you die." These same concepts her friends Bo and Kit from Sweden had shared with her on their channeled teachings. Gayle didn't have a clear understanding of what "die before you die" meant or felt like. Letting go was becoming increasingly obvious as the next lesson to learn.

This time Samuel's teachings were less interactive with the audience though he smiled gently at the lady wearing angel wings. Samuel taught that death was simply a change of state. It was not the end, but simply a portal to a different place with a different purpose.

Since the mention of death brought fear, Samuel framed his teachings with the concept of ascension.

Death was a way of letting go and seeing the old pass away. Samuel taught the creation of a simulacrum as a nonphysical vehicle. As he lectured, once more Gayle had the sense of Egypt again and lying within the sarcophagus. She had never exactly understood the purpose of that experience. The chamber shafts were aligned to stars so that their light might shine upon the candidate. Light, the fascinating duality of being both wave and particle, was part of the Egyptian mysteries. Ron had said that light and water were the elements of organic life on this planet.

Plato suggested two steps of reproduction – faithful and intentionally distorted. The simulacrum was the substitution of a depiction of the real for the real. Samuel suggested the faithful reproduction without exactly explaining why they were creating them. Gayle remembered Ron's admonishment not to mistake the map for the territory. The evolution of the simulacrum led to little distinction between the real world and the simulacrum.

Gayle wondered if the light beings who visited her during the white wolf episode were visitors who lived on the edge between worlds. She chuckled realizing that she sounded like Castaneda's account of inorganic beings. But light itself was not organic and from a different dimension. They could just as well be a figment of her imagination or a past life bleeding over.

"The old processes and the old foundations for knowing no longer work." When Samuel's eyes met hers, Gayle felt his presence resonating deep within.

Samuel's work was not all aerie faerie. He recommended a Victory Journal to create a trail of small consistent successes while a more complete relationship with Source was built. Again, Gayle saw a similar pattern in Ron's "trail of crumbs." Just as Hansel and Gretel left small markers to find their way out of the forest, both of these teachers were suggesting the same thing.

Samuel also suggested that the group give up its old way of doing things through control and manipulation. The shift here was to let go of the known to jump into the pool of the unknown. Samuel talked of angels and higher beings and when he made an obscure joke, Gayle laughed. Samuel leaned forward to say to her personally.

"You would laugh. After all, they call you the Angel of Death."

The Lion Path with Bo and Kit

When Bo and Kit visited Athens, Gayle contemplated their connection. Bo was the only other person she knew that had access to the kind of energy that Ron did. Bo's own physical and emotional frailty rendered him unable to cope in the world. As Ron had said, what good was it to have access in the world, but to be dysfunctional in it?

The couple offered to do a trance channeling for Gayle in exchange for their room and board before they left. As they sat quietly in meditation before Kit went into trance, the images of Uxmal, Mexico presented in Gayle's inner vision. Having visited there years before, she recognized the nunnery, house of doves, and the Mayan ball court. The name Imhotek kept coming to Gayle. She felt responsible in some way—for all that went on in Atlantis or in Atl as she called the ancient island. She knew how to implant crystals and she could read them. Yet, while she was doing so a musty smelling beast-like creature with shaggy hair monitored her every move. She brought her focus back to the small living room where Kit began her trance journey.

"There is fear/darkness inside. I wait until Bo gave me energy to go on. There was a lot of pain and symbols of all ancient kinds. This is from a deep, deep past—memories of power and strong, strong power. They are coming to tell me I could reclaim this power. I had thrown light away."

Gayle shot a look at Bo and mouthed, "Who came?" However, Bo shook his head and let Kit continue.

"They offer me the crystal. But I must throw away the pain that is only useless here. Where do I go? There are no open stairs, but a dark archway. I don't want to go in there, but only in there can I have light."

Kit's eyes were closed and she trusted the guidance of the much younger Bo to take care of her. They were an unusual couple, but they were well-suited for each other.

"In tunnel, I found stairs and went down. Came out to this place. I hear a drumbeat, same rate as my heart. It is strong. There is a crystal cave and Lion met me here and showed me an open plain. This is an unfamiliar landscape. There are tipis one after another. A certain calming. I walk past them all and stop at my own. My power is there."

Kit described several scenes–a primitive face etched in white lines against a dark background, faces of ancient Egyptians and a very high being. This high being had been here since the beginning of our existence on the planet. She recognized the eyes from across time.

"The business in Egypt is not finished. Follow your dreams. This is not knowledge for knowledge's sake. Now it looks like a blue-white sphere helper is coming toward you. It is a penetrating knowing. You will get help to know, direct, teach and wonder where it came from. There will be instant knowing when it is needed."

Gayle felt comforted. She too relied on Bo to ask the right questions and allow Kit to remain in trance. Kit was frail, elderly and blonde. By remote chance this Swede had been married a man who lived in the farming community Gayle's ancestors had settled.

"Kahotek. There was a power struggle, teaching power with this name, but also, was something unresolved. It's an Egyptian feeling and a place where you can go back in time. Now I am back at my tipi. Here, I sit down with my drum and trying to match my heartbeat. The sky beings are dancing. You will have a lot of love and help. It will be needed and you will have it. Gather your gifts. Declare your intention. Make sure you really want it."

Gayle watched as the couple got into the car to leave. The path they had chosen was not an easy one. Their lives and work often depended upon the kindness of strangers. Their work had crossed paths and once completed diverged shortly thereafter.

Splitting Light

Throughout Gayle's graduate school notebooks were drawings of scarabs, suns, hieroglyphs, and pyramids. Thoughts from the first Bonclarken week bled over into her mundane academic world. Her fascination with Egypt was at the point of distraction. A vision of a small pyramid's door kept showing up whenever she closed her eyes. The door position split the rays of the sun on this day to illuminate two painted signs inside. The land outside was lush, green and neither desert or jungle. The only pyramids Gayle knew were the ones in Egypt and in Central America.

In the UGA library, a book about a small pyramid in the South of France used in the 13th Century by the Knights Templar on their return from the Middle East attracted her. The book reported that on the autumnal equinox of Sept. 21, 1969, the pyramid projected no shadow on the ground. Gayle recognized this pyramid as the one from her vision. She knew the building and its layout.

This was not the first time that had happened either. Days before her move to Louisiana, she had nightmares about an old Southern mansion and people screaming in agony there. During a detour off the interstate highway, Gayle made a wrong turn and found herself parked between that Southern mansion Beauvoir and the Gulf of Mexico. The home was formerly occupied by Jefferson Davis and used as a hospital during the civil war. When she entered the house, she immediately knew the layout and what each door opened to. Yet it was the private library and study outside that intrigued her. She knew this place. Perhaps she had been the architect. That would explain her doodling house plans habit.

Gayle further neglected her academic studies to delve into *Isis Unveiled* by Madame Blavatsky. Having become acquainted with the Theosophists through Leadbetter years before, the leap to the more difficult to read Madame Blavatsky seemed inevitable. Blavatsky stated a candidate for initiation was placed in a deathlike trance at the initiation ceremonies of the Great Pyramid. When awakened after wandering in the world of the ghosts, the candidate was considered reborn. Others suggested the sarcophagus in the King's chamber of the pyramid of Cheops was used as a coffin. Some claimed it was a ritual device to simulate death and a journey into the underworld. On the night of the approaching third day at the entrance of a gallery where at a certain hour, the beams of the rising sun struck full on the face of the entranced candidate awoke to be initiated by Osiris, Thoth, and the God of Wisdom.

While the Manly P. Hall book version suggested similar theories, he stated the illumined portal where candidates went in as men came forth as gods. The candidate was laid in a great stone coffin for three days. His spirit, freed from its mortal coil, wandered at the gateways of eternity. His ka, as a bird flew through the spiritual spheres of space. All the universe was life, progress and eternal growth. The body was simply a house he slipped in and out of without death. The candidate achieved actual immortality. At the end of three days, he was an initiate.

Gayle remembered a dream of sleeping in the pyramid only to awaken with her father nearby in another sarcophagus. This paralleled an experience when she spent the night in the hospital with her own father. He too seemed to have been part of an Egyptian past life.

A psychic in Atlanta had once picked up on her paternal line to metaphysics. Viewing a family photo, the psychic pointed to her grandfather and said he was the reason she had picked this family to be born into. From this family lineage Gayle had a connection to a Cherokee fire talker, a person who could take the heat out of burns. Her own father was a dowser able to find water with a simple stick. When the Army Air Force personnel had shown up at her grandfather's home to say his only son was missing in action, Gayle's grandfather had gone to a psychic cousin. Calling upon Billy's gift of prophecy, her grandfather pleaded to know his son's fate. Billy said her father had gotten out of the plane before it crashed and was OK, but was a prisoner of war. He had been correct.

So despite the conservative views of her Southern heritage, Gayle had some support in the paranormal gifts. When she began to have back problems, she used her sixth sense to diagnose it. She felt a dagger in her back, not a real dagger, but a pain that never healed from a long ago war injury. She had been a warrior of some type, but betrayed by one in her own group. She literally had been stabbed in the back.

Random insights permeated her awareness not just in dreams, but also in waking reality. She knew about music and color, and planets and cycles, and light with water but most of all, she remembered Egypt. The week of teachings with Ron was fading, but she had new tools and new insights.

Sometimes at night before she fell asleep, Gayle dreamt of Egypt. There was a long, shallow lake that led to the labyrinth to her temple. Steps led down into the water. Initiates drunkenly struggled in the water instead of swimming through the underwater entrance to the innermost chamber. Gayle gradually gleaned bits and pieces from Deb and Janet from Ron's group about the rites done at Dendera, Egypt. Both friends remained guarded in what they told. It probably didn't matter. What wasn't shared in words, Ron shared with her in dreams.

Gayle found herself most nights in an Egyptian pyramid. However, when she exited, she would inevitably end up in Central America. The pyramids were a time portal. Unlike her visit to Stonehenge, there was still magic and mystery in the dreams. Not all the dreams were enlightening though. Then there was the horrifying dream of having secretly gained access to Ron's laboratory where he encoded crystals. The hallways weren't straight, and the rooms were not numbered linearly. She kept getting lost in the laboratory while trying to avoid Ron. It was imperative that he not know she was there.

Even in the daytime, Gayle could not escape the onslaught. Behind her eyelids, she could see Ron's form in the shadows, but his eyes glowed with white light when she caught his gaze. At night, she found herself soaring as a bird with him.

"Haven't you had enough for one day?" he asked.

"NO! I want to learn."

Chapter 8 – Reopening the Search

Samuel's Time for Magic

Gayle's hunger for knowledge meant that she delved into astronomy, numerology, and poetry. Her weekly Pathfinder meetings provided a reason to create classes around her exploration. Her group developed friendships and often walked downtown for dessert after the classes. Their group was often the loudest and having the most fun as they burnt off the chi they had created.

When the next Samuel channeled meeting in Atlanta date arrived, Gayle decided to attend and her friend Angela tagged along. They had gotten a very late start and neither of them was comfortable about walking in late. As it was, even speeding and no traffic jams they would be a half hour late.

"We'll have to shift time," Gayle said. Angela looked surprised.

"What do you mean?"

"Well, Samuel said in his last newsletter that time could be shifted since it flowed at different rates. Let's just find a place where it will get us there before the seminar starts."

With the setting of intent and some good luck, they arrived at the hotel ballroom with a couple of minutes to spare. Neither questioned their good fortune nor were they surprised at the topic, "Time for Magic."

Samuel provided a nice counterbalance to Ron's teachings. His loving gentle spirit often taught the same principles, but in a far different manner. While Ron confronted egos, Samuel's mission was to encourage humanity to uncover and make practical use of its power. While Gayle had always been adverse to using magic to control others,

Samuel's definition was a bit different. Samuel wanted magic to raise one's own spiritual vibrations by forming a more conscious connection with deeper levels of the self. Perhaps she understood it best when Samuel said, "Magic is a tool, magic is a way of seeing, all of it designed to allow you to manifest your entity in synthesis in this world."

Both Gayle and Angela embraced Samuel's exercise of carving symbols into the candles that when lit released their magic. Magic seemed much more of Angela's destiny than Gayle's. Angela already did shamanic journeying, drum circles, and moon lodges. Gayle knew that for now, magic was not part of her path. However, she sensed it had once been a very big part of some previous life.

After the seminar, they stopped to pick up Deb's large crystal that she said needed to go home with Gayle. Deb was taking an active role in Gayle's life now by calling more and sharing some of her own experience. When she asked if Gayle was going to continue with the Bonclarken training, Gayle replied that she didn't know. Deb just nodded and said she was available if she wanted to talk.

Angela placed the large quartz crystal in the back seat and they headed down the road to Athens. As they drove down the familiar four-lane highway, they were stunned to see a tower of an ultramodern home shining in the distance.

"What is that place?"

"I don't know. I've never seen it and I've lived here all my life."

"Let's go find out."

The turned off onto some small two-lane roads until they found the glow of the home in a remote area. There were no cars around. The gravel drive led them to a modern home out of place in the Georgia countryside where clapboard farmhouses were more likely. They sat dumbfounded even as they realized that they were probably trespassing.

"Oh my god, can you believe this place is here?"

Then before either could think another thought the beautiful home was just a microwave tower surrounded by chain link fence and lit by small guard lamps. The two exchanged looks. "Let's get out of here."

They drove in silence to drop Angela off at her home. However the magic wasn't over. When Gayle got home, she found her car's interior lights were on. Even after she turned off the engine, removed the keys, and got out, the indicator lights were still on in the car. Worried that the battery would wear down, she unplugged the battery cables. The lights remained glowing in the dark. It was only in the morning did Gayle realize that the crystal was still in the back seat.

The Noble Truths

Gayle shoved the fifteen books stacked on the empty side of the bed aside. There was just too much to learn and it was impossible. No matter how much she read, she couldn't put the whole picture together. Einstein had searched in vain for the theory of everything. Her quest for the truth was along the same lines.

She had found teachers, but the teachings conflicted with each other, and the teachers came from entirely different perspectives. The academic, other worldly, and mystic overlapped like fireworks in her brain. Determining priorities had always been an issue in Gayle's personal life. She hated letting any idea slip away or to close any door. This failing had to be overcome or she would flunk out of graduate school. Today her focus had to be catching up on her studies in Buddhism.

Buddhism grounded her memories and visions with a simple structure of four noble truths. The world was full of suffering was the first. The cause of suffering was desire. The way to end suffering was to end desire. The eight fold path was the way to do this. Four simple instructions comprised Buddhism's Four Noble Truths. They were simple, but not easy to do.

Gayle reflected on her wandering path. Pain had served as a catalyst for change. There was a reason for pain-there was something awry in the system and a person must change to alleviate the pain. For many, the pain carried was not in the physical body and therefore not easily seen. The emotions, thoughts, and lack of connection led to states of illness as well. Thoughts could make one sick as well. Human nature was to not fix it if it ain't broke. Professor Kirkland said you could use ain't if you had an advanced degree.

Gayle was still having back pain and serious headaches focused behind her right eye. Pain was a stimulus to fix something-to seek help, knowledge, or solace. Endurance, patience, acceptance were among its gifts. When in pain, Gayle remembered that the crack was where the light gets in. When walking through hell, keep on trucking.

Judgment of Humanity

As Gayle studied Judaism, Christianity, and the early mystery schools, the theme of judgment of the race recurred. The misfortunes of mankind continually placed them at the mercy of the gods who created them. The theme of a great flood was found in several sources and Gayle began to think all religions conveyed the same event in their own terms and myths. Yet it was the Sumerian mythology of the Nephilim, or "Those Who from Heaven to Earth Came," whose tales felt more suitable than some of the more patriarchal religions.

The Sumerian creation myth began with the arrival of beings from the 'Planet of the Crossing' called Marduk to create the human race. The gods were humanoid, bird-headed with wings, or reptilian in appearance. In other texts, they are considered the Shining Ones. Sumerian history was divided into two epochs divided by the Great Flood which was the judgment of mankind. The gods had ordered the destruction of the human race.

After the waters receded the chosen ones had been saved to begin the re-population of the earth. The sons of gods took human wives. Thus, the hybrid race of god-humans was born.

Gayle Seeks Another

Ron's awkward sexual overture bothered Gayle. She wanted a spiritual teacher, not a fling. Gayle was no prude, but she wanted to know the mysteries more than the man. The universe had made a mistake in sending her to Ron.

Rumors and accounts of Ron's earlier sexcapades with his students offended her. Passion and power were an explosive combination. The mismatch of power often meant the exploitation of the woman involved. Patriarchy shaped male sexuality with domination. In the masculine world, size equates to power. Sex was not only an act of dominance, but also exploitation. The women's liberation movement had changed societal concepts on reproductive rights, domestic violence, equal pay for equal work, and sexual violence. A balance of power had always been part of her belief system. Involvement with her so-called spiritual teacher was out of the question.

The quest for a better teacher began at once with the New Age Expo in Atlanta. As a faculty assistant, Gayle gained access to several workshops. She heard Dan Millman, Hank Wesserman, and others whose books she had read, but none of them inspired her. She empathized with the hungry crowds seeking some unknown path. Pathfinder's name represented its mission to feeling that the name would spin people out to the right paths for their own spiritual destiny. There were teachers out there. If the sayings were true, everybody got the teacher they deserved.

Yet the New Age conference left her more disappointed than ever. Though many of the authors wrote an intriguing and compelling story of their own enlightenment, none of them were really teaching it. Their intent was selling more books rather than conveying what they knew about the path to enlightenment. Many were not teachers, but storytellers. No one emerged as the right teacher for her.

At the same time, a much recommended author of a best-selling book admitted to making up the tale of her walkabout in Australia. The book went from being classified as non-fiction to fiction. The tales of many seekers were now being questioned. Even the existence of Castaneda's Don Juan was questioned. Internet connectivity was in its infancy and people were comparing notes from all over the world.

Still, Gayle's immediate problem was she needed a real spiritual teacher. While Samuel provided tools, insights, and energy in a group format, Gayle didn't like his group very much. Many of the egos were manipulative and bossy. While Samuel did offer private sessions, they were expensive and hard to come by. The tape of the one she had done the last time provided a surprise to her. At the end after she had left the room, but the recorder was left still running Samuel had added, "How I love that soul. She has so much courage."

Although both Janet and Larry from Ron's group kept in contact, Gayle never told them the reason she was so troubled about Ron. Ron's proposition of her tainted the entire thought of him as a teacher and his Bonclarken training.

The letter arrived that day giving details of the next Third Wave training. She left the deposit form on the table. When the due date for the deposit arrived, Gayle did not send a check. A decision was made by omission. On some level her inaction left the decision to fate. If the universe wanted her there, Ron would make contact with her. However, no phone call ever was made.

When the day the second week of Third Wave training began, Gayle rode with two friends to the Franklin gem show instead. Her friendships were based through the local Moon Lodge so the significance of her deciding to not attend Ron's training was wasted. She felt a twinge of regret, but no remorse at her decision. Even as the week passed, Gayle did not inquire as to what happened. It was better to leave that door shut.

The Dalai Lama

The door did not stay shut. Deb and her partner Bob from Foundation called. Bob often shared invitations to different Buddhist teachings and initiations in Atlanta. Through them, Gayle learned of His Holiness the 14th Dalai Lama, Tenzin Gyatso, who was both the head of state and the exiled spiritual leader of Tibet. The Dalai Lama was a manifestation of Avalokiteshvara, the Bodhisattva of Compassion. Gayle had already learned in her Buddhism classes that bodhisattvas were enlightened beings who postpone their own nirvana and choose rebirth to serve in bringing all conscious life to awakening.

When the Dalai Lama entered the auditorium at Emory, the air became palpably richer, the crowd hushed, and the radiance of a man filled with holiness filled the room. His talk was with humor, compassion, and enlightenment. The Dalai Lama spoke while his translator remained at his side. When the spiritual leader of Tibet looked out over the audience it felt as if he was talking directly to her.

Gayle sat in the far back. She had arrived late. The Emory area was unfamiliar and she had gotten lost in this quaint part of Atlanta. There were no parking spaces when she arrived, but there was no traffic either. So she had taken a chance and parked the car in the unmarked space near the road.

Her spirit was hungry. She wanted to meet the Dalai Lama. She thought nothing for the handsome actor Richard Gere who sat on the front row of the audience. All Gayle wanted to do was to meet the Dalai Lama. Suddenly she felt his gaze fall upon her during a pause in his teaching. There was no doubt that he had felt her request. Tears filled her eyes.

The event was drawing to a close and she knew she had to leave to beat the traffic. She slid out quietly through the back door and headed for the parking lot. As Gayle came around the corner, His Holiness the Dalai Lama was being ushered out the side door by his bodyguards. Gayle stopped and gazed longingly at the back of the robed man.

He suddenly stopped and turned toward Gayle. Obviously against his bodyguards' advice, the Dalai Lama crossed the grass to meet her. It was only a moment, but a moment of so much clarity and understanding that it instantly transformed her state of being. She smiled as he left. Gayle made her way to her trusty Honda car where she discovered that she had jauntily parked in the middle of the exit lane of the parking lot.

The Guru

The encounter with the Dalai Lama inspired Gayle to seek out local Buddhist meditation groups. However, she was disappointed at the level of consciousness. The teachings were disciplined and the crowd attentive, but they did not reach the same level the Dalai Lama, Ron or Samuel had.

Ron's human weaknesses made Gayle reticent to continue training with him. The abuse of power was something she had been a warrior against all of her life. Gayle rebelled against convention to work on her own car, attain an engineering degree, and become a national account sales manager. Now, however, she had hit another wall. No one else seemed able or willing to work with Gayle to teach what she needed to learn. She had no idea what it was she needed which complicated the search even more.

She had learned one thing though. Perhaps the best indication of a guru was the ability to share their higher awareness with others. The average teacher was teaching what they knew. However, Gayle was looking for something more. She had received a taste of that from three separate teachers who each had a contradictory and paradoxical way of presenting the same material. Her own answer lay somewhere in the crisscrossing paths.

Perfection was fortunately not a requirement for attaining these levels of awareness. Yet the traditional Buddhist path was not open to her nor was the quarterly teaching of a disembodied teacher enough. That left her to the crazy New York Italian teacher and his Foundation group. Gayle's heart sunk to a new low.

The Prodigal Daughter

When Marcia invited Gayle to Ron's seminar on the tantra of relationships, Gayle reluctantly attended. She liked Marcia and this would be a good test of the waters. The group welcomed her without comment. The tension between Ron and her, however, was palpable. She listened with interest, interacted when necessary and knew she would ultimately go back. It had been inevitable. When the workshop concluded, Gayle left without talking to anyone.

She checked the mailbox when she arrived home. The usual bills had arrived along with the airline frequent flier statement. Later that month her miles were to expire. The perk of free travel was not going to go unused. The availability of flights was limited, so after several tries to book a trip the agent suggested Italy. Gayle agreed.

In short order, Gayle had reservations for Rome during the school break next week. Out of habit, she dialed DJ's phone number realizing that it had been some time since they had talked. But the phone went to voicemail so she left a message to join her in either NYC or Rome if he could. She didn't get a reply.

In Rome, Gayle entered the Vatican's Sistine Chapel with great anticipation. Michelangelo's depiction of creation had always been a favorite painting. The iconic gift of life extended from God's outreached hand to Adam was a wallpaper on her computer. The slow moving line to the chapel led them through hallways with artwork on the walls and ceilings. Everywhere she looked there were hidden signs of excommunication, esoteric landscapes and symbols, and goddesses in the forms of angels. Her eyes had been opened after all.

The Roman Forum presented a familiarity of layout. The style of the Vestal Virgins temple with columns and graceful arches appealed to her. At the Coliseum her vision was taken over by things that were not there anymore: the covered basement, the lions, and the screaming throngs of people. Outside, she had been warned about the gypsies so she did not linger.

The trials of being in a foreign city made it time to move on. She had done the prerequisite tourist activities. When a stranger mentioned that a train to Pompeii was an easy trip, Gayle booked it. The volcano Vesuvius dominated the landscape outside the train window for miles. Gayle had planned to stay in Naples, but the short stop in the city convinced her it was too dirty, crowded and uncomfortable. She would make her base in Sorrento, a British tourist vacation spot high on the cliffs above the beach further south.

Her morning walk revealed her suite was in the midst an olive grove. The view across the bay looked toward the ancient volcano Vesuvius. Gayle took the train to the ruins of Pompeii. Gayle's Italian was rusty, but English was spoken everywhere here.

In Pompeii, the tile work, pornographic murals, and marketplaces fascinated her. When she came to an outside altarpiece depicting a white bull being slain by cutting its throat, she knew the whole story. There was a staircase behind the ruins of the wall that could not be seen. She climbed it. She remembered the initiates who had been bathed in the blood of the bull. King Arthur had been initiated into the Mitra's warrior religion. She knew more than words could convey. She had been drawn here to remember and she did.

Further down the pathway, a small sign pointed to the Villa of the Mysteries. A short walk took her outside of the main site to a small private estate. A wedding was finishing up in by the small gazing pool in the center courtyard. Off to the side were the red painted murals within a single room that told the story of a woman's initiation. The guard waved the only visitor there in past the red velvet ropes. She could see the murals in detail.

The woman was bathed and prepared for a marriage to the god Dionysus. Dionysus, the intoxicated god whose wild followers danced ecstatically. The marriage to Dionysus would enlighten a woman. Gayle was fascinated. A woman married to a god. When she exited the building, there was one last mural of the same theme. Against the deep red background, the dancing god smiled at her. She noted that he looked like Ron. Of course, Ron was of Italian descent.

A Private Session

Deb drove to Athens to see the photos of Gayle's trip to Italy. They discussed the temples, initiations, and religion of Italy as it compared to Egypt. Deb and Bob had recently returned from an extended tour with John Anthony West in Egypt. Deb's facial expression changed from friend to woman on a mission. Deb asked her, "So what is really going on with you and Ron in the Bonclarken sessions? Why didn't you go back?"

"He propositioned me."

"Oh that. Yeah, he has problems with that. Some people view him as a fatherly figure and others as a lover. It has happened and it has caused a lot of problems within Foundation with jealousy, rivalry and rumors. For my own part, I want a teacher with human frailties-a teacher that can sit in a hot tub and put away a few beers. That means it may be possible for me to attain what he has. I don't have to be perfect after all."

Gayle nodded, but was relieved when Deb left shortly afterward.

Chapter 9 – Third Wave's Third Intensive

The Third Time is the Charm

When the invitation came for Ron's third wave's third meeting, Gayle knew she would attend. At the same time, there was an invite to spend the following week with Foundation as a way to bridge the two groups. When she called Ron to ask about both weeks, Ron was reluctant to let her attend. In missing the second meeting of her group, he thought she might be behind. Two weeks later, he approved her to do so as she was the only one who requested it.

This time Gayle felt a bit more comfortable at Lookout Lodge. She knew the layout and a few people. When they asked why she had come back, Gayle replied, "Because Ron asked me to." Ron quickly challenged her on that as that indeed was not the entire truth of the case. Already the ego dynamics were in play.

There were marked changes in the group this time. Even Gayle's own group claimed that she was an entirely different person after meeting with Ron. This time, too, Ron did not seem the same. There was more mindfulness and a quieter demeanor. While they were setting up the meeting room, he indicated that this week would be about transcending the ego and lots of meditation work.

Ron positioned his pillow embroidered with the udjat or Egyptian Eye of Horus on it at the space in front of the bay window. He placed his recorder to his right, his pile of notes, and the books he would use as resources on the side table. He pushed off his leather loafers he wore under the chair. This time he borrowed Sandi's reading glasses. Ron was aging and he was now walking with a slight limp as his hip joint was in the initial stages of deterioration.

Ron spoke of the *Hero's Journey, Holy Blood and Holy Grail, Genisis,* and other mystery material as being on the week's agenda. The information was still underground and had not reached mainstream consciousness as it was fated to do. Ron claimed to be five to seven years ahead of the crowd. He spoke of Gurdjieff, DeRopp, and Ouspensky's work on the ego transcendence. Since the ego was designed for the body's survival, Ron explained that one did not want to lose the ego, but to transcend its unconscious effects on one's behavior and psyche.

"I'm glad you decided to come back," Patty said. "It wasn't the same without you here."

"Thanks. The universe didn't give me much choice in the matter."

Gayle slept soundly for a change. Awakening late, she opted to wear her pajamas to meditation. Others had done this, but usually not on the first morning. She sat quietly feeling the presence of the others as they joined her. The meditation was nothing special and Ron didn't bother asking for comments before lecturing.

"I can't believe I didn't tape last night's lecture," Ron said to open the morning's lecture. "None of that material had ever been said in quite that way." Ron fiddled with the chords until he realized that he had the microphone switch off.

"This morning, we are working on building a collective meditation." Ron explained the exercise in constructing a sandpile of chi. The combined energy of the group laid like granules of sand on the floor. The metaphor was to sweep the sand into a pile in the center to a collective oneness. Some would be at a higher place simply because the group supported that tower.

This time he insisted that the meditation process be of an organic nature versus forced meditation on his part. There was no doubt that he could shape the group into a whole, but it would never be learned until done by the group. At break, Gayle sought out Ken who was again sitting in on this session with the group.

"I heard you think that you wished someone would answer the damn phone," Gayle told him.

Ken laughed uneasily. No one likes to think that their thoughts can be read so easily. However, there were no secrets at that level of awareness.

At break, Gayle noted that Ron slipped out the front door. It was cool outside so the porch was the one place one could be alone. She wondered at the ease at which other students talked with him. Her own dynamics with Ron involved slammed doors, ignored questions, and deliberate avoidance. Marcia had told her more than once that she was glad it was Gayle he picked on and not her. Gayle was driven. This was the only thing in life that had any meaning for her at all. She would do almost anything to soothe what was burning inside of her.

The morning began with a lecture on the triple brain as being holographic. Fetal development began as a fish, frog, and then human. All of evolution could be experienced within the womb. Ron explained how the different parts of the brain stimulated different responses. The reptilian hind-brain was the genesis of the flight or fight response. He then explained how different parts of the brain could be implanted in other parts of it to serve new functions. These were all a part of the Atlantean mysteries. Ron informed them that this week's work would be dealing with the concept of shadow or the unacknowledged part of themselves.

"After all," he said, "you don't know what the back of your head looks like do you?"

When they next meditated, Gayle decided to look at the back of her head. She was surprised to find purple energy pouring from outside her body into the hind-brain. When she reported this to the group at the discussion of meditation, Gayle realized for the first time how easily she slid out of her body to see what was behind her. Ron simply referred to the purple energy entry as where he stimulated past life memories.

The lecture turned into more of a personal sharing or encounter group when they returned to lunch. Ron awkwardly explained he wanted it to be more than just personal sharing. He also wanted us to share our discomfort with others' personalities, traits, and coping mechanisms.

Some of the stories dealt with domestic abuse which during the telling was held in a sacred space. There was no one offering advice or attempting to control the emotional content. The deeply personal sharing was not a bonding experience, but one of observation of pattern. One by one people opened their psyches into the group. Yet, Gayle remained silent.

"While this is all good stuff what I am looking for is someone to speak to their issues with others in the group," Ron stated. A long uncomfortable silence followed as no one wanted to discuss another person. However, this was the third time Ron had asked this to be done and it seemed that the process would not progress until someone did. Gayle decided to plunge ahead.

"Well, I am not sure this is what you want, but I am having a problem with Jane. Every time you open a topic, she is the first to speak. At each joke, whether it is funny or not, she laughs and looks around for approval and consensus." Gayle spoke slowly and with consciousness. She wasn't trying to hurt Jane, but she wasn't trying to protect her either. She was reporting a dynamic.

"As I observed this, I began to recognize this as a reflection of myself. I wouldn't be aware of it unless some part of me resonated within."

Ron nodded. In some way Gayle had not only observed some one's behavior, but had enough self-awareness to realize that it may be her problem as well. That had been the point of that exercise. At break however, Jane avoided any interaction with Gayle. Jane's ego was wounded and bruised.

The lowering of personal boundaries continued throughout the day with the promise of that type of sharing to continue throughout their week's meeting. Gayle wasn't a fan of people dumping their psychological baggage into the group. Yet, she was back here after some tough decisions. So while she did not know Ron's full intent, Gayle learned to be an active listener for longer periods of time. She also began to use the sacral pump exercise to keep her mind open and aware. When the group energy dropped, Gayle watched Ron manipulate the group. When they broke again, Patty came to sit by her on the couch.

"You're awfully brave to have done that."

"I'm not sure it was brave or a way to deal with my own aggravation. At least it brings things out in the open and can be dealt with on some level."

"Yeah, I am not sure I want to open myself up to that dynamic. I mean, like last night, I had this dream of being a Native American shaman. I stood in the hall, feathers and all, and knew I had to take a stand."

"That's ironic since I dreamed you were standing outside my room with your blanket still wrapped around you." They both laughed. "However, I hope Ron moves to another topic this afternoon as my next share will be to wipe that smug grin off of Ken's face. He thinks he is superior because he knows the mysteries already."

As they moved off the couch into the kitchen, Gayle was dismayed to see Ken arise from lying behind the couch. He had heard every word.

Maskmaking

In the warm afternoon, Ron had them out on the front porch of the lodge. From time to time a car would pass or a college student would walk by, but they mainly had the stream sounds babbling across the street as accompaniment. Ron chose the exotic looking Nancy for the model of the first plaster casting. He cut strips of plaster as he explained how building the mask was a process of infusing one's essence into the crystalline structure.

"Just meditate while we do this, Nancy," he coached in a soothing voice. He instructed the rest of the group as he began to place wet plaster strips on her Vaseline covered face. "The person you are making a mask on must be touched and reassured as they will no longer see or speak as we cover their face. This is a very intimate project of touching and being present as we form a three-dimensional representation of their true self."

Ron deftly smoothed the plaster against Nancy's skin until it conformed to the shape. He built the main structure with long thick pieces across the forehead and chin and along the jawlines. Then building upon that base, he cut pieces into angular shapes to make a better fit along the nose, eyes and lips. He took care to cover the lips and eyes last so that Nancy would not be isolated from the world as long. Once complete, he sat by Nancy's side holding her hand while the plaster dried. Five minutes later, he released the mask.

"Now you will make a mask with your partner and then switch roles," Ron encouraged them. "Take your time and if you need assistance, let Sandi or me know."

Ron had announced Sunday evening that he and Sandi were in a relationship and she would be moving down from NY with him to North Carolina.

"Tonight, we will have a special ceremony with the masks."

Gayle chose to make a mask first rather than undergo the process. She found the smoothing out of plaster strips took more finesse that she had first imagined. She worked in a meditative state and stroked her partner's face with great care and attention. She was amazed to see how a person's face changed when they were no longer holding the personality's expression. When it was complete and dried, she called Ron over to release the mask.

Ron carefully worked the edges enough to break the seal of the mask. Then carefully running his fingers under the edges he began to tug the mask away from the face. Suddenly, the mask was free and Patty was liberated. She laughed as she proclaimed it to be the best facial she had ever gotten.

Now as Gayle waited for Patty's return from washing the gel off of her face, she felt a bit apprehensive. She didn't trust easily and she would have no way to communicate her fear. When red-faced Patty returned, Gayle closed her eyes and let her begin.

The strips felt cool on her forehead and the hands gentle and warm. She was reminded how her grandmother stroked her face with a washcloth when she had been sick. When the plaster began to harden, she realized she couldn't move any of the muscles of her face.

Fortunately she had relaxed many minutes ago and she just let the work continue. She heard Patty ask Ron to check something, but Gayle felt that she had withdrawn into some dark personal cave. She simply breathed and let herself go into the process.

When her mask was done, Patty sat with her and talked some silly words to her which at the same time seemed so reassuring. She was not left alone. When Ron finally came over to release the mask the tug pulled small facial hairs, but not in a painful way. She now knew why Patty had called it a facial. They were the last pair to finish. After scrubbing her face from the plaster and Vaseline residue, she wondered back to the porch to look at the works of art. Gayle could recognize none of the faces.

The Mask Ritual

Dinner was good, though Dot the caterer seemed to recycle most of their leftovers into soup. There were still a lot of beans on the menu and despite Ron's encouragement to fart proudly, Gayle could never bring herself to do that though others did.

The tensions of self-revelation in the morning had dissipated through the creative mask making. The white plaster faces were drying in a circle around the candle in the center of the room. While the night sessions were generally for ritual and energy work, it was great to have a break.

As soon as everyone settled in to the established seating circle, Ron sent Sandi out to change into a robe. She came back in wearing a simple satiny violet wrap robe. She stood directly in front of Ron who gazed intently at her. Obviously something transpired, but it was undetectable by the group who only knew there was a change in Sandi. Her facial expressions were gone and all personality had disappeared.

"Let her choose," Ron said as Sandi who seemed to be in a trance circled the masks looking for the one with the right feel.

She finally settled on one, stood in front of Ron again and placed the mask on her face. Suddenly she moved in an entirely different way, dancing or moving with great agility to express the energy of the mask. Her previous skill as a gymnast was evident. Some of the poses were acrobatic. When she returned the mask, Sandi circled the candle again to select the next one.

Each time she returned to Ron to place the mask on her face. Sandi appeared as if in a trance. Each dance had its own flavor – animalistic, birdlike, temple dancer, goddess, and fairy. Gayle did not recognize her own mask. Later she found out that hers had not been selected.

"It's incredible what you do," Gayle said to Sandi when she returned.

"It's not me at all, but thank you," Sandi responded before wandering off in a different direction. It had been a good session. When Ron wished them sweet dreams, they thought they might just get them tonight.

Sweet Dreams

Few slept peacefully during these intensives as Ron called them. The work on ego and the subconscious continued on through the night. The dreams brought up mythic tales, archetypal beings, and Gayle would wake up in the middle of the night speaking with someone. Sometimes she would awaken mid-sentence.

Ron had taught on different types of dreaming: the arising subconscious to dramatize themes in dreams, archetypal stimulus, and then open awareness throughout the night. However most people could not remember the dreams, but were tired and grumpy in the morning. For Gayle, one night she was treated to a buffet of the most wonderful desserts she had ever imagined. She knew she wasn't supposed to have large quantities of sugar, but she was tempted. It was a dream after all. Who would know? Yet as she reached for a cross between coconut layer cake and chess pie, she was pulled backwards out of the dream. It had been a tunnel. A tunnel that she had recurring dreams about. This tunnel she called the Myrtle Beach Pavilion exit. In order to get out of the dream, she had to exit down this huge slippery slide in the dark. She laughed in her bed at the dream. However, if she could process in dreams it sure would be easier than having to deal with it in reality.

Lowest Common Denominator

One reason Gayle detested groups was they often fell to the lowest common denominator. When she was training sales representatives, some in the class would never get it and some already did. As a teacher, she had learned to aim for the middle instead of catering to specific levels. Gayle had observed others struggle to lift the worst up only to lose the focus of the rest of the class.

The Third Wave group assembled for morning meditation and it flowed well. They built a metaphorical sandpile with their own awareness into a collective structure. For the first time this week they emerged out of the dreamy astral world in to the land of the golden sun with clarity and memory. Everything was clearer and lighter and Ron was pleased with them. The vibratory level was comfortable and the bird outside sang his pleasure at their accomplishment. Ron rang his bell.

"Sometimes, like good horse trainers after only five minutes of schooling, they get off the horse. The creature performed it correctly. There is no further need to school that day. Mission accomplished."

They broke for coffee, toast, and eggs. Jane had volunteered to cook a batch for all of them. Gayle grabbed coffee, but wandered out the back door for some privacy. She wondered down the road to the lake. At the edge she watched the pair of swans swim in widening circles. Crows roosted in the trees admiring the students and the tidbits they might drop.

There was a strange sadness today. Even with the good meditation, she felt a longing for a place she did not know. She used to teach. These meditation spaces she knew in other groups, in other lands, and maybe even other lives. The levels were markers for her students long ago.

She let the screen door shut gently behind her when she returned. No one had missed her. The circle was mostly settled in the living room as she entered. Ron moved his microphone cords, adjusted his socks, and found Sandi's reading glasses to use before beginning the day's lecture.

"Physical work during processing engraves the animalistic psyche. You do not forget something during the experience of pain/strain in the body. Gurdjieff used to make his students work at the Priory–in the gardens, fields, and house. That was part of their teaching."

Ron had previously talked of movement and energetics. Gurdjieffian dancers had to maintain perfect balance. Their game of freeze meant a test of their consciousness. Likewise, Ron demonstrated micro-motion and how the use of different muscles created an awareness of a different type of consciousness. The body works at levels both above and below normal awareness. Gayle knew from her classical ballet training how to use the body to convey feelings and emotions. Movement was her best form of expression. To use dance to attain enlightenment would be a valid path for her.

"The problem with students is that they want to teach what their teacher taught. You cannot do that. The work moves on. Integrate it and teach what you know. Novelty wakes you up. Once you think you know something, you will revert to your lowest common denominator of understanding."

Ron ran down a list of exercises to generate enough chi to become the higher self or aspect of self. One could press down on the knees while seated to create tension in the body. The sacral pump could generate energy to be moved from the base of the spine to the mind to bring more alertness. By breathing through a different nostril with each breath, the mind was affected by the excitation of oxygen moving through the body in different patterns. Conversely, Ron said that the focus on meditation starved out the lower self to become the higher self. Another tool was to become a watcher and observer of all the processes.

"The spiritual warrior takes life seriously with only one consideration–to do what you need to do. There must be discipline before anything. Remember Castaneda's laundry list? Trungpa and Gurdjieff's student deRopp have only one consideration–to do what you need to do. Discipline before anything. Just as in the martial arts, the teachers demand unfailing obedience."

Jumping up to his easel, Ron flipped through the large pages until he found the drawing of brain mapping. By energizing several angles within the mind, the brain activated different portions. When enough of these lines were activated, Ron promised that something magical would happen, but he would not tell them what. One immediate result was learning how to work with headaches. By pulling energy through the line where the headache was located, the pain could be released. The exercises of mapping parts of the brain and noting some resultant stimulation was interesting, but not earth shattering. Yet Ron insisted that as a sick child limited to his bed for long periods of time, there was a result if one practiced it enough.

The group practiced moving energy in their minds along the indicated paths. However, other than discovering they could do that, there was no great revelation. Still Ron encouraged them to practice it as one day it would show results. Gayle tucked that information in her memory bank in case she ever had those debilitating migraines again.

During the long break as was intensives tradition on Wednesday afternoons, Gayle opted not to go book shopping with Marcia or to impose upon Nancy and Bruce's budding relationship. Instead she opted to catch up on some much-needed sleep. With all the psychological releases, the dream time was filled with unresolved issues. Some of them were hers and some of them were those present here. She saw herself at age eleven months being displaced by the arrival of a new baby. She no longer got the coddling and attention that she so desired. Realizing that this was one source of tension, she quickly forgave all those involved in the situation. She herself could heal that wounded child within as the popular cliché went.

She awoke suddenly from that bit of work in her nap with a vague feeling she was supposed to be somewhere. The sun streamed through the window and she could hear no one milling about. Marcia had promised to wake her when she returned so it must still be early. She was about to allow sleep to overtake her again when she suddenly found herself on her feet and then walking down the hall as if a somnambulist. Upon entering the meeting room she was surprised to see everyone waiting for her to arrive.

As she got seated, Ron said, "Now we can begin."

He had jumped into her body. Gayle realized that. Just as he could use Sandi's to enact the personalities encoded into the masks, he also had the ability to enter Gayle's body.

Last Night Ritual and Party

Ron's requirements for rituals were fairly simple. He often lectured about thirty minutes before sending the group off to do some form of purification ritual. Some took showers; others anointed themselves with oil; some went out to gaze to the stars. When the group returned they gathered in silence and stood in high awareness.

"Tonight is Halloween, a time when the veils between worlds are the thinnest. So tonight when you walk through this ritual, I am going to ask you to bring a loved one from the other side with you."

There had been relatively few deaths in Gayle's circle in the last year. She vaguely remembered a high school friend who had come to say goodbye when she died of cancer. Then, without provocation, her grandfather's voice came to her just as it had on the New York Thruway when a blinding migraine in Friday afternoon traffic incapacitated her. He had taken the wheel and driven the car across the Tappan Zee Bridge and down to her New Jersey home. She came to only as the vehicle turned into her drive. Her grandfather would walk with her tonight in this ritual.

Ron was dressed in all white with his large turquoise pendant against his bare chest exposed in the deep V-neck shirt he wore. The energy was flowing into him and his words were delivered faster and with more charge. He described an ancient Egyptian ritual of judgment. He asked them to enter one by one.

The group waited nervously out in the hall in the dark. Sandi stood at the door to prompt them when to enter. A deep rhythmic drum paced their individual footsteps. One by one they would make their way to stand before Ron seated at the far end of the room.

As Gayle passed through the doorway, the golden light filled the room. She stepped towards Ron with some apprehension. Imaginary pillars filled the room, but the path to the front dais was straight. When she reached it, she realized that there were three chairs at the front. Ron was seated in the center and two barely visible Egyptian gods stood on either side. She met his gaze and stood unadorned to be judged.

Her fate depended upon the weighing of her heart against Maat's feather of truth. If her heart was too heavy and the scales tipped, she would be devoured by the monster Ammit. If the heart was too light, she had not engaged enough in this world and would not be able to return for a long time. If the heart balanced Truth exactly, then she would pass through the door to eternal life.

Meeting Ron's eyes was easy. Gayle simply dropped all ego to stand metaphorically naked in front of what was now an Egyptian priest. There was movement from the figure on his right as if to make a comment of a judgment already. In a moment, Ron nodded. She had passed. One by one each of them walked to be judged and then stood silently at the opposite side of the room until everyone had completed the process. Ron's only comment was that he wished the timing had allowed the candidates to stand longer than the brief drumbeat. Regardless, it had a profound effect on each of them.

When the brief sharing was done, the party began. On Thursday nights at Ron's intensives, beer and wine flowed freely. The group let their hair down. Per his tradition Ron made homemade pizza for his group. One of his favorite lines was 'I eat the bread I bake' from Normandi Ellis' translations in her *Awakening Osiris*. There was laughter, music and loud conversation. Gayle didn't drink anymore. DJ's alcoholism had turned her off to drunks.

Instead, she observed the crowd from the corner of the kitchen. Even as they partied, Gayle noticed that Ron injected pointed jabs at their egos in the midst of their playful conversation. Yet, the atmosphere where their boundaries were lowered and their egos unleashed kept them from feeling it immediately. Most of those comments went unnoticed, but yet she could see the words enter their auras. Perhaps that was how he seeded their dreams. The week was over and they would be leaving in the morning. Only Gayle would return for the following week with Foundation.

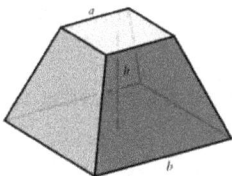

Chapter 10 –Foundation Inspection

Foundation

Gayle drove the four hours home for the two days between intensives. Her own home seemed foreign and familiar at the same time. She was glad to be alone though. So much had changed and yet nothing here had. She stretched across the king-size bed exhausted. She needed a minute before she unpacked the car.

When she awoke Gayle stretched and rolled over to the bedside table reaching for her knife. She fastened it with the leather belt about her thigh. Then she slid the simple woven dress down over her head. She walked to the door only to stop abruptly. Something was wrong with this picture. The room wasn't quite right. She didn't wear a knife in this reality or this kind of dress. She was in an alternate reality. Her fear was not what lay beyond the door, but that nothing did. Remembering Ron's teaching on Castaneda's dreaming practices, she backtracked to the table, undressed and crawled back into bed. She found the exact position she had been lying and closed her eyes. Either she fell back asleep or she split because when she opened her eyes again, she was in the correct space–time.

Michelle, Julie and Angela met her at the store on Saturday. They had covered her classes in her absence and wanted to update her, but in reality they wanted to know what had happened in the Third Wave training. She had needed this touchstone in reality.

"So is Ron talking to you yet?"

"Not really," she sighed. "He's not as rude now though."

Julie nodded. Gayle had shared with her how distant the relationship with her teacher was. Somehow Gayle had expected having a teacher in the physical would be easier. Her expectations of picking up a phone and asking questions that got a response seemed overly idealistic now.

"It's almost impossible to describe what goes on there. So much happened-like Ron jumping into my body and making it move down the hall." Angela's eyes widened and Michelle gave her a look of disbelief. "I will tell you all more about it when I get back. New exercises for the group as well."

Her friends left Gayle alone in the store. She picked up one of the black quartz crystals she had for sale. The unusual shape of crossed double terminated crystals within a third intrigued her. She closed her eyes, held it against her heart, and remembered all the events of the past week. The energies and teachings were now grounded in her home and local group.

The next morning Gayle left at sunrise for the trip back to North Carolina. The magic, energy and place called to her. This time as she exited I-40, she stopped at the Ingles market to get provisions. Dot's food was not always to her taste and she already had gone through a week of beans. Gayle already knew some of the people coming to this week–Larry, Janet, Deborah, Bob, Patsy, Joe, Julia, Ken, and Martin. This was going to be a new adventure.

When small clusters of people arrived, the energetic impact increased. The house was fuller and the energy escalated. Gayle panicked. She had no idea of the routine, the people or schedule. Their familiarity with each other strained her ability to cope. Mentally she called to Ron for help. A minute later he appeared leaning out over the stairwell peering down.

"Here, Gayle, this is the blueprint of how I want the room. Gather the troops and make it happen." Gayle breathed a sigh of relief. She had a chore, a mission and a purpose. Small as it was, doing something comforted her. There were more people arriving–and there were more men here. The interactions should prove interesting as the Third Wave group was primarily women.

Throughout her life, Gayle's friends were men. As a small girl, she sat on the side porch where the men smoked after dinner while the women gossiped in the kitchen. She chose engineering as a field of study which had been dominated by men. Men discussed more interesting things in her opinion.

The first evening began much the same way it had with the Third Wave. Ron opened with his agenda for the week. The major difference here was that this was a somewhat established group. They knew each other, the lodge, Ron and the former teachings. The camaraderie and teasing made the group more relaxed. Yet the underlying anxiety or expectation was there as well since many came back for the evolving experiment. Most agreed that their weeks were seldom boring.

"How far do you want to push yourself?" Ron asked. "Your group is yourself and your tool. If you don't know the difference between your tool and your rifle, you are in trouble." The group laughed at the oft told joke.

Ron brought the group to focus by reminding them of their stories and shared experiences. He encouraged them to teach, transmit and share what they had uncovered. The time distortions the group had experienced came with the persistence of memory. Ron reminded them that they remembered things they had never lived-such as Atlantis. Eight out of fourteen of the original members came there to release the myth of Atlantis.

Memory could be inaccurate as well such as in the case of familial abuse. The mind can be contorted. Ron recounted a news story where after one daughter spoke of being abused, her sister also began to remember incidents. After a short period, the father even remembered that he had abused his daughters. However, none of it happened. Time and memory distort each other.

"There will come a time no one will remember Ed Sullivan and his variety show. Who were the Beatles? The effects of memory in this case of abuse were distorted by the power of suggestion. The entire family had been interviewed by psychologists. Suddenly when asked questions that the interviewers knew never happened, the family begins to remember details about the suggested imaginary events."

Gayle was horrified as were others. Some laughed, but some had wounds from their own past. She remembered Nancy's personal story from the week before. This morning as Ron discussed the Inquisition, he reminded the group that when tortured not only did the victim release the secrets, but also details were simply made up to appease the torturers. The mind was subject to self-preservation.

Evidently meditation had run long this morning because the caterer was already setting up for lunch. Before the break, Ron decided to read an account of the death process of the mother of one of his students. The process was one most resembling a Tibetan Buddhist's perspective as Ron described it. He had a knack for bringing higher insights into whatever was presented to him—a letter, a movie, or a dream. Gayle remembered his analysis of her own dream that got her an invitation to join this exclusive group. The letter was long, intimate and full of details. Ron read through it without comment. Uncharacteristically, there was no discussion either.

After lunch, Ron picked up on the theme of conscious dying referring to the *Tibetan Book of Living and Dying*. The Buddhist principles of impermanence and the true nature of mind were combined with Ron's experiences of letting go, detachment, and meditation. The Buddhists have an elaborate understanding of the Bardos, an interim place between lifetimes, and other realities. The teachings were to help a person who was in the process of dying, from the moment of death, the Bardo of Becoming, and then on to rebirth if not final enlightenment.

One member of the group was creating a non-profit organization to work with those in hospice or otherwise in the process of dying. Ron sat on the Board of Directors. The theme of death and dying was continuing in the mystery school tradition.

The Akashic record as Ron described it was a library that recorded every action by every being of consciousness. Just as in the ritual completed the previous week, everyone faced their own karma at death. The methods of judgment varied according to different religious traditions. The ideal situation to avoid rebirth was to have the heart as light as the feather. Gayle was amused at Ron's pun back to the Egyptian rite of the dead and the insight it gave her. She assumed that his Foundation group had undergone this same ritual in their own First and Second Wave training.

Ron blended science and parapsychology in a language that redefined how Gayle interpreted the world. Ron had lived in the sixties while a relatively young man and according to his stories enjoyed the experimentation of that decade. He recounted how in the 1960's research experiments on the effects of music on the growth pattern of plants were conducted. This stimulated the talking to plants into popular culture.

During that exciting decade Ron described how his own energy at high enough levels changed the color of the precipitate in his laboratory. His day work as a chemist echoed his past recollection of the Atlantean experiments. Gayle continued to wonder if there was really anything new under the sun.

Ron reviewed the hundredth monkey theory to Foundation where rats on the opposite side of the world from the experiment were using the critical mass of enough monkeys in the collective consciousness that had run the maze to grok the pattern from them. Grok was a word Ron interjected frequently. Larry told Gayle at break that it came from the book *Stranger in a Strange Land* and meant to grasp understanding intimately and completely.

The next section of Ron's lecture reviewed the theoretical physicist David Bohm's work with the nature of light that contributed to the Manhattan Project. The double slit theory was part of the studies required when Gayle and Dana had attempted their long ago hologram experiment.

Light had a dual nature; it was both particle and wave. Wave nature was displayed when the light passed through double slits interfered to produce bright and dark bands on the screen. However, light on the screen was also absorbed as if it was a particle.

"The dual nature of light is a pair of ducks." Ron waited expectantly.

"Quack, quack," the group responded to his pun.

"Consciousness creates reality."

Gayle's mind was whirling with past information and new insight. Schrodinger's cat was another experiment in physics that boggled her mind. She knew the outcome of the experiment was determined by the observation of a conscious observer. There was only one consciousness no matter how many observers there were.

"Space and time are both relational. An electron could appear to be in two places simultaneously."

Gayle's mind was spinning out the current space-time. Boehm's interview with former Theosophist leader Krishnamurti in Shanta's course on Eastern philosophy came flooding about. The juxtaposition of physics and theosophy brought science and religion closer together. Gayle's schedule next quarter included an intensive study of Krishnamurti's teachings.

Next Ron introduced Rupert Sheldrake's morphogenic fields that theorized as more and more people learned something, it became easier for others to do so. For example British biologist Sheldrake experimented with three short, similar Japanese rhymes. One was a meaningless jumble of disconnected words, the second was a new composition, and the third was a well-known traditional and popular rhyme. None of the participants knew Japanese or which verse they learned. The most easily learned verse was the most well-known in Japan. Sheldrake postulated there was a morphogenic field containing habit patterns and it replicates easily. These fields influenced the pattern or form of things.

Having set the concept of collective consciousness and its use within creation, Ron returned to the discussion on dying. He encouraged the members to share on the process of dying. Gayle listened to Janet's account of the early loss of her mother that shaped who Janet was today. Joe spoke on the loss of his parent as well as others. By listening, Gayle was beginning to learn who these people were and how they worked psychologically.

"Pain is not unending unless you die in fear. People in the last few moments just don't feel the pain the way they did before. The big issue is when one feels the disintegration into the bottomless pit otherwise known as the black hole."

Ron suggested that meaning, faculties, and skills all were created to avoid emptiness. Gayle recalled the book in the UGA library suggesting that all religion was created to explain death. Death was inevitable, but most people lived in denial of it.

Ron explained that the death of the physical body ended how a person knows their existence. That frequently was the real fear as a person approached death-the question of a true identity that existed beyond life in a body. The body and mind were the tools to know yourself. To know yourself was the secret of life as written at the entrance to the Oracle of Delphi's cave. When dying, as intellect dissipated and metabolism slowed, within a minute or two there was not enough energy to support self-awareness. Ron stated that was exactly what happened when one encountered the black hole.

"However, what would happen if someone could connect at that level?" he asked not so much as a question but to provoke internal reflection. "Meditation without thinking would be just awareness. There is a residue of awareness. I could connect within half an hour after Georgie died. I could pick up memories and essence energy. If I am not delusional, after they were biologically unable to think and had no personality, there was still something with a level of awareness. There is an energetic form of self after brain function died."

Another of Ron's students shared a similar experience. She stayed telepathically linked with her dying mother to ensure that her fading awareness would have presence. Her mother's essence merged into the Foundation group soul.

"How come she got a free pass? She did not get there on her own." Ron interrupted. "In understanding the process of dying, there is great learning. Yet, I want to know what this group thinks about taking a role in the process of dying." Ron sounded almost humble at his role in people's deaths.

"A process now exists that anyone who can be contacted in this non-verbal state can be led through dying and placed in whatever level they are capable of understanding. A person can be placed in a higher level above their comprehension, but it will be meaningless and they will dissipate. Almost everyone can be placed in the light. Light is not the end."

At a break for lunch, Gayle noted this group talked more about the lectures than the Third Wave did. Perhaps they understood more. More of them shared experiences about their meditations which jogged Gayle's own awareness of fleeting events within those sessions. She interacted where she could, but her own shyness made her more of an observer. In sales she had developed an outgoing and confident personality, but when it came to sharing of herself, Gayle held back. She was relieved when the lecture continued.

Ron shifted topics into how quantum physics accounted for creation and the beginning of time. He proposed his version of how consciousness came from the Big Bang. Much of it was beyond the group's comprehension, but he insisted that it would be in their minds and one day they would grok it. Gayle had to trust that would be the case.

Perhaps building on the lunch conversations, Ron analyzed the entire meditation process with shifts. He described each stage and pointedly indicated that after light, there was absolute darkness. However, that darkness was not the end. There was a place where there was neither black nor light. The map was whole and comprehensive. It all came full circle where the end was the beginning. However, unlike the Third Wave, Foundation was not interested very much in meditation. Many came for social-spiritual interaction and for the energies Ron generated. As was his style when the group was intellectually saturated, Ron changed the subject. He reverted to the previous subject of conscious dying.

"Dick said last week that the light became almost painful. I can relate to that. When my father was dying, I could have done more than I did. My excuse was his inner nature was to be tough to the end. The only way I could help him was to expose his breaking down. Instead I helped him after he died. My brother picked up on his exit and said 'I can feel him leaving.' Guilt doesn't do much for us–forgive yourself."

Gayle listened as members conveyed their own near-death experiences or being present at the death of a loved one. She wondered whether it was their ego speaking or whether this was the way they processed new information. At times though Ron denied it, this was a re-creation of the encounter groups of the 1960's and 70's.

"...however the point is going beyond being present and actually lifting them into a higher awareness, is this one of the functions this group should be doing?" Ron asked. "I want to know what the internal resistance is to this idea? Are we playing god? To what degree do you feel the taboo?" While the group responded to pragmatic concerns, most remained silent about internal concerns of manipulation and responsibility. Ron moved on.

"The real question I have here is about the karmic displacement. Much like the original Bonclarken experiment where the Atlantean myth was displaced on our group for resolution, so will be the karmic debt of any person we midwife through the death process."

The group had little reaction despite of hearing the accountability they would undertake. Gayle feared the recklessness of the group. The group was claiming some function that most religions undertook to resolve. There were some new glimmers of awareness stated in a few comments, but overall there was little reaction or questioning. Gayle remembered that long ago dinner when she met Ron and the group hung on his every word. Despite his encouragement to question everything, they seemed more likely to simply accept his words and directions at face value.

Ron's lecture on the meditation levels returned to the Foundation work on the twelve essences. Ron was attempting to create the Twelve in the room for the sake of humanity. Ron had commented on Deb's experience of seeing multiple faces coming before her and its negative affect on her energy. Al had commented on the same thing happening to him the evening before. In fact the group was reporting what came to be called karmic sludge, a lethargy and an inability to deal with life.

Faced with the group's accounts, Ron suggested this was a human reaction to the archetypal presences making themselves known. He suggested Foundation was the emissary and had assumed the role of what humanity was going through.

"We must deal with the cultural horizontal band of experience– or all of the things in past lives. We may call upon ourselves in that we are going to work for a massive group of people instead of just our group. Deb, Maria and Brenda are not sitting here for this session; they can't deal with the massive karmic weight. As we open to massive spiritual change, the physical system will react with sickness, toxicity and the desire to sleep and hope it all is forgotten or goes away." Ron shuffled some papers as he sought to change the direction of the group. Ken spoke up in the temporary lull.

"The group last week was easily moved and lifted. I returned this week expecting to pick up where we left off. Yet, we are where this group was a year ago. I couldn't sleep last night. The energy was discordant and I was caught up in that. The movement in meditation this morning was slow, but I was aware you were doing something to bring this group together. There weren't enough people to hold it together," Ken offered.

"The group may be too large for this room. Like a party when the space is too large, people and everything is dispersed. If the space is too small for the participants, then there is a party. Like Goldilocks, we need a place that is just right for our number. I want to release being the lion-tamer or the watchful parent who keeps it together. It would be nice to dance with you and have you hold yourself as a capable partner."

Gayle was seeing how the group worked. Write Ron letters, call him about paranormal events, and he would teach about it. She could see how each topic shifted the focus to another individual drawing upon their issues and knowledge. When Ron had done the ritual the evening before, he noted that he had gone to the archetypal level. He called the Twelve down and energy filtered through each individual according to their makeup. This was not a conscious decision, but rather the energy sought the patterns most compatible to the original archetype. Most people were part of two or three families. It was a rare occurrence to find an individual with only one pure untainted essence.

In that circle where she stood between the two sisters, Gayle felt huge amounts of energy flowing through these older women and into the room. She had looked at Linda first then at Carol in astonishment when the circle ended. She was used to such energy, but she had never stood between two such powerful channels at the same time.

"Now you know why people choose not to stand between us," Carol laughed.

Gayle did indeed. The tantric energy between the group and Ron made it pleasurable and orgasmic for some. As its creator he most likely had designed it that way. Heavy breathing, a few fainting people and some sweet smiles were the general reaction. However, a few did have their moans and escaping sighs. The energy circles of her own group were not as easily generated. Perhaps that was because she was a woman in the center of a circle of women. She may have needed the polarity of a more male energy. From her long ago electromagnetic courses, she remembered that energy going around in a circle whose center contained a pole would create a current. She didn't need to understand Ron's ritual intellectually, but she felt the need to know how to do it.

Limits of a Universe

Ron alluded to Gayle's presence by indicating that a single individual could easily be absorbed into the group. Indeed part of the reason he had invited Third Wave participants to visit a Foundation meeting had been to begin the integration of the two groups. He was now balancing the natural tension of group and its energy to correct the course of events that made a few of its members ill.

"You create a reality back and forth, going here and there, if it continues long enough, it creates a rut that you may not be able to break out of. If you maintain the balance carefully, you use up very little of your vital energy. You will live a long time. You will stay vital maintaining the tantric tension. Learn how to extend lines of awareness and cause charismatic force and bring forth awareness of the long life. When you can observe both sides of the tension as being equally necessary and be in balance, you complete the system. You complete a reality. The action of being aware of the equal value of both sides of the tension completes a system which in turns generates a vital force that enables you to go to another system. There is an end of the systems."

Ron's theory was that human development followed a progression. If the development was smooth and natural, they found the boundaries of their universe. That was true if nothing interfered with it. The path of the initiate was to create a personal universe. A classic magician created their own universe by going as far as they could in both directions.

"My teaching process has been consistent in that we address events in the physical, then emotional that leads to intellectual layers. When the absorption is complete and integrated, we are ready to move on."

Standing at his easel, Ron turned to a new page. Gayle chuckled softly as she realized that this was the first time she had seen him use a new sheet of paper on the pad. Ron reminded Foundation that the shaman's journey began as a point which he placed near the top of the page. He then drew two diverging lines from it as in the creation of space-time.

"A universe expands to its personal limit until it encountered an opposing universe. The point at the beginning knew nothing else but self. At the end it returned to a point but with the knowledge of opposites and complexities of being. In understanding the boundaries of the personal universe the point had become self-aware. All in all it is Uroboros, the snake eating its own tail."

The lecture continued with modern psychologists' theories that consciousness works similar to crystal growth. Expansion continues in a different direction until confronted with a barrier, trauma or a fear it cannot deal with. The initiate had met the immovable object held in consciousness.

"Perceive the opposites in the furthest bounds of your universe. If a growing child cannot deal with a situation, it retracts from that barrier. It keeps returning to the uncompleted universe until it can let go. The human mind needs content to make a symbol for what it cannot understand. It doesn't remember historical events, but it remembers the fear and the pain."

Jen related how hearing a particular song brought her back to a particularly painful place in her life. Every time she heard it, she felt the memory of the events, the hurt, and the wound reopen over and over again. As Ron counseled that while the song was a marker, the wound itself could be healed. With that accomplishment, the song would never provoke the same symbolic pain, but only a memory of the power it once held.

"A being that can perceive over lifetimes is an archetype. An archetype extends through realms and brings back pieces to teach. One has very few tools to check what is illusion and what is not. Whatever you have, use them. In the end, you have a sharp intuitive knowing of whether this will stand questioning or not. Having gotten through the stages of intellect and feeling, I have experienced what some call sainthood, an absolute outpouring of unconditional love and compassion. I've just stood naked in front of you; are you willing to do the same?"

Some of these statements brought a reaction from the group. Gayle wondered if it was the claim of sainthood, Ron's perceived arrogance, or simply personal button pushing. Ron was great at stimulating parts of others' egos to bring areas needing work to light.

At break Gayle walked back to the tennis court that she and Nancy had visited the week before. The wind was blowing more, but also the sense of magic was not there. Perhaps it was her fear. Given what she was hearing about Ron's relationships with his students, maybe that was what was required to attain to achieve enlightenment. Perhaps she had been too hasty in rejecting his advances.

"Is this a price I am willing to pay?" Sex had become less important after leaving DJ. She wanted more than just physical intimacy; she wanted emotional and spiritual intimacy as well. If a sexual relationship was part of the package, did she want to continue? Gayle contemplated that and then remembered Deb's counsel that some thought of him as a father and some as a lover. Gayle mused that some probably did both. She walked slowly down the hill back to the lodge.

Still there was that suggestion that they be willing to stand naked in front of the group. Now she wondered if he meant that literally. Salacious behavior to satisfy egos she could not do. Lust was one of the deadly sins. She never could list them all, but she knew lust was one of them. As soon as she entered the hall, Judy grabbed her elbow.

"I've been looking for you. You doing okay here?" Gayle looked into the elderly woman's wise eyes. She had been one of Georgie's friends. There was compassion here.

"I guess. We don't really have to stand naked in circle, do we?" Gayle's words slipped out.

"No," Judy laughed. "You don't. But I did want to tell you that during that long ride with Georgia from Atlanta to Mississippi, Georgie told me about your reading."

"She did?" Gayle wasn't sure whether she wanted to hear this or not.

"Yes, it gave us time to plan. While I'm not sure that she knew it was imminent, the reading opened the door for us to discuss her death and burial wishes. It was a gift for her, Gayle, a gift."

Gayle was relieved that her revelation of Georgie's impending death had served a greater need. However, it would be a long time before she gave another reading.

A Visit with the Twelve

Ron was late for the evening ritual. Of course, the others were used to him not being on time so there was little concern. They just gathered when he showed up. It had been dark for a while when he did. He offered no explanation.

"We're not going to do much in the way of lecture and move directly into the evening ritual. I'm going to set a pattern in the room. Once you perceive it, use your intuition to determine where you should stand when I invoke the Twelve."

The group formed a standing circle around Ron who stood in the middle of the room. He closed his eyes and Gayle immediately felt the type of energy the Third Wave had finally achieved the week before. This Foundation group could access that level immediately. To her surprise, the pattern was instantly visible in the astral. When looking for her own position, Gayle was astounded that her mind placed her in the center with Ron. There was no way she was going to stand there. Instead, she opted to move into a place where few stood. She would allow the energy to connect there.

The room was pregnant with expectation. Gayle worked to simply remain open to whatever might happen. As Ron stood in the center, he observed the pattern and made a few slight adjustments by asking a few people to shift their positions. Satisfied, he raised his arms in a chalice position and called upon the archetypal essences. Within moments Gayle saw silvery columns of light descending into the room. Looking up, she noted a convex colander-like container above streaming light. When a single silver column overshadowed her, Gayle was no longer able to observe, but was totally consumed with a flood of golden energy filling her. The energy pushed her slightly off balance. At one point, she wondered if she could remain standing. She held the position until minutes later it all faded away. The room returned to being an odd assortment of people standing around a man whose face glowed from the experience.

Beyond the Twelve

The group sat down in whatever spot that was near. No one talked as most seemed profoundly affected. Even those few who weren't waited to hear what Ron would share. Ron's voice was shaky and he uncharacteristically searched for words. Gayle sensed this was a new energetic experience for Ron and hence the description was original.

"In opening the door for the descent of the Twelve, the archetypes were quick to respond. I had perhaps two solid minutes of satori, a Japanese Buddhist term for enlightenment or knowing. Two minutes may not sound long, but most people don't have that within their entire life span. The experience was mind boggling. Beyond the Twelve, I could get there and yet could find nothing there. There was no light and there was no darkness."

The group remained silent. They were fatigued, but they also didn't want to interrupt the account of the experience. They knew that state specific consciousness would not allow the details to emerge in the same way if there was a dialogue. They listened intently.

"Within the last nine months while I could push through this space, it took me a while to find a description of it. It includes creation. My only experiences there indicate that I am no longer in anything contiguous with human consciousness. There is an unchanging plane of dimensional potency that is a release of all meaning, all hunger, and all expectation. There is no intellect there. Don't mistake intellectually projecting what should be there as it is based on nothing known. Whatever drives me is to bring more awareness and consciousness to matter."

The people in the group were beginning to act normal again. Some got up and went to bed. Others lounged in space. Some gathered their belongings while others moved back to their original seat in the room. Gayle sat.

"The black hole is filled with fear. Everything ended in nothing except that I had gone beyond to a place where everything comes into being, lives and exists, and then extinguishes. There is no linearity to this and as I felt my way through I realized it was a circle–the great circle of meditation. There was no longer any up or down. I had sent the thread through and met it coming back to me. I'm the prow of your ship. You will all pass through these same waters."

Ron paused to find his microphone and turn the recorder on. The tapes served him as well. He knew how quickly mystical experiences could fade in the mind.

"There is presence without content. My reaching your collective unconscious and connecting to where most are linked to the collective super-consciousness opens the door for each of you. The barrier in the middle is ego, time and space and all. Your identity will exist both above and below the ego. The ego keeps you a working member of society while the other levels will contain it. Sub and super consciousness meet in a dimensional shift.

"In completing this great circle, is this the end of an evolutionary line?" Janet asked.

"Do you mean have I killed a lot of archetypes? I hadn't considered that. It's possible." Ron pondered that a moment. "But the archetypal realm may disappear as I have a prediction that I have always made which is that if the Bonclarken experiment does not self-destruct or run out of steam, it may serve the next stage of human development as archetypal presence. The human essence has to be strengthened enough to hold an archetypal realm. A sure way to become insane is to be touched by a god."

Gayle was dumbfounded. Perhaps Mark's experience at Pathfinder with Gayle's group had been an encounter with a god. Death and insanity accomplished with one touch. When Ron left, others dispersed as well. Gayle wasn't sleepy, but knew it was time to rest.

The Others

At break after morning meditation, Gayle glanced over the eclectic selection of books the infamous Marie-Claude had displayed. Others in the group, besides Ron, had told of the enigmatic Frenchwoman who drew symbols and worked the energies with her body in dance. Her French accent and speech patterns gave her words a different slant when she spoke. Marie-Claude had no problem objecting to what seemed to be arrogant statements made by Ron or questioning why he interrupted the flow of energy to talk. Gayle began to put herself in Marie-Claude's path. She wanted to know this woman who seemed to intimidate Ron.

"Well, Bambina, what do you make of this so far?" Marie-Claude asked her on the porch. The porch was the only place where smoking was allowed and many of the outcasts gathered there to discuss events, smoke, and commune.

"I'm not sure yet."

"Ah, one who is wise enough to know she doesn't know everything," Marie-Claude giggled at her own pronouncement. The woman wore a long skirt, with simple t-shirt blouse, and yet appeared stylish in a European way.

"I lived in New York. I flew." She giggled again in her own unique style. "I used to watch ze man with his zig-zag energy. You watch out for that."

Al, Wade, and George were at the far end of the porch. They were natural rebels. Gayle didn't feel it time to make conversation, but she made a point to sit near them at the next session. She had always preferred male energy.

9 PM Meditation Lecture

Some time back Ron had requested that everyone tune into the group consciousness at nine o'clock each evening. Most chose to meditate at that time. Now he wanted feedback as to the effects it may or may not be having.

"Some will feel the call regardless of looking at the clock or not, they are called. There is no message, but only awareness to subliminal consciousness. This is a non-verbal and non-spatial area of being. When I tuned in to you, most were not consciously participating. This was an exercise to be conscious outside time and space–it opened the door to the collective unconsciousness. After some reported minute and hours delay, I realize that this was the time it took to propagate through individual awareness."

The group had little to offer beyond what Ron had stated. Gayle sat among the men in this session. George, Al, Ken and Wade eagerly embraced her into what they called the dark side. She sat content snuggled among the men and they welcomed the presence of a light goddess. So many dark goddesses in Ron's group kept him a light god. Her presence in the smaller inner group allowed them to be dark and seductive. Ron eyed them a bit jealously.

Bob had started snoring and Martin had been asleep for some time. Most of the group was dozing or lounging. Gayle couldn't keep track of the discussion. However, she did hear a consensus to continue to experiment with group meditation at 9 PM.

Three Graces

Gayle dreamed that she and Ron were in a large formal room fully conscious and awake. A child approximately six or seven with golden blonde hair was bought in. 'This is your daughter,' the disembodied voice informed them. 'At twelve, she is more aware than either of you.' The beings led the nude girl down the hall. Gayle noticed that her hair had never been cut and was unusually shiny.

When she awakened, Gayle realized there were people out on the porch talking. It was not as late as it had seemed. She had gotten very little sleep at the Bonclarken week. She eavesdropped on the porch conversations for a few moments, but didn't find the conversation of interest. She slipped out the back door just to be away and among nature. Even as a child she found nature as a refuge—whether she built hedge forts in the woods behind her parents' home, or watched her dog leap above the straw in the dormant farm fields in search of rabbits, or even when she pulled the grass out of the dirt driveway. Nature and animals were kinder than people. Nature did involve the survival of the fittest. There were no head games there. Instincts and wit prevailed. Gayle drank in the starlight filtering through the trees. When filled, she headed back to the cabin. A figure was running uphill toward her on the deserted road. Turning, Gayle was surprised to meet Janet returning from a run.

"Where are you headed?"

"Actually just into the sacred grove of little trees here," Gayle pointed to the twisted shrubs that had called to her. "I have to dance. Words are not my first language; dance is. Want to join me?"

Gayle wasn't sure when Bea showed up, but the three of them were in the woods late at night under the light of the moon. It was a courtly dance, one made for three.

"Do you think Ron's aware of what we are doing?"

"Of course," Gayle said. While Janet wanted to go and awaken him to get his perspective, Gayle felt Janet's ego was too involved with the situation so she and Bea returned to the lodge. Gayle reflected on one of her favorite paintings, *The Three Graces*. In similar form, their dance had innocently created magic out in the woods outside of Lookout Lodge.

Karmic Sludge

In the morning Ron admonished the group for not getting it together meditatively. Personalities were acting out and members were not able to focus or blend in meditation. There was not enough energetic force or chi to make the group work at the higher levels. Gayle wondered why they did not do sandpile to coalesce together as the Third Wave had done last week. This group was different though. Some were there for social reasons, some to learn, some not to miss something and some to evolve.

"The current astrological energy could also interfere by providing too much psychological energy for the group." Ron said, "Simply put, the group was overwhelmed by too much presence."

"I am finding it very hard to be in the group and it is overwhelming me and making me feel toxic," said Jen.

"Toxic energy is being liberated through some of our work. Excess energy must break out. Others can look at you and say, 'You're getting sick.' Toxins are excreted and you get achy muscles-the white blood cells are fighting the virus or foreign and toxic invader."

A Lecture on Meaning

Ron's lectures often presented new perspectives on the same topics. This afternoon's was no different. Perhaps this was why a lot of the group dozed or daydreamed through them. However, Gayle found new things in old subjects no matter what Ron talked about. This time he appeared to be addressing the malaise of the group through the process of the great meditation circle.

"Meaning is the last bastion of the intellect. The encounter of the black hole in the spiral often results in the individual finding no meaning in life. The person can never find pleasure in the world anymore. While there is meaning in existence, a true identity extends beyond intellectual realms."

Ron further explained that a master magician or mystic generated meaning in the emptiness. The intellectual process, however, was destroyed. Either through intellectual arrogance or intuitive knowing, there arises meaning without beginning and end. This precise point allowed a person to see through all illusion. At this point a person understands personal karma and finds mystical awareness. A person falls into the heart.

"Meaning, emptiness and mortality–you refuse to become all you may be because you can't deal with the responsibility or it may be meaningless. You end up in negation of self because self is meaning. Am I real when I am not doing and being anything?"

Dark Night of the Soul

Ron used everything in his awareness as a teaching. He questioned the value of living an ordinary life without being suicidal. The larger question was how to recreate meaning or find it. If one failed to find meaning, then one entered into the Dark Night of the Soul. The Dark Night of the Soul was having touched the divine in a mystical awareness and then falling back without the content of that mystical awareness so that everything became meaningless.

The second Bonclarken training had been about Re-member and the ability to remember the mystical awareness the group had attained.

If the validity of the mystical opening was not remembered, then it all became meaningless.

Gayle noted a marked difference between the Foundation group and the Third Wave. Most of the people at Foundation had been with him from the beginning when evidently the meetings were more experiential and much more lax. In the porch discussions, stories of loud parties, dancing and drinking emerged. Some people left the group after the initial training. Many didn't make the transition from the Bonclarken phase to join the working Foundation group. By the time the Third Wave group came into being, Foundation had evolved into something quite different than its original intention. The results of the Bonclarken experiment had already been determined. The second group confirmed it. Now Ron sought to put more discipline and ego work into an established, but resistant group.

"You may develop extraordinary psychic abilities and not to be trapped by the power you manipulate. You must live in balance with body and emotions. Are you being inflated by the energies beyond capacity? Are you human or are you god? You are not big enough. Your entire system has to be redesigned to allow the energy to flow through it. I want conscious aware human beings extending beyond normal operation. You need some working system to deliver what you have found back here or you are on a one-way trip. The only reason I want to do it is that I must complete. I like earth. I like spirit. I love bodies. Anne Rice has been writing my biography in Lasher."

Gayle took this lecture personally. She had already been without meaning for some time. Ron's description of the extension of self into the mystical realm had already brought her to a fork in the road. His expansion was to create a decision point of whether to locate her identity in spirit or matter. The matters of the world no longer had the same significance.

"Should one become a wandering ascetic forgoing the material desires of the world? The state of being without meaning is an indication of processing," Ron finished.

There was little discussion of this quandary. Perhaps others had not yet encountered the mystical realm. Yet, Ron had promised that if he had experienced the mystical state, then everyone in the group had experienced it with him to the best of their own capability. Gayle was left with more questions than answers.

Spirit Matters

The natural quandary as Ron described it was to balance the desire to be spirit and matter. Everyone would be faced with that dilemma in their own structure. The side effects could be body or mind manifestation that expressed as strong pathologies. The physical body went awry, but a person could treat its dysfunction without resolving its dual nature. Even if duality was balanced as he explained it, another part of the system could malfunction. The hybrid human nature created a floating physical malaise. However, when the mystic emerged with the realms properly aligned, there was an aged, scarred body, but it no longer caused many problems. If unlucky, then the overload of archetypal energies generated issues in the emotional realms.

"As I worked with a member of the Third Wave group last week, I gave him a good coping mechanism as a kick into the system. Initiates must become physically and emotionally stable. Of course that spirals into mentally and spiritually as well since only then does the integration of body, mind and soul occur. The place of integration insures that the human system is no longer an impediment."

"Bo greshe ba." Brenda interjected with strange language that given the lack of reaction by the group was seemingly part of her past acting out of energies. She made a quick apology and Ron moved on.

"You are an archetype–god and human. Both and neither. You are capable of being an avatar. You have become the completed magician having built the perfect universe. If at that stage one is not complete, then one must destroy oneself and begin again."

Gayle realized that she fit with this group. The training level of her Bonclarken week was too easy, but now she had a place where she wasn't some freak of nature, but a valued peer. She found that the people in this group while diverse, all shared experience in the energies. Indeed that may be the only common denominator they had. The members included lawyers, doctors, clerks, massage therapists, students, psychologists, retirees and a mix of other statuses. Each had their own connection to Ron and their own reasons as to why they were part of this rather eclectic experiment.

"In order to find wholeness, you must break down your universe. You must go into the space that has no boundaries. There is a place that cannot be known and nothing you can extend to find contact or reaction. You cannot even push against yourself. There is no longer a universe inside you. It is an impossible place to go into the Great Death–death of everything even death of death. The fall of heart can be blocked by fear or by desire. No balance is found with form. Let go of everything without it being despair. You integrated form, matter and awareness and you are complete."

Ron's technique mapped the stages of a process with relevant markers to reassure initiates they were making progress. This sometimes was the only thing that kept them going through some tense moments. Ultimately there was an end to every journey. The end was where the student doesn't identify with what arose. The ultimate quality was experienced and the initiate, now mystic, had become nothing but the process and the drive. Only then was the journey through the spectrum of consciousness complete.

"Be careful of creating your opposite, in my case this group, whose tension you use to push through to the next level. We'll talk later about the position of the evolutionary process–the tree of life, how to create soul, long life, and adeptus exemptus. I hope this is real to you."

Dinner was filled with animated conversation, a few teachings and lingering over dessert. Gayle got up and began the dishes. She washed methodically. Washing dishes had been her chore at home. Her year younger sister had managed not to do a good enough job to be in the rotation. Yet, she liked the physical movement, hearing the others talk without having to participate, and finding that space where she could be alone with others. In NYC she had learned the ability to have privacy among millions. Perhaps it was the privacy that kept her sane from the insanity of her life.

"Who's signed up for dishes tonight? Gayle is in here alone doing them by herself," Ron bellowed to the group.

Within moments, others arrived and moved her out of position. Not feeling useful any longer, she headed back to her room on the second floor. There was a different vibe on the second floor of the house. However, she preferred the bathrooms downstairs. Her life had marked the places of good bathrooms. She preferred clean and modern, and much preferred those of her own than public facilities. Now she wondered why she was thinking of bathrooms. Oh yes, the recurring dream of an open bathroom filled with overflowing toilets had been part of the previous evening's dreams. Lots of stuff was not going down.

Spiritual Hierarchies

Sometimes Ron's histories sounded more like memories. His description of where humanity had begun and where it was going included a lecture on intermediaries that served as the liaison between gods and humans. Wise women, shamans, or priests and priestesses attempted to personify what human beings were looking for. These people specialized in providing a link between matter and spirit. While they may have known nothing of medicine and psychology, they could serve as a channel to mystical knowing that would elevate the person. The elevation alone could bring clarity and insight to heal.

Intermediaries built systems among themselves. This psychic force made them know that they were more than animals. There became a hierarchy of beings. Higher consciousness and essences build knowledgeable systems, knowing which buttons to push within themselves and people who could extract it from their aura.

For example, Eskimos were among the first to ingest a spiritual source of hallucinogenic mushrooms. After their process, some were allowed to drink the urine that still contained some of the properties. Yet in one step removed, others could drink the second generation urine and get less of a high. There was a similar chain of transmission of energy and awareness with a hierarchy of priestesses and priests. Of course, the purest substances were given to those most capable of handling it.

How the energy was channeled whether through tantric mysteries, rituals and sacrifices or though patterns of energy created by a group changed people profoundly. People refined it into religious ritual using external symbol and internal energetic awareness.

Christian mass was an old mystery school tradition. What is now known as the Eucharist involving the bread and wine becoming the body and blood also related back to you are what you eat. If you wanted to become Christ-like, eat of his body and drink his blood. This was also practiced long before Christianity as part of the warrior religion called Mithraism. The blood of the bull figured prominently there. It is not unusual for religious traditions to borrow from each other. Mithraism was the Roman religion before Christianity became the state religion. The son of the Sun, the date of Saturnalia, was adopted as the birth of Jesus, and the Eucharist were adapted from Mithraism into Christianity.

Gayle felt the connection. The trip to Italy had opened many doors for Gayle. Perhaps the most important, other than the rituals of bull sacrifice, was that there was a mystery school for women. While it was true some cultures such as the Navaho were matriarchal, most western religions focused primarily on men. Some religious traditions denied teachings to women. Even most of the ancient mystery schools had limited access for women. Within the mysteries of Dionysus, the dichotomy between patriarchy and matriarchy could only be resolved in the sacred marriage. The symbolism of the art, the balance of the rituals and the esoteric teachings for the divine principle spoke to a more equal status. The signs were there for those with the eyes to see.

"Many know the external symbol without the initiatory energies. Over time the loss of the higher energy and knowing turns many rituals into simple repetitions of an act without meaning. There are higher mysteries reserved for the initiates and the lower mysteries are what the public would practice. Yet, there are always those prodigies who could intuit higher energetic principle and serve as channel."

Chapter 11 – Blueprint for the Future

Creating a New Energy Pattern - School

The days blended one into another as the lecture and experiments continued. Gayle sat like a sponge trying to absorb as much as she could. She noted the patterns Ron created and the group's reactions. Some day she might need them.

Foundation, according to Ron, needed to create an energy pattern with no relationship to past patterns. Much like creating a new universe or founding a new religion, the new pattern required the incorporation of karma as cause and effect, the chain of causation, and perhaps a Buddhist Pure Land where souls could be uplifted in order to continue to learn without falling back to their former status. Ron's interpretation was that the first effort should begin with real small boundaries. Then the group could build upon it in small stages.

"This way when you slip, you don't fall as long a distance," he reminded. "A hierarchy of people is not what I am talking about."

"There have always been schemes of energy and ritual," Sue added. "An internal clarity will disappear as we disappear. There must always be a relationship of vital energy and force and a constant replenishing of the foundation of the structure."

"The more sensitive part is to have pure intention. Determine the pattern for you to weave it through. The intention needs to be approached with clarity. No matter what you do, if you act in total consciousness you can make no mistake. No matter what, Foundation has to consider the nature of our responsibilities."

Janet had once mentioned that one of Ron's driving forces was to create a school to pass on the techniques Ron had developed as well as the access to the higher energies. In his mind, Ron's success with his first experiment and then repeating it to make sure it had worked fulfilled the obligation that had driven him. At the same time he felt it important to create a structure for those who had given so freely of their time and energy to push him through.

"If you knew the moment of your death, you would not fool around. Even as I talk of school and have primed this Third Wave to come in hot, all that seems really important is to transmit the energy right. Then it doesn't matter what else happens."

Ron's sessions as well as the mystery schools he referred to all involved bringing a person to the point of death. That pivotal point is where the ego drops away, all superficiality fades to black, and only the most important truths are faced.

"I've faced death many times. My parents were told I would be dead before morning, then I was told it would be before twenty, then before forty...and now I know I am going to die soon. There are a lot of things involved when I tell you that–get this material out of me while you can."

Gayle heard this–and she made a commitment. She had to know. While Ron seemed to pride himself on never having a teacher, she did not share that aspect of ego. She had three major teachers and yet it was Ron who addressed the issues she needed to know most. There was no tried and true path, but an ever-evolving spiral. She would get as much as she could from the man.

"We're on a suicide mission–none of us are going to get out of this alive. The more successful you are, the faster you will die. I am becoming ripe for the Eagle. Foundation must build a state of heightened awareness; you must begin to feel it. We have to come up with a plan before the oxygen runs out."

"The group must learn to trust itself. We can use the Tupelo Pledge to call each other on glitches," Martin offered. The women from Tupelo, Mississippi had pledged to be honest and real with each other in order to stay clear of the ego traps and to remember those higher states of awareness.

"We must scrape the bottom of the barrel for all awareness: consciousness, spirit, soul, intellect, emotion, and body," Ken said.

"When I first contacted this high energy source, I fried every tape recorder within 50 feet of me. It isn't what you say, but how you hold the tensions of the dynamics to resolve that is important. Barb, Jill, and Patsy all left Foundation and then came back. School is not a thing, but an energetic principle," Ron concluded. Al, who was already teaching within his own school, wondered how his own would be incorporated.

"Of course your work is a part of this, Al. Any physical thing can carry the principle. School is an energetic principle. The people in this room are conscious fortune cookies. There is a concept that is real–a platonic system. We are boiling down people down to their bones. We are not going to be transmitting the flesh, but the structure. The people here are in a heightened state which we try to reproduce as often as possible. Understand the ladder and the transcendence. You are digging your rut deep enough to bury yourself in. You must overcome your ego."

Gayle noted that the answer seemed to satisfy Al, but she wondered how individual schools could effectively bring their groups together for a larger work. Already an attempt with bringing Barb's students into Foundation had not worked satisfactorily. While Al's school was more psychologically based, others worked with magical systems or within other traditions. So at the moment Ron's statements to start a school seemed more of a statement of desire rather than a plan to move forward.

"I hope I know when I am going to die. It would be nice to know that before it happens...we need to be ready."

Posture, Movement and Meditation

The meditations for Gayle were becoming less of an endurance test and more of enlightenment. The visions came fast and there were times she simply stopped mid-meditation to jot down a note or two so they would not be forgotten. Some were sketches or lines while other times it was just a key word to jog her memory. Despite Ron alluding to

Castaneda's obsession with writing things down as being totally unnecessary, Gayle was compelled to establish her own vocabulary of symbols and reminders. After being clued in that Ron did not record everything said, she also began taking her own notes during the lectures.

After observing a teaching by Barb, Gayle noted her precise use of mudra in meditation. She knew that Buddhist art often depicted a quality by the position of the hands, fingers, and spine. Her own experiments showed that the language of mudra as expressed in Hinduism and Buddhism worked well for her. The palm, held upright and facing a person, expressed the sentiment of "fear not." If she brought her fingers together as if drawing a thread of energy down from above, the focus came together in the room.

Now in meditation Gayle found a position where sitting was perfectly balanced and almost effortless. By rocking gently back and forth or using the sacral pump to generate energy, she could sit for long hours. In those moments of correct alignment, Gayle often felt her neck or back crack as if in a chiropractic adjustment. It felt good. Only when she got up did the muscles protest staying in one position for too long.

The meditations were more interactive with Foundation than Ron's Third Wave training group. These people were less disciplined and obviously were untamed in their interactions with Ron. There was more feedback, more conversation, and fewer were intimidated by Ron. Their past shared experiences bound them in that relationship. In the Third Wave Ron had established himself as a dominant force. He had an agenda with no karma with the training group.

Dreams

At the beginning of the next teaching session, Ron read an account of a significant dream by one of his advanced students who had just recently returned to his teaching circle.

I am going back to a place not seen for many years. Others do not want me to go, but I pay no mind. I am transported by moving sidewalks to a field where there is brilliant green grass and a bright blue ocean beyond. There is an unusual humming that makes a beautiful strange music holding this place together. I arrive at a glass crystal building where there are lines that separate blue and green. Inside there are no ends to the lines. This perfect harmony is made by lines. I was rather dispassionate. There was equal regard for any and everything. I hold one of the lines, a filament, in my hand, and it brings a drop of blood that becomes part of the network.

Ron made no comment, but recalled a dream of his own that had awakened him at 4 AM. The outer memory of the dream was vaguely anxious. He was in an office building with limited or restricted access since it held confidential material of some sort. Metal detectors lined the doorways. However, he was leader of a squad with a mission to acquire something vital–to recover a computer disk or something with more impact.

He now knew the elaborate plans made weren't sufficient to get the group out. Alarms were tripped. There was one scheme where one punched a number sequence to exit. However, it was too late. Guards permeated the building to find the intruders. There are only two ways possible to get out now: evade metal detectors or by the use of a long strange cord. This cord was a strange metal device about ten inches long shaped like a spike-like dibble–a device used to plant seeds. Ron twirled the cord to a point to stick into the other end. Although the anxiety woke him at that point, when he got back to sleep the dream continued.

Other people had broken out of the building and dashed out in all directions. Ron was being chased. One identifiable strong young man was going to wreak havoc on him. He had a mesomorphic face and was a member of the dark intelligence forces. This muscleman was trained to hunt and he was after Ron specifically. He had only one grim purpose: to destroy him.

"A hubcap which was mentioned yesterday in conversation came into the dream. Something appears on the street–a gold hubcap, saucer-like, and I maneuver this. My antagonist is trapped in the saucer. He has shrunk to the size of this bowl and he is lying there helpless. He is holding either pan pipes or the shamanistic rattle. I slowly turn the bowl over and shove it to the sewer opening. It is large enough to slide them into the underground. Dream resumes. I am held captive, but without violence by a group of four beings whose faces and actions are neutral. The older man with authority is determined for me to confess and giving up some bit of knowledge. I must confess and yield which I don't want to do. There is more threatening energy. The fourth was a distorted man who was evidently called in as the torturer. He laid out implements that would cause exquisite pain. The expectation was painful, but he can't hurt me. The threatening man says of course there is no way we can actually hurt you, but you better give me what we want before we hurt you."

The dream itself was full of symbols of laboratories, restricted access, and shamans with dark magic and voices that murmured that they couldn't hurt her that reverberated in the memories of Gayle's dreamy astral world. Yet it was the four beings that triggered Gayle. She had forgotten how horrible her predicament had been in New Jersey. She loved an alcoholic, she hated her job, she hated the cold weather, and her soul connection was lost. In her despair one evening Gayle cried out for help as she fell down an endless well. Four beings showed themselves at the top of the well and leaned over placing their arms inside as if to catch her. Their arms began extending faster than she was falling. They caught her just as she was about to hit the bottom. Even as that long ago memory surfaced, Gayle resonated with the comment that they couldn't hurt him. The beings from the UFO hypnosis session had said the same thing to her. Ron continued with his own dream account.

"Then they let in someone else. It was Samantha, my former lover and partner. Evidently since I was not going to yield to them, they will torture her. The energy of unbearable agony was in the air, but still I could remember them saying 'No, they can't hurt anyone.' Samantha came out sobbing deeply and told me what they had done. She was terribly frightened. Maybe someone will interpret this later for me."

Ron shook his head as if to shake the memory of having caused such pain to his former lover. The group was rather disorganized so the rather quiet Buddhist, James, spoke up.

"I loved hearing the Gregorian chants this morning as we came in for meditation. My dreams were rather dark last night as well as if they came from a really dark, dank place. I was on a table surrounded by several members of the Inquisition. I was being tortured and about ready to die. Just as I was screaming in agony and pain, I woke up." James seldom spoke up during the week. This is the first time Gayle had heard the gentle artist reveal anything personal.

"Oh, I forgot to mention something, Ron. They were taking apart a stone building to use for rebuilding a new place elsewhere."

"We are enacting karmic lines for people–valid outside of this room. Between Barb and James, I thought this was worth bringing up," Ron said as he concluded the session.

The Twelve

"Integration destroyed the archetypes just as forgetting the gods caused the twilight of the gods. You are all aware of the trinity and the four which makes up the twelve. There are four sets of three in the twelve: three bright masculine, three bright feminine, three dark masculine, and three dark feminine. The bright goddess may contain all three at one time or they can be separate. A trinity is three in one or one in three."

Ron explained that within those twelve, the principle of point, spiral, and pattern applied. The naming, for example-maiden, mother, crone, as a trinity was not the point. The spiral destroyed in order to create. The process began with a simple identity and evolved it to become more complex. Some archetypal presence broke down existing pattern. If done correctly, the patterns collapse on their own. Sekmet, the Egyptian lioness goddess, destroyed intellect, illusion, and hubris for example. In the Hindu tradition, it is Kali who destroyed illusion. Ron explained the trinity more in the Hindu terms of creating, sustaining and destroying aspects. The group was looking blankly back at Ron. He changed up the style to inject an example.

"A mass murderer is a person whose ego structure is so weak that he is taken over by the desire to assume an identity. I use the example with a man since women have too much of the nurturer aspect and do not destruct anything except for themselves." Seeing the group was now paying attention Ron continued.

"If a man is fearful of dissolving into nothing, he seeks a substitute identity in the sense that 'If I kill someone famous I will acquire their identity.' John Wilkes Booth killed Lincoln and absorbed his vitality. By nature a President is archetypal as he contains something of everyone in the country. They find the destroying principle easier to assume than the creating one. A tremendous amount of energy must be focused to create. This person, seeing themselves disintegrated, knows that if they will kill enough people that it will end the desire within themselves to destroy themselves. They will take on a new archetypal energy. A mass murderer faces emptiness and is afraid to die. They take this tension within them from this archetypal energy and turn this drive outward. They end up with a rifle on a tower and shooting people. Some underlying core belief is enacting a ritual sacrifice or sexual mystery taboos that will redeem them."

On that note, they took a break.

Embracing Archetypal Energy

It was Thursday afternoon and the group was fatigued. Some were visibly ready to go home, but no one wanted to miss the final night's energy ritual. The pattern of Ron's intensives meant a first exposure on opening night to determine where the blocks were, releasing the barriers, sharing experiences and on the final night to put it all on the line again. Most of the time it worked.

"Both Jennifer and Catherine expressed that they feel more alive here. People change at these weeks. Stay conscious and create a self-memory in the back of your head or somewhere of an enhanced presence. Enhance the tantric dynamic between self and others without it being an intellectual exercise. Keep waking up. Keep remembering. Watch the process going on as well as being in it. Create a conscious observer."

Ron expounded on how the archetypal energy encourages growth through dynamic tension. The tension existed between light and dark and then male and female. However, the tension of the trinity was self-resolving and self-creating constantly like the dynamic version of the yin-yang Chinese symbol.

"So what is the difference between the archetypal realm versus the twelve?" Charlotte asked. Gayle observed Charlotte to be very clear of ego. The petite refined lady was also known as the "harlot" and could tell the best raunchy jokes. Whenever Ron needed levity in the group, it was Charlotte who held court. Despite or perhaps because she was hard of hearing, she listened carefully to the lectures and was quite knowledgeable.

"The archetypal covers the bottom of a range of energy that at its peak is the twelve essences. Archetypes do change in our perception. They have been known in the past, but are they are difficult to find today. It is possible that archetypes won't be known until the far future. You think there are more than twelve, but those twelve are fundamental aspects. The twelve have a crystallized purity." Ron stood to draw a pyramid of dots on the easel pad.

"The pyramid shows three and four as one of the Pythagorean mysteries. It is a symbol of a hologram. If you know this, it gets simpler. To the degree intellect is left behind it becomes simpler, but also fuller and richer. It's simple, but not easy."

In the meditation that followed Ron was attempting *darshan*, a type of energetic immersion versus a formed structure or configuration. While he did this in the original Bonclarken training, it seemed very few could soak it up. Consequently he had created structures that could lead to higher structures. Eventually his plan was to infuse awareness without the structure in it. He expected the group to be able to transfuse the subtlety of that level and become master teachers there.

Unlike most meditations where there was no talking, Ron slowly brought the group into each realm, described the barriers to it and the techniques used to move beyond them. He asked the group to become aware of more subtleties at each level of awareness. The emphasis was on manifestation and the basic fundamental nature of that level of energy. The demonstration was to teach how one coalesced energy from the lowest level that contains personal vitality and then pushed it through to the next level.

"This process is similar to diving. We are at the bottom of a great ocean. The temperature increases as you rise to the surface. Reach out and collapse chi–it crystallizes, elongates and penetrates different levels. That is the form that Kundalini moves energy from the base up the spine until it arrives higher in the spectrum of consciousness. If not from the bottom, it would have a different effect completely."

Gayle could feel each shift and see each marker. The painting of the inside of her head she had done so long ago in her den now manifested in more dimensions. She now understood that she had always been able to achieve mystical awareness. That awareness was the source of her intuition and foreknowledge. Now she could break it down to teach others. The long hours in meditation with Ron were suddenly paying off.

When the meditation ended, Gayle opened her eyes to a different world. Everything was made up of lines. She could barely make out people since the energy lines that comprised them overlaid her vision. However, when she looked for Ron, he had disappeared at the front of the room. Behind him, the stones in the fireplace wall had become waves of energy. She could hear him talking, but his physical form was fading in and out of physical reality. The last time she had observed the transparency of rocks and reality had been on the only acid trip she had done. She really could achieve these states. No drugs required.

Last Ritual

As Ron reminded them, a ritual could never be done the same way twice. Using the tree of life structure borrowed from the Cabala, he had people sort themselves for the proper station to stand in. He sent a test signal to see if the pattern would conduct energy.

"Stuart, could you move to this side of the room? Barb, will you join Jan at the base of this structure as part of the mirror?" After they moved, the pattern was tested again and passed to his satisfaction.

This time Ron evoked the energies in zigzag pattern. The energy came down from the top moving from station to station until it reached its target recipient who sent the energy back up to the top. It took a couple of attempts until it worked and it appeared that Ron had reached some kind of exalted state. He tried to share his experience with them.

"It was a successful experiment. Yet, the pattern did not work as I had thought it would. Once the energy could be felt returning to me, the whole pattern moved from the horizontal position to the vertical. There were other trees appearing in both directions."

While the group appeared to have had some experience of the energy, personally Gayle noted that she had little reaction to the different pattern. Either the intent was different or the reactions or possibly both, but she just noted it was different. For a fleeting second, she felt a large being out there, but it soon passed.

"The other sensation I had was a being with rays of light projecting from his eyes. If anything, it reminded me of the Seth channelings and the concept of an oversoul. This seemed to be a primeval soul containing all human souls. Hmmm, a blueprint of man if you will."

Ron soon realized that the group could no longer hold focus. He took a deep breath and dismissed them. Uncharacteristically, he went to his own room instead of participating in the last night party. The music was changed from New Age to classic rock, beer emerged from behind the milk cartons in the refrigerator and people partied on the porch and in the living room. The same ones who just participated in a spiritual ritual were now whooping it up. Gayle interacted with a few, but drunken parties were not her cup of tea. She went back to her room to pack and get some much needed sleep.

Foundation Farewell

The last morning of the intensive meditations was the best. The tension generated by the interactions of the group had been resolved and Gayle could simply sit in a place of bliss. The feeling of energy moving through her spine and surrounding her kept her in a high state of awareness. This morning, however, that shared space only lasted a few minutes as someone began gasping for breath and obviously was in crisis.

Ron rang the bell and jumped up quickly to be at Charlotte's side. There he simply held her for several minutes as Charlotte gradually moved from some emergency state to normal awareness. No one moved or spoke. It reminded Gayle of the aborted airplane takeoff quiet. Obviously class was over for the morning. Ron continued to hold Charlotte, but waved us to move on about our business.

People packed their cars and a few started putting the leftovers out to eat. If there was time afterward Ron would give a short closing teaching. In this case, it would be necessary to alleviate the group stress from Charlotte's reaction.

After the house was put back into its original state, Ron rapped on the meditation bowl sharply three times to call the group back together. The group had not yet shared on the meditation experiences of the morning, but Ron decided to speak only about the experience with Charlotte.

"Charlotte was overcome this morning. The energies directly affected her. You are not yet in a state to feel it. The animal body resists. As Charlotte will explain, she is fine, but I would like to hear impressions from a few of you. I have a good twenty minutes left on the tape."

Ron was serious about the recording. He hated to leave blank spaces on the cassettes. He prided himself for being able to complete concepts right before the tape ended. That meant he was in the flow.

"I noticed that your face became serious and almost stone like in meditation. As I focused a bit longer, I realized that your head was the one on the sphinx," Stuart said.

"Someone had to model for it, Stuart."

"I kept seeing a face looking at me while my eyes were closed," Martin said. Ron nodded.

"This one was difficult as I was not going up as I expected, but to another place. It was difficult to keep chatter down. There was a constant stream of stuff though from another level and it was aware. I was left with a warm fuzzy glow," Joe said.

"Joe often runs off in the mind. I'm describing this for you, Joe, to deal with it. You always want to respond to what others need, etc. and you are pulled out of yourself." Ron explained.

"This was the first good meditation all week," Jen said.

"I found a mythic connection that created a flow within myself. There was some level of balance, but it felt like the body and group energy was being infused in me with very soft warm energy," Gayle said.

"Being lacks ego which makes it gentle. I apologize," Ron responded.

"While the verbal chatter broke down, what disturbed me was the content of the imagery–sadistic pornographic images. Very disturbing. It's unpleasant," Martin shared.

"Things have been working on you, Martin. You are experiencing your shadow. You have kept your universe intact and orderly. Your buttons are being pushed internally versus intellectually. Our toughest warrior is beginning to crack. Did your experience include some people here?" Ron asked.

"I'm a bit ashamed," Martin said.

"Last night I evoked the dark male energy. Before it was over I had everyone's dark energy engaged. It will be going back into the earth. I think we have gotten to a place where it can be amusing and harmless. There are only twelve faces in the world," Ron explained. He nodded to Ken who had raised his hand.

"I need to recap. This morning I realized I had absorbed as much as I could. This morning mediation was already fading. But after Charlotte's experience, I was trying to hold focus. An internal voice chided me: 'How could you not be paying attention? He has given his body and his blood for us'," Ken said. Ron nodded as he contemplated his final comments for the week.

"I believe we reached the saturation point. The point of fatigue...and if one can focus at that point...pushed to the edge, that is where the greatest work is. I've gotten less sleep this week than I ever have. I pull myself into focus and the energy and power flows through. Forcing something to overcome the animal fatigue and to build chi builds soul. I plan to sleep a lot. You may go home and blank out, but don't sever your connection here. In this bag you take home, you may be too tired to unpack it. Later at home, unpack it."

"What happened to me was proof you are getting it even when you think you are not. I reached a place where heaven and earth were the same. There was a glory that filled my body and I was aware that I was carrying that package of energy within me," Charlotte said.

Ron ended with a ritual reading reminding them to keep silent about his mysteries. She wasn't too surprised when she received the tapes of the sessions a few weeks later that Ron had written her a note-"It felt right for you to be here the second week."

Chapter 12 – After the Thrill is Gone

Emails from Wade

Wade contacted her shortly after the conclusion of the Foundation meeting that Gayle visited. He copied these emails to only two or three select individuals. She had no idea that he had been married to the quiet Kira before her association with George. Through some long cigarette breaks on the porch with the mysterious Marie-Claude, Gayle gleaned some of the past history of the group. The Foundation group seemed less like a spiritual group and more like friends sharing some vacation time in an unknown inward adventure. Still, the group was loyal in not sharing the mysteries prematurely with her. Ron had made them all take an oath to keep silent about his mysteries.

Gayle had sought out both Wade and George during breaks as Ron's energy was both perturbed and stimulated by each of them. She made a point to ask them questions. So it was not too surprising to get some teachings through email from Wade. He was one of the few to keep in touch after the week ended.

Wade writes Nov. 7 - The assemblage point exists because we change our reality to include it. When you move into another world, you can perceive energy any way your intent and will dictates. Re: Don Juan's whereabouts – I recently sent you a reply about twirling eyes with music. Carlos' 360 degree total perception is the same thing. If you twist to the right, you access the right hand path. If you twist left, you access the left hand path. Mangravite has abandoned them to say keep to the middle path.

Wade writes Nov. 9 – Gayle, I read the article you sent on Castaneda. Even Don Juan told Carlos he was stupid when he took the drug. In my opinion, Don Juan never told Carlos about the other students.

Gayle writes Nov. 10 -Wade, Ron has not taught anything about the three paths in the Third Wave. Why is there so much tension between the two of you?

Gayle writes Nov. 28 – part of the tension I can speculate to be jealousy. The formation of a school is a goal he will probably not live to see. Ron still has the macho Italian manner. Being challenged is not of his favorite situation. Since both of you like to be in "control" there is conflict.

Wade writes Dec. 4- Gayle, the third attempt to get back to you is the charm. I learned early about the Foundation people. They were selected because of their energy–not by their knowing. I'm hesitant about talking about Ron and my conflict because it reveals aspects about me that are not generally known and puts me in a position of revealing things about Ron that would be detrimental to his.

Gayle writes Dec. 5 - Wade, I understand selection by energy lineage, but it would be more effective it seems if they also knew. It's black magic to use individuals without their knowledge. However, it seems those in Foundation give freely of their energy and trust to Ron.

Ron is cautious of discussing his purpose with me. Sometimes we have a level of trust, but it blows up after a very short while. It is hard for me to remain in the group. Regarding the access to the twelve–most of the time I don't bother with them and just go to other levels if I am working the path. This is illusion for me unless I am teaching. Even then, I am split into being and the teacher.

Everything exists as energy to me. I see lines that make up people, places and things. They interact and I may interact with them. It is easy to read when a line pattern is seen. These higher than normal vibratory levels I have learned from Ron by watching the patterns he creates. Whatever chores that present to me, I will do. I'm getting more Buddhist every day.

As to sharing your conflict with Ron, it is your choice. If you are worried about damaging my opinion of Ron, don't worry. I see him fairly clearly and have no desire to hurt either of you. My quest is for freedom.

I am very aware of Ron's past indiscretions and his arrogance and insecurity. It does intrigue me, but there are other worlds than these. Ron and I have a tenuous link. We do share mind occasionally, though I do know some areas where he does not have access.

Anyway, the air is purple whenever I shift slightly. This is somewhat like astral colors, but more present. People glow in little white eggs and I can touch the links making them up. They react in strange ways.

Dreams continue to be fun and interactive. I am very aware of Ron's dreams, but he seems to be sleeping of late. He looked very old last time I saw him and had little interest in anything. Oh, well.

Gayle did not receive a reply back from Wade. When she asked Deb about him, she replied that he had his own school rivaling Ron. Gayle appreciated that Wade had shared his experiences and perspectives with her. For her, Wade represented the dark magician energy. He was more accessible than Ron had been with her to date. Yet, she was being solicited as a student and that was not the path for her. The conflicts between Wade and Ron were part of a dynamic she did not wish to participate in. When Wade did not return to Foundation and did not respond to her emails, she let him go.

The Grit's Golden Bowl

The events of the intensives faded fast from everyday life with little fanfare of their departure. Mundane life just took over: academic classes, Pathfinder Bookstore group, overdue papers, and catching up with her new friends. Gayle regaled them all with tales of her experiences. Even though she found her experiences to push credibility, the group accepted them without question.

Gayle felt better about her decision to return to work with Ron after Foundation. There were others like her there sharing similar things. Even if she had to endure another week of the Third Wave, she would to join Foundation. Ron was much more open there as well. Deb and Bob called her more frequently to invite her to group dinners when someone from the group came to town. Gayle was now understanding a bit more about the group closeness. If there was a workshop somewhere, people frequently sacked out at the host's house. If there was travel to another area where a group member lived, people opened their homes as if the group members were family. Gradually she was feeling a bit more comfortable with the whole Bonclarken experiment. Besides, Janet had made her promise not to miss the unveiling of the mysteries the final Third Wave week.

At the university, Gayle was studying Islam and Sufism with Dr. Godlas. Gayle enjoyed his stream of consciousness lectures and unorthodox views. Godlas had studied under Huston Smith, author of *The World's Religions, in* California. Smith had experimented with Ram Dass and Timothy Leary in what was called empirical metaphysics. Godlas was a liberal breath of fresh air in the conservative Bible Belt school.

"He went to Berkeley," her friend Christina explained. "That explains everything."

Dr. Godlas was likeable, approachable, and encouraged debates in his classroom. On this day, Dr. Godlas had invited fellow UGA professor Coleman Barks to recite the Sufi Rumi's mystical poems for the class. While Barks did not read the Persian language of Farsi, Godlas had provided some literal translations of Rumi poems for Barks interpretation and were long time coworkers.

When the unruly-haired bearded man entered the class room, his presence quickly over took it. Barks only made a short introduction about himself and his love for the mystical poetry. The rhyme, rhythm, and bodily movement induced a state he called Mast, a state of intoxication. Instead of wine, though, the catalyst was the love of God. Within moments after Barks began his recitation, his intoxication led him from the outside world into the immersion of the inner plane. Gayle was astonished with the result of his process. Her path was opening into new realms of spiritual work. She buried herself in the academic process seeking to know and experience more.

When the intensive tapes arrived six weeks after the meeting, the insights of the training intensives emerged again as Gayle listened. Ron had said it would take six months to integrate all that she had been exposed to and was the reason his training weeks were spaced six months apart. There were entire sections on tape that Gayle seemingly heard for the first time. Knowing that she had not missed any lecture sessions, it was surprising to realize that in the energy Ron emitted she had not taken in the words or intellectual content. She also noted gaps where Ron had surreptitiously turned off his microphone so not to record some of the more esoteric material. She was thankful for her notes and memory to fill in the missing gaps.

Gayle admired the cover insert that Ron used for his cassette tapes. The sepia tones depicted the stained glass window of him with eagle wings walking through a winding river valley. That scene was a powerful marker of his own demand to move events forward to become enlightened. She had not forgotten her own pain in her search for a teacher-the loneliness, fear, and constant craving. The truth was closer; she could feel it.

However, the excitement of those training weeks made mundane life almost unbearable. There were times Gayle knew she lived only during those weeks. Other times it was the memory of something beyond every day awareness even if she could not access it. She had written Ron asking him to come do an evening meditation at her store. Her motives were not all altruistic; she needed a catalyst to shift the group and she wanted him to teach more. He and Sandi frequently left their rural North Carolina home to visit Atlanta for entertainment. Athens was a simple stop on their route and Ron agreed to come teach.

Today at Pathfinder Bookstore, Gayle was pricing her fairy and angel jewelry. She hated tagging items even though it was necessary. She fingered the star-burst cross, a fairy sprite, a peace sign, and an ankh. The ankh she didn't really want to sell. She made cards for the rocks she had purchased. There were stones used to bring abundance, confidence, grounding and healing. Marie Claude had invited her to the next North Carolina gem show. Gayle planned to go.

Ron was to demonstrate his meditation and energy circle style at her bookstore that evening. She met Ron and Sandi at the local vegetarian restaurant, the Grit, for dinner. The Grit had good healthy food at a price the students' budgets could handle. Ron and Sandi were delighted at the choice. Gayle suddenly looked up highly aware and conscious. Something had touched her.

"Don't ever forget that," Ron said. Sandi looked at him questioningly, but he did not explain it to her.

Later at the store there was a marked difference in the relationship between Gayle and Ron. As she sat there in a clear place, he acknowledged Gayle not only as a student, but also as a teacher. The thirty people there enjoyed what he called his cheap trick which was to influence people by manipulating their aura. Ron's lecture covered the spectrum of ghosts, UFO's and spirituality. The group was suitably inspired.

Yet it was Gayle who was most impressed. As her students raised their hand to ask Ron a question, Gayle sent the name telepathically to Ron who used it to call upon them. He didn't miss a name. They celebrated the event with coffee and chocolate decadence cake afterward.

On the Home Planet

As Gayle fell back into the routine of school, papers, the store and her teachings, she also began to realize that she enjoyed teaching. At Pathfinder Bookstore students showed up because they wanted to learn. The classes were entertaining, but also were building a sense of community that she had longed for. She was in the proper rhythm for a change.

The heavens provided the calendar of the mysteries with its rhythmic movement of stars, planets, comets, and moon. An observer hears the music of the spheres and the symphony of life. As Gayle taught the lesser mysteries, she taught the patterns of planting cycles, measurements of the moontimes, and the rituals honoring the equinoxes and solstices as markers of transition of the solar year. The heavens were ruled by the stars, those eternally glowing beings affecting all who lived beneath their lights.

Yet whenever she taught, Gayle's identity shifted back to ancient Egypt. She drew upon the teaching there to establish in this time. The destiny of the pharaohs of ancient Egypt was to transform one's human status to being a star. In part, that became the mission of the store.

The small New Age bookstore planted itself on the outskirts of the downtown area of Athens, Georgia. Taking Pathfinder as its name, the spiritual community had formed around spiritual exploration and blended into the diverse perennial student population. The art and music vibes of the town balanced the staid colonial educational structures across the street. The historical Arch marked a transition from the university and the town.

After the retail season and tiring of being confined to physical space, the focus began with creating a working spiritual group. The exploration of ritual, movement, and intuition gathered various cliques of students on several evenings each week.

On a rare free day one of her students, Michelle, drove Gayle out to the Georgia border to visit the Guidestones. Many years ago, a strange man going by the pseudonym R.C. Christian had commissioned large granite stones from the local Pyramid Quarry for a monument. On each of the stones, the same guidelines were engraved in many different languages. The remote hill top had the highest elevation in the county and just as in England the standing stones appeared from the road suddenly in the pasture as the American Stonehenge.

There was more magic here as well. The Athens group had started annual solstice rituals at the small park. Even in winter they would encounter odd winds, sandstorms, rain, and hail. However, despite the weather they gathered, did a ritual and then had dinner in one of the local dives. Over time, local reports of pagans doing strange rituals made the newspaper. The religious right planted beds of white and red roses little recognizing how prominently both roses and those colors figured into the esoteric mysteries. Gayle was somewhat concerned that the presence of her group would cause protests or controversy. However, most of the time their only accompaniment was the lowing of the cattle in the surrounding pasture.

However, this time drought caused farmers to lose their businesses. Deep in meditation, Gayle and Michelle decided to shift the current weather pattern to bring water to the southern part of the state.

They sat among the huge stones with the sun warming them. Only a few cars passed on the rural road about a mile below them. Without a word spoken, they both came out of meditation simultaneously knowing that the work was completed.

Days later, southern Georgia was under water - literally with river flooding from excessive rains. It's not nice to fool with Mother Nature.

The Zodiac

"Hey, I have two comp tickets for Richie Havens tonight at the Georgia Theatre if you can use them," Angela said holding out the pair.

"Love it, thanks," Gayle said. She gave a call to Deb to see if she wanted to drive over from Atlanta for the concert. Bob and Deb were no longer a couple and Deb could use a night of distraction. The venue wasn't crowded so they headed up to the balcony where they could be more comfortable. The acoustics were great and while Richie had aged from his Woodstock days, he was mellower and wiser with incredible songs. Gayle had just begun to wonder why she had been led to this experience, when Havens began a song with the story of a secret that had been kept for 2000 years. She and Deb looked at each other and burst into laughter. The song was the Zodiac, an ode to the Twelve, Ron's current teaching theme.

> "*These are the twelve people who inherit the earth*
> *You are one of them and there are only eleven others*
> *And if you get to know the eleven others*
> *You will be able to get along with everyone all over the*
> *world -All over the world.*"

The next morning when walking the sidewalks to open the store, she met Richie on the sidewalk. Gayle held her hand out, introduced herself.

"Loved your concert, man."

"Thanks."

Athens was a magical musical place.

Three Rivers

Gayle's writing struggles continued in school. She just didn't understand what her professors wanted from her. Consequently much of her writing was the reporting of boring facts from ancient, seldom read texts. Although Shanta encouraged her to draw upon her experiences with Ron in her writing, Gayle found it difficult to write about it. Fortunately Shanta was gentle with her and encouraged her to teach in his class and speak more often. She continued to meditate in his classes and formed a telepathic connection with him as well. There was always a feeling that he had been waiting for a student like her. If only she could write like she talked.

In Hindu philosophy class, Gayle broke out of her clear meditation space. Shanta described the Triveni Sangam where drops of nectar fell from the pitcher held by the gods. A bath in the Sangam washed away all of one's sins and cleared the path to the heavens.

While the Christian reference to "bathed in the blood" immediately came to mind, it was the name that captured Gayle's attention. Triveni Sangam meant the confluence of three rivers. Three rivers again-the confluence of three waters reminded her of Medicine Bear's instruction long ago. Just as in Warwoman Dell, in the Hindu version one of the rivers had been invisible since it flowed underground and joined the other two from below. In January, it was said the gods themselves came to bathe at Triveni Sangam making the place of the three waters a redemption of the gods. The pieces of the puzzle were beginning to reveal a hologram.

The Sirian Agenda

While Gayle was pushed to her limits, sitting with Samuel was like bathing in warm love and compassion. From the first time she had felt the channeled entity's energy of unconditional love swirl throughout the room before inhabiting Lea's form. Gayle wasn't thrilled with his followers, many of whom were so enchanted with the experience and caught up in their own egos, but here she was back again. Samuel's teachings often followed Ron's topics. In her private session with Samuel she could see his body in what she called a reptilian form.

"Well, that's not quite the word I would use, but I could see why you would say that," Samuel answered.

Somewhere in the past couple of years Gayle had gotten comfortable talking to disembodied entities and the idea of alien intervention with humanity. In fact, many people considered *Close Encounters of the Third Kind* and *ET* to be forerunners for future events. Despite her own experiences Gayle wasn't sure what she thought anymore about alien beings, but she had become much more open.

The last Samuel seminar was "The Sirian Agenda" which was closely aligned to the mystery materials. According to the agenda, the gods from Sirius built the Great Pyramid and the Sphinx on earth to keep the geometric portals to the stars open. This structure was an inter-dimensional access to the human cellular memories of their Sirian roots. The memory of this extraterrestrial origin was to be awakened in August 1987 at the Harmonic Convergence.

The Sirian story predicted a dual sun or binary star for winter solstice 2012. Most stars were binary systems and for the sun to be the exception did not make sense to Gayle. Several of the New Age books in Pathfinder talked of the earth moving into the photon belt at the time of the galactic center alignment in 2012. She remembered the vision she had of the gatekeepers energetically holding the earth in light. Samuel used the terminology of guardians. The seeds of the flower of life would bloom in Orion's light.

Samuel spoke of a time when matriarchy and patriarchy co-existed in balance. Balance did not mean perfect static harmony to Gayle anymore, but a dynamic version of the yin-yang. Gayle thought it was still idealistic, but a good goal. Samuel said the Sirian connection was the process of energy being turned to light.

"Einstein must have been Sirian," Gayle thought. Einstein had translated higher knowledge into his own equation which was mathematically stated as $E=mc^2$.

While Spirit was often described as pure light, Samuel reminded that in this dimension there were all sorts of unseen vibrations of light. From light came sound. Samuel said that the energy would come from Sirius and some individuals having achieved mastery there would reconnect with those memories. He suggested that his group begin to find a connection to that ray of energy and to remember their responsibility to this planet.

Academic Shamans

Gayle borrowed an outline from an article in the *Encyclopedia of Religion* that Dr. Kirkland had shown her. She vowed to own the volume set someday. Eliade wrote that in addition to shamans having special relations with spirits, ecstatic capacities of magical flight, ascent to the sky, descent to the underworld, etc. they could also transit through space-time into other dimensions. The encyclopedia gave her fundamentals to base her paranormal and mystical studies. Her professors drew the line at New Age teachings or books as valid academic sources.

Gayle felt comfortable in the Eastern religions such as Hinduism that embraced a male and female aspect of the creator. The dance forms from that culture were to inspire the spark of consciousness. Still, in her personal life Gayle hungered for a culture that was more spiritual and more embracing of the feminine aspects of god. Otherwise, as some religions taught, she would have to be reborn as a male to become enlightened.

The rise of patriarchy had suppressed the original knowledge of the goddess. Perhaps this was part of the wisdom the Templars and other mystery schools protected through the ages. Patriarchy, Gayle theorized, was afraid of the divine feminine energy. Perhaps it stemmed from accounts of an original battle involving the men overthrowing a primordial and feminine chaos which some call the battle between the cosmic serpents.

Gayle learned shamans often received their calling through a serious personal illness where visions of spirits and beings emerged. Other cultures believed the abilities were inherited or transmitted through biological lines. Gayle's uncle was a firetalker able to talk the heat out of severe burns. Firetalking could only be transferred from male to female to male in alternating patterns. In genealogical research, Gayle uncovered a Cherokee great-grandmother who may have passed on her heritage. Her father had been a dowser and her cousin had the gift of prophecy.

At other times as Eliade's writing stated, being struck by lightning was a more direct calling to be a shaman. The Greeks believed a person struck by lightning possessed magical powers. Gayle noted that the theme of light emerged through most of her religious studies and much of her personal life. She had been within twenty feet of lightning strikes at least ten times in her life. Already Black Elk had taught her to sing and dance. A local medicine man sent her off to find a mysterious place where three waters flowed. Visions showed a native in the desert who moved through the stars. The pieces of the puzzle were beginning to fit together. Perhaps the universe could be trusted after all.

The Solar Disk

The Pathfinder working group had progressed rapidly. Gayle easily saw where each person was and yet was able to do some work herself. They had become a stable foundation. Tonight she had a few minutes of simply being aware. The meditation was deep and full of awareness. It was deeper, richer and more aware than ever. Then on the horizon, rays of light emerged. They became brighter as a huge golden orb slowly rose on an imaginary horizon. The brilliance of this solar disk filled the inner vision and began to flood into the group. When Gayle opened her eyes a slit, she could see the golden light permeating the room.

"202 555-3764." Gayle heard the number clearly. She used to get phone numbers in her head. From time to time, she would dial them.

"202 555-3764" She was puzzled. The area code was for Washington, DC, but she did not recognize the number.

"Please call 202 555-3764." At the third repetition Gayle ended meditation to write the number down to call later. That night, she dialed wondering what in the world she would say to the person who answered. The ringing phone was answered by a crisp professional woman's voice.

"Thanks for checking in." The line went dead.

Pathfinder Energy Circles

"It was a cosmic orgasm," Christina boldly proclaimed.

The Pathfinder group laughed. Christina, a relative latecomer to the group, was adept in the astral and higher levels. Her statement alone could have gotten her arrested in the 1930's. Back then, Dr. Wilhelm Reich used orgasm as medicine. For his efforts, Reich was imprisoned. A government setup shutdown the building of orgone boxes that collected cosmic energy for healing. Ron's older brother Tom had been charged in the government's case as well. Gayle knew there was more below the surface, but for now she knew sacred sex was a gift of the gods, the universe and all there is. Ron's techniques allowed her to charge energy circles. Sexuality was known as a path to enlightenment in Hinduism, Egypt, mysticism and meditation.

Gayle enjoyed Christina's reaction and statement. Orgasm was called Le Petit Morte-the little death at orgasm that opens to cosmic awareness. The flow of energy was life. To be in bliss required nothing but remembering who humans were in the first place.

Chapter 13 - Revelations

The Last Week of Mystery School

Gayle wrote the check for the full amount for the final week of Ron's Bonclarken training. She stamped and mailed the envelope. She knew she would attend so she gave up her drama around it. She had invested too much time and money to miss the revelation of the greater mysteries. Patty wanted to ride up together so making that commitment already meant she was attending. Though Patty missed the turnoff from Atlanta to Athens and arrived hours late, Gayle temporarily gave up her controlling nature and just went along for the ride.

When the circle gathered for the first time, they were surprised to see Ron wearing black instead of his usual rotation of white yoga pants with either a white, royal blue or mauve polo shirt.

"It is Halloween week," he reminded them.

Conserving Chi

The first lecture in the last week of the Third Wave training was on the importance of conservation of energy and chi. Ron stressed that wasting chi and mindless chatter was a leak of personal basic energy. The process of self-preservation was difficult unless people were stimulated. As initiates, Ron reminded them to keep themselves in a state of balance.

Gayle remembered at the last meeting how she felt looking at Ron in the kitchen. After the Saturday night ritual, almost everyone partied. Their energy had quickly gone from heightened awareness into having a good time. Ron observed them all from the corner across the room by his revered compost pile. Yet, there was no judgment in his face as the group lost awareness; just a twinge of sadness. Perhaps this was why he began this final week with conserving energy.

"When you complete this process you find integrity. You can see people as they are and not hold judgment. You are a mirror. Do not feel sorry for them. Once you achieve a level of consciousness, you can offer yourself as a mirror, but it is pointless trying to enlighten a person who doesn't want to wake up. It is a waste of your time and energy."

Gayle wondered how he felt about his own students. Some obviously had been at his intensives for the drama while others for the socialization. A few were serious students while others seemed to dabble in their religion of the moment. Ron had said he looked for a representative slice of humanity and it appeared he had gotten it.

"Don't confuse pity with compassion. Compassion should be extended to those who are not awake and are aware of it. Never extend pity. The subtle difference between pride and fear keep you from a clear space. Look at who you are without fear or shame–never consider that you are going to be perfect. Be aware of what you are at all time."

Ron was beginning the week with cautions. That was not something that Gayle had observed before. He asked them not to succumb to peer pressure, but to retain their own chi and identity. There was a tendency for group acceptance to revert to the lowest common denominator. In some way he may have hoped this more grounded group could hold its identity when it merged into the more rambunctious Foundation.

"When your chi is lowered you are reacting at the lowest realm where you operate efficiently. If you are suffering, you need to get more chi. Find the center. If necessary, hide. Practice structure and a way of being so that you can be in the presence of another without losing your own self. How much of your reaction to the world is shaped by it?"

Ron related how at his annual work weekend and birthday celebration that he had become over fatigued. His tradition of having all his students gather to exchange hard physical labor for meditation and his expert cooking over the birthday weekend had gone on for years. This time he realized that he had a lot less chi than he was used to. Fortunately he knew techniques to gain access to more chi and used it to restore his true identity. Ron also noted that some of his behavior patterns had shifted. He had become aware of some of his own glitches in personality and was working toward change. Gayle remembered him as saying that from time to time he had to kill his old self off again.

"You need to evaluate yourself. Until you have practiced this, you will never be sufficient. Those who believe themselves to be sufficient are probably so egocentric there is no room to grow. In believing to be insufficient, a person is probably so distorted that they don't have enough capacity to grow."

Ron began recapping the subjects of their training process. He once again even in the introduction overloaded the intellect with stories from the Knights Templar, Christian Mysteries, and occult magic. He kept providing small tidbits to be woven into a holographic crystal for the process of self-knowledge. He foreshadowed what was to come.

"When you know you are good, you can take criticism. You need to have enough confidence to be open to criticism. If criticism is undeserved, then ignore it. You can take a jealousy, go to a high place and watch it disappear."

Gayle looked at the others. Neither Marcia nor Patty had changed the expression on their faces, but both had turned toward her. Gayle had taken the brunt of Ron's criticisms. Gayle had learned quickly that if Ron could get an emotional reaction from her, there was something for her to address. She noted when she reacted. Tonight she also noted that the old buttons had been disarmed. Things that would have upset her last year no longer even got noticed. Ron smiled a private smile to her as if he could hear her thoughts. In fact, Gayle knew he could.

"Sacred geometry transcends the differences and limits of language. We'll do more work with that in ritual and in explanation. Die so you may be reborn is the ultimate mystery–there must be a shift in identity. The ultimate act of creation is to see order in chaos."

Those associated with Ron's local groups knew that Ron had done a lot of work with magical groups. Yet he did not introduce much formal magic in the Third Wave. Several of them discussed whether or not it was because Ron found himself more of a mystic now without the use of tools. While occasionally for ritual he used the ankh, Tibetan knife or his large turquoise pendent, there were no altars created or tools required by them.

"The difference between a mystic and an occultist is using a tool whether it be a spell, a wand, or a sacrifice. Magicians apply formulas which are memorized and grind them out like trained chimpanzees. We will be replaced by chimpanzees who will be enlightened by a transfer of genetic material. I have a folder that lists the mysteries from Atlantis that are already revealed today. Polymeric transformations that replicate RNA are only one. Occultists finally only use catalysts. Yet eventually they don't even have to use that. When the catalytic element maximizes, the person becomes a mystic. The ultimate tool is not the object, but the consciousness itself. The occultist becomes a mystic."

The group was exploring how to use the tools he had given them. The more clearly the magician knew the tools the better the universe he could create. Using the example of how a good science fiction book created an entire universe, Ron explained that it was good due to its self-consistency. In the same way a magician must have an internally consistent universe.

"When magicians are capable of being clear, they go through their magical universe and take care of inconsistencies. Their world is impregnable—it doesn't matter if others agree with it. However, the real trick is to overlap others' universes so that it works well together."

Each world must contain the necessary physical factors to make it work well. Ron emphasized that one had to take care of the body, communication with others, handle emotions, and still allot room for what makes a person a god or goddess.

"An insane person has an inconsistent universe," Ron said with a broad smile. "A teacher shares their universe with you. At the end, your teacher must die. The universe that enables you to come to life is their universe. You must create your own universe so that you can destroy it. If you create it successfully, it is invulnerable. If you do it in my methodology, only a god can destroy it."

Ron explained the energetic methods to build it by beginning with the understanding of why everything happens. He offered that the evening ritual required each of them to destroy their own universe.

Holographic Mysteries

Realizing that the moment had long last arrived, Ron did the classic approach to the mysteries which was to reveal them from all directions from the same time. As previously stated, the mysteries could not be known linearly-to be told them linearly was a monstrous destruction of the hologram of the meaning of life for the last twenty thousand years or so. Despite knowing that the revelations would be distressing and frustrating at times, he followed the traditional model. Ron promised that while he would tell random tidbits throughout the week, he would integrate them on the last day.

"You will know the key secrets, but it will take many meetings and questions and references before you get the significance of the entire package. So shall we begin?"

The group beamed huge smiles back to him. Ron had successfully dodged their questions with half answers and boomerang questions over the course of two years. While he admitted that his teacher code required him to answer properly formed questions, few people had enough luck or awareness to ask a proper question.

"Why is it that in many significant works of art and paintings is it that women cover their faces from the sun? Women are white on the outside and red on the inside. This has governed social traditions for ages. Red, white, and blue and red, white and black is the tantric tension of men, women, and death. Black of course signifying death and the blue transcendence. The colors of the United States flag, chosen by the United States founders who were Freemasons and descendants of the Knights Templar, are signals that the founders knew the secrets. Red and white are the secret to many things. The fairer a woman's skin, the more she embodied the principle of the woman."

Well, the group wasn't astounded with that revelation. Yet, they knew better to press Ron who was intent in doing things his own way.

"King Solomon consorted with the Queen of Sheba whose name means Isis. In the scriptures it was said that she was black but comely. The black Madonna sect is part of that." Ron took time to pass some old postcards around the group. They were supposed to depict the mysteries, but the group still remained clueless. Ron looked at Marcia.

"Your husband keeps asking about the Jolly Roger, the skull and crossbones flag the pirates used. The original pirates were from Gibraltar where the disenfranchised Knights Templar became the first mercenaries. The Knights Templar had disbanded in Europe and fled to Malta. Knights of Malta, now a heavily Christian organization, were where the Knights Templar maintained an outpost and launched their ships. However, they had lost their fortunes in condemnation. The secret aim of the Knights Templar was to purchase the world. However, they were destroyed. The nature of all secret societies is the mysteries."

Ron then revealed how the Rothschild family who secured funding for national governments acquired more money in one or two generations than any other. Part of the secret was the use of carrier pigeons. The changeover in French structure and government was imminent. The Rothschilds rented a home next to the government official. When Rothschild saw someone kneel to the official, he sent word by carrier pigeon to London. The arrival of the carrier pigeons in London with the battle results at Waterloo allowed Rothschild to plant rumors that the British had lost. When investors adjusted their bond and security positions accordingly, Rothschild released the true news that Wellington had vanquished Napoleon. The Rothschild bet both sides from the middle with their foreknowledge. Nathan Rothschild successfully manipulated the stock markets to his advantage.

"The Knights Templar lost all of their gold and fled for their lives. Like good Buddhists they chop wood and carry water. The Knights Templar had been initiated into why they were sons of the widow, but most of them were simply fighting men who worshiped she who must be obeyed. They were also accused of worshiping the skull, a talking head. And they flew a flag who only the initiated would know the symbolism of the two crossed bones and a skull."

Ron waited expectantly, but there were no takers on his lull to jump in with questions. Most of the group just wanted him to reveal the hidden secrets as everyone felt they had paid their dues.

"The origin of the Jolly Roger stems from the Templar legend where a young knight fell in love with a young lady. Unfortunately she died early and on the night of her burial, the lover dug up her grave and made love to her body. An inner voice told him to return in nine months to find his son. At the appointed time, the lover opened the grave and found a small skull on the thigh bones of his love. The inner voice told him to take and guard it as it would give all good things. The man was able to defeat his enemies by showing them the magic head. Later, the possession was passed to the order. Some say it is the focal point of a secret ritual by Yale's secret society Skull and Bones."

Marcia was relieved to have an answer for her husband Jim even if she couldn't reveal it to him in its full significance.

"So where does the name Jolly Roger come from?" she asked.

Ron offered that an old English word roger meant wandering hobo or possibly Old Roger was a synonym for the Devil. In French, "jolie rouge" meant pretty red and the meaning could have been extended to flags of all colors. Then Ron did an uncharacteristic thing by seemingly getting a revelation in the middle of his answer. "Asian pirates called their captains Ali Raja, a title meaning King of the Sea. Hmm-I had not remembered that before."

The Helix

"After this morning, some of you came up with a few questions at lunch."

Standing at the pad Ron flipped the pages until he found where two figures were already drawn. There were two pyramids pointed one into another. "Some patterns may become a pyramid or as in this case a progression from the upper one into the lower one. Others see a pair of sine waves with a border. Does this resemble anything you know?"

"A helix," Patty said.

"Right. This becomes the interaction of RNA and DNA in a swirl. People in a line dance called the Virginia Reel mimic that pattern.

The Virginia Reel was created in Virginia, of course, by the founders of this country. Men and woman would line up opposite on sides and dance toward each other then pull away creating sexual tension. They were constantly making and breaking the electromagnetic connection between them. That produces a tremendous amount of potential energy. The Shakers shook, but knew that it had to do with the denial of sexual energy. They built this dynamic charge and became the designers of some incredible inventions. In the Virginia Reel male and female participants would crisscross and form patterns reminiscent of DNA and RNA double helix pattern."

Ron's linking of subjects seemed endless. Gayle hoped the tapes they received later would slow it down long enough to be understood. Ron continued talking of the Shakers. The Shaking Quakers or Shakers were taught it was possible to attain perfect holiness. The founder, Ann Lee, taught that shaking and trembling were caused by sin being purged by the Holy Spirit. Mother Ann's followers believed she embodied all the perfections of God in female form.

"Speaking of shaking, the inventor Nikolai Tesla had a brain fever that caused some strange breathing patterns. Actually, it was the rising of the goddess Kundalini within him. Tesla's brain was flooded with alien ideas, visions, and creations. His visions would come to life before him. Yet I was talking about pyramids. The joining together of the pyramids is the symbol, not of evil, but of spirit moving its force down into a point. Like Michelangelo who drew the extended finger of god to give life to man, this is matter striving to come up and meet god. When they finally touch which is one unit of the dance or it is the Star of David whose number is six opposed to the pentagram whose number is five. Remember every bit of that and start to put it together," he laughed. "Very few people are capable of generating a concept that has never existed."

Gayle remembered her Religion 870 paper where she mistakenly thought she had achieved an original insight. Dr. Godlas never asked a question that he didn't already know an answer. So an old seldom checked out book in UGA's arts library revealed the same insight over two thousand years ago. There really was nothing new under the sun.

Even at the Sistine Chapel, secret society symbols were incorporated into the ceiling paintings. In the corner of one panel was a Sibyl or oracle. These esoteric figures and symbols were incorporated everywhere; the popularity of the symbols bound by some overriding yet not recognized meaning. Gayle's daydreaming ended when Ron looked at her. She felt his gaze.

"Piroget rises in his scale to meet the average human being. Initiates must go beyond there. Humans create their universe by speech. Remember how it all started. The Logos speak the Word and thus begin the creation of the world. Children fall from god and don't speak. It is all so innocent in a beautiful way. Humans are pure in believing that the universe is sufficient for everything. A child falls when they learn language. They face the limitations of being in physical form."

Old religious history kicked in for most that had a Christian upbringing. 'Let there be light' was an unspoken refrain. They had also been taught that Adam had been given the power of naming. Ron must have picked up on their thoughts.

"A child must learn each thing has a name. Patty will learn that soon since congratulations are due to the adoption of Tyler. God gave Adam the power to name which ticked Lucifer off. Little children know that. Call out the name, get the object. When you learn the laws of sentences, you reach another level. Make up sentences and relationships and you gain control over a higher realm of reality. Then, learn about the entire nature of language and well you are about midway up the scale."

Ron sipped the tea he had by his side. "If you look at this simply, it is a glass with ripples filled with liquid half way up the sides. It appears to be iced tea in a Coke glass. See how once you name it, it has less information."

The discussion ran through a kaleidoscope of subjects. Mostly now Ron was focused on the rules of the game. Whether it was the game of life, the magician's game or the laws of physics, Gayle wasn't sure. However, it all seemed so very profound. Maybe he stressed certain things knowing that some of the group would never return.

"When you can understand the rules of how these things are governed, then you can make up rules on how to govern the games. Make up rules of systems that dictate the systems and games. The highest functioning available is to understand how to govern all the systems–some of which are language, color, sound, relationships. The final stage is total holographic information. These statements of laws are what mystics have. The canon is that which binds the laws together in patterns of meaning. Patterns of meaning are where it is at."

Ron emphasized that those who understood patterns understood the universe–physical and spiritual. Further training was suggested. Facts were only markers to see the patterns. The Pythagorean mystery school was the greatest school that has ever been. The Pythagorean secret of the simple triangle formed by units of three, four, and five provided the Freemasons a way to form a proper or right angle. Ron opened Lucy Lamy's Egyptian Mysteries book to a drawing of a figure with an erect phallus within the pyramid.

"Note that the bird is leaning backward," Ron pointed out. "Thoth brought writing and allowed remembering. Thoth became Merlin. The ultimate mathematics is the number of the circle that is 360. Three hundred sixty is the womb of the universe and totality of creation. Femininity is complete within itself. Male is an extension and is a perfect companion to the goddess. The squaring of the circle is one of the fundamental secrets–the relationship of a straight line between the outside to the center of the heart-though I may be on a tangent."

Ron sighed when none of the group got his pun.

"Here are two magic symbols: Pi–two uprights and a cross piece and it is the altar to the goddess. When you sit upon the bench, your seat is on the throne of Isis – Pi is the symbol of Isis."

Ron was on a roll and the group was taken on a ride. There were a few questions, a few points of clarification, but there was simply too much to take in all at once. Gayle overheard Sandi tell Ron at break that the material simply did not have the impact it did the first time he revealed the mysteries. There was no real drama, but there were a few good discussions in the bathroom at break. Yet Ron had promised and he would deliver.

"The fundamental relationship that governs the universe is the impregnated goddess. The masculine energy is never totally contained. Phi–stands for ½ symbolically, 1.168 or half of pi. Phi or the golden mean governs the growth of systems or the helix. In Egyptian murals, the body of the pharaoh represents the golden mean with his body. Also note that Isis stands between Osiris and Set to make a major magic symbol. 101 is binary number. Zero and one are from the Arabs who taught that 10 is the combination of emptiness which is Isis and one which is the secret to all counting."

Ron introduced a new concept, the six levels of sexuality, but did not allow questions. The group was fascinated, but Ron realized it was a mistake to open a new topic when there was so much material to be completed.

The Correct Use of Pain

"How do you not allow pain to fix you into the history of what surrounds it? How can you do that without missing the lessons?" Andre asked during this brief pause.

"The only thing that matters is what did you do–that is the lesson–the actions. The pain needs to be done as soon as possible. Physical pain–two things can't be in the same place at the same time such as your bedpost and toe. Emotional pain has to do with illusion. You wanted everything to stay the same, but it changed. Change is the constant in life. You must be prepared for everyone in your life to leave you. Everything you have and believe in will go. This makes it richer while you have it."

Gayle recognized some Buddhist concepts within this: detachment and impermanence. When Ron said to expect things to disintegrate and be prepared she saw the value of no expectations not as a way to avoid pain, but to be clear and unattached.

"The lessons are the things you did not expect. You can learn it without pain. For example, every teacher lies. Every lie is an adaptation of reality to suit the immediate need. Good lies are ways to form a relationship with an interpretation of reality."

Ron ran his hand down the microphone chord. Gayle who was wearing the recorder monitor felt chills down her spine and shiver.

"You felt that?"

"Yes." He did it again as a test. Gayle's automatic response was the same.

"Necrophilia -it's not about undertakers, think about Osiris–sex with a dead man with a wooden phallus. Remember the jealousy between the brothers Set and Osiris. Set ended up dismembering him and poor Isis went about Egypt picking up the pieces. However, Osiris' penis was never found-supposedly it fell into the river and was swallowed by a fish. In order for Isis to mate with Osiris, a wooden straw was used to replace the penis. In that union, Horus was conceived. Myths have been shaped to astronomical events as well as to psychology and emotional content. Some celestial body came close enough to earth to change its orbit. The days in a year used to be 360, but are now almost 365 days."

Ron jumped back to a tidbit regarding the Jolly Roger.

"If you remember, the man so in love with a woman who died before they could consummate their union made love to her corpse. Nine months later he dug up the grave and there between her thigh bones was a skull. Evidently a baby born then died in the coffin. Remember how in the movie The Omen instead of a body of a child in the coffin, it was a body of the dog which was a horrific rip-off of the mysteries. The dog-like Anubis is a symbol of Sirius. Instead of a monster or the son of Set, this was someone from Sirius. The being from Sirius is a god-like being. Damian was swapped for a normal child who when buried turned into a dog underground. The dog is a being of light. Damian was a being of darkness."

The group then was dismissed for a break, but Gayle sat dumbfounded. The white wolf was a being of light. The dog form could have simply been a screen memory that she had seen through. Beings from Sirius had visited her to adjust some of the neural connections in her body. Now she recalled that they had come back months later as well. She had been lying on the couch and they stimulated neural pathways in her brain. They told her they were rewiring her circuitry.

There were more neurons firing today than normal. The sheer amount of connections being made was fatiguing. Finally Gayle got up for a glass of water before the lecture was on at full speed again.

Create Your Own Universe

This time, the work began with them standing up which was a welcome relief from the long hours of sitting. Ron stood in the center as usual.

"We are beginning the create your own universe energy work. When we stand up, we automatically form a circle. Now put your arms around each other's waists. The circle represents wholeness and Isis. The skills involved require exploring the inside of your head. There, you will organize a conscious center, move it, and alter its frequency. A lot more can be done. You can move across space and time without there being intellect. You will sense the reality of alternative spaces. In order to go through the transformative states, you will go through dimensional shifts. The richness of the magician's universe consists of setting boundaries and populating it."

The description of the process of beginning a new universe began by preparing the essential elements for each individual. Since magicians failed by not including the necessities, Ron reminded them to overlap the common universe. Ron suggested allocating territory for elements keeping them alive-for such processes as breath, health, and nutrition.

"The creation of a Tarot deck is a side exercise of this as it contains the entire universe. You design your own pictures. When you read someone, you allow them to trespass in your universe and you can then tell them what paths they may choose from. You lay out the pattern of the universe. To tell them, you show them where they are on the map of the universe." There was a quiet time as individuals began the rudimentary aspects of their personal universe. Ron sensed when it was time to go on.

"Building a universe–let your mind range the universe. You understand how things relate to each other. You touch it and see what it feels like. You arrange them into a pattern. Intellect finds no rationale, but your gut knows it.

You can begin or end with the significant events that form markers. Anything that came to mind without intellectual cause marks a spot where something is too difficult or too painful to keep in memory. These are highly significant things and not just random memories and associations. Markers decide the universe. When you have gained some control over your psyche, you can set boundaries by reaching out as far out as you can. Do this internally and not with your eyes. Minimally use four directions while you have a body. Four describes the square and the cross and all things of this earth. Six markers. Master magicians of this plane use eight or 16. The numbers of Isis are 2, 4, 8, 16 and 32. The male is the external or $32 + 1 = 33^{rd}$ degree magician or master mason. The masculine is the bridge between."

The group had their eyes closed though Gayle peeked every now and then to see what Ron was doing. His voice energetically charged the group with its tone, intensity, and faster pace. Occasionally he did a mudra or held his arm at an angle to invoke more energy.

"In energy, reach out to the boundaries of your known universe, forward, back, up, down, create energetically a universe you can now begin to encompass. Your past universe happened to you–bounded by your parents, lovers, body and emotional karma. These set the boundaries of your universe. Reach inside of you to your identity, rise above and observe. You come before the throne of Anubis. Between the two of you, the universe has been created by tension before resolution. What can you feel–span your life, every second, event, and moment-was written on stone. You encompass it and surround it with a membrane."

Ron paused letting the energy fill and inspire him. No one in the group moved. The energy acted to plant their feet firmly in place.

"Every time there is a major incident in your life, perfect the magician part which is the foundation of the mystic. Every conscious choice is an action used to populate your universe. You will acquire great power. When you destroy it, either at death or in transcendent places, it will be impressive and the universe will know it. Of course, it is not destroyed, you abandon it. Other lesser beings will continue to inhabit it."

Now that the circle exercise was finished Ron reported seeing petals multiply on flowers that were now hidden. Gayle could feel every single member of this group including those of Foundation she had met. Evidently she had served to bridge the groups together. While everyone was separate, they were all contained within her universe.

"When you can contain the reality of everyone that is aware or in the mystical sense you have dissolved all boundaries. If you achieve a high enough state of your own identity and the dissolution of all boundaries, the only boundary you have is perception. Like Wigners's solution to the Schrödinger Cat problem, there can only be one universe. The person who finds that becomes the same person. I will be making my traditional pizza for you on ritual night and we will celebrate with wine."

The Taboo

"There is a barrier to the ultimate realization. Everyone seems to encounter the taboo against knowing who you are. The taboo is that if you think you are as good as god, you will die. Many people will get very close and then they self-destruct. Just before they cash it all in, they gamble it away. There is only one cure–to die. Many yogis are born in America. Yoga teachers don't necessarily have "it"-they may be good teachers, but they are not gurus. Gurus all have it. Many of them had died in their childhood."

Gayle knew that she had not transcended the taboo despite her many near death experiences. She felt a bit of sadness in that since it seemed to be the key to the ultimate achievement she desired.

The Sexual Mysteries

The days were filled with information that finally made sense as Ron drew lines between the dots. Finally the time had come to reveal the sexual mysteries. Janet had cautioned Gayle not to miss this week and its final revelations as it would have been worth the wait. Others appeared anxious as well. All of them were over eighteen and while sex was not new to them, the concept that there might be something new intrigued them all. Ron was radiant. There was no doubt that he enjoyed this revelation.

"Arthur got his sword from the Lady of the Lake. The cup is the earth or body of the water. He got his sword from the fluids. Another version says he got his sword by pulling it out of the stone. The Lady of the Lake is between a great rock and water. The stone is said to be magic. Arthur's scabbard is magical and will heal any wound." Ron paused to sip his Earl Grey tea. His voice was getting hoarse from the hours of talking.

"The hanged man has his legs crossed. What does it look like–an inverted 4, the number of Isis, and also the origin of the skull and crossbones. A man is hanging by one foot–remember Achilles? Achilles was immortal all except for his heel. Isis in making her young charge immortal held him by the heel within the eternal flame. So what is it about hanging upside down that cures all wounds? These are the clues, folks. Clues are association."

Ron paused and glanced around the group seeking inspiration for the next direction. Marcia sat up straighter, Patty curled up on the couch, and Gayle mused about the hanged man position. The light beings who had rearranged her body into that position at the time of the white wolf visit had changed her structure. Could they have been making her immortal? She didn't have time to consider it further as Ron plunged deeper in the mysteries.

"The Atlantean event is occurring in cycles–humanity has certain things happen to them periodically. The evolution of conscious life on this planet is not a straight line progression. Every one of those jumps or leaps in evolution fits into the esoteric rhythmical cycles. Progression is of some entity building force until at the right cyclical the force explodes into a nonrandom mutation. Other beings say every 25 or 26 thousand years, they come again. These beings claim the responsibility of converting Neanderthals into Cro-Magnum. They enlightened them and genetically modified them."

Neanderthal became the dominant species on the planet according to Ron. In less than a generation after Cro-Magnum appeared, they replaced Neanderthal who faded away by interbreeding and otherwise.

"When you encounter a superior species, the will to procreate disappears. There are no more babies. Yet, the writings of the Sumerians almost 13,000 years ago recorded the descent of the gods. In periodic cycles of 2,600 years thereafter, there was a rash of sightings of flying saucers and of strange beings."

The group was attentive but still unable to put the pieces together on their own. Ron glanced at Sandi with an open palm shrug indicating that he was doing the best he could. However, she seemed disappointed.

"What was King Solomon doing? Why did he have the son of Cain, Tubal Cain, or the son of Set who murdered his brother, building a temple? Jerusalem was the source of the great mysteries protected by the Knights Templar. Abel was Neanderthal and Cain was Cro-Magnum. Cain had the elements of higher consciousness. The mark of Cain is the scar upon the brow or literally 666, the number of the beast. Alister Crowley called himself the beast because he knew that the Beast was the source of all that humanity could call its own. Crowley was a sexual degenerate–he did the right things for the wrong reasons." Ron was on a roll.

"Solomon, son of the sun, had built a great brazen bowl where he created half human, half beast animals. He got away with it. Solomon had so much of the blood no one would refute what he did. In the fluid in the bowl, Solomon created experimental life. Around the great brazen bowl were drawn designs of pentacle, twinned circles – vesica pisces, ankh, and what is now known as Solomon's seal or the Star of David. Solomon was a descendent of the Atlanteans and the Egyptians."

Ron described physical looks as a reflection of inner being. Gayle's own students had said that after each visit with Ron, she came back looking like a totally different person. The body begins to reflect soul; animal vitality fades by 50 and a person begins to look like their inner qualities.

"The greater mysteries are about back-breeding. Secret societies seek people with the blood and begin back-breeding them. The interest in genetics has exploded in the remembering of Atlantean and Sumerian techniques. The cytoplasm is the fluid around the genes that can be changed. The people who were royalty were assumed to be of the blood. You could prove it by healing with the king's touch. How do I pick people? I pick the ones that shine. I pick highly charged sexual people–they have the blood."

The Prime Directive

Time was rushing by. Ron moved faster now to finish the material. Their week was nearing the end. Ron cautioned them to never mess with natives.

"A woman violated that directive. She made the animals of Sumeria conscious. Where is Sumeria? Sumeria is heaven, the Garden of Eden, was centered around the fertile golden crescent. There are memories within me of not only Atlantis, but also Lemuria or Mu. Those who were exiled went into the underworld. Remember, it's not nice to fool with Mother Nature."

Ron announced that the final ritual would be with the corn god who was the sun god. The king must die because he was only necessary to fertilize the queen. The queen was always represented by the circle which was Isis.

Ron wove music and its role in the genetic blueprint of life. The source of all life was music or vibration. Melodies could be Baroque or from the romantic periods. In particular, the canon was a term for the approach of natural law.

The Ark of the Covenant

"The ark is constructed to be an energy capacitor like Wilhelm Reich's orgone box or an electrical capacitor. The ark is an agent of destruction of the lord. If the armies of the righteous carried it before them, all enemies would be destroyed. King Merovee when spotted in front of the army caused his enemies to lay down their arms."

Gayle remembered that the King of the Franks had two fathers-King Clodion and some strange smelly beast of the sea that mated with his mother. Ah, Ron had alluded to the beings from Sirius as having to live in the sea. When they emerged, they were said to have a horrible stench. That same stench was attributed to Bigfoot and the Abominable Snowman as well. She was proud of that connection, but in the meantime Ron was continuing on.

Ron relayed how the Grail Stone was both cup or chalice and a stone. Peter, the name, meant rock. In the painting of the Bergers of Arcadia, the question was what was in the tomb. Did the tomb hold the stolen temple treasures, the body of the son of Jesus, or some other genetic material? The symbol that Jesus used was the sign of the Fish.

"In the 1940's the SS were dispatched to Mont Segur, the mountain hold of the Cathars, looking for the treasure. There Mussolini was rescued from his prison on a mountaintop. The SS had a project to find a secret horde or information. They searched in Greenland. They searched for a sample of the body and blood of Christ. A wafer turned into the body with the cellular material from the blood, the fluid. The search was for a return of the blood."

Ron was smiling broadly. He didn't need to consult his notes. The information flowed seemingly assembled in some holographic pattern in his brain.

"In these modern times as well as the time of the crystal skull, it was possible to transplant part of someone's brain via a crystal into another and the consciousness was moved from body to body. There was no separation between bodies. Mystics inhabit all bodies. Some are always dying and some are always being born. The archetypes are a higher body. Jesus could come back. Just as in the movies when the dinosaurs are recreated."

"DNA of any origin can be analyzed to discover the reproductive chain, amplify them, and then transfer these sections to a living cell in the body of a donor. When the female gave birth, it could be anything-either the ark or body of Jesus or descendants. If any part of it could be recovered, it would be a genetic twin born from the body of any mammal. Solomon and Frankenstein were both involved with creation of a new body out of bits and pieces of dead flesh."

"We have the means for the Second Coming, but it has already come. The anti-Christ is a mirror of Christ. The second half is logically, woman. What beast slouchest towards Bethlehem to be born? Plantard and Godfrey of Boullion traced lineage back to Jesus. Jesus had children. Consider the daughters and intermixing. Secret societies manipulate bloodlines looking for this quality of the blood. They could back-breed."

This was the secret goal of the Priory of Sion which Ron had intuited long before the book *Holy Blood, Holy Grail* was released. It made sense for a Jewish rabbi to have married and had children. Gayle just had never considered the possibility. Celibacy seemed antithetical to Jewish law. If royalty was considered to be above the status of normal human being, could this be traced back to an extraordinary birth? After all, Jesus, the Buddha, and Merlin all had extraordinary if not miraculous conceptions. Gayle's mind was whirling with all kinds of new possibilities.

"The mysteries of the Goddess who enabled all of us to sit in this room imply that a woman had all the control. She has the essence. Man is an extension and servant to the woman. She controls what generates a child or what awareness. A conscious woman controls conception. A human egg is not a sleeping beauty. The fluid in some women's ovaries acts as a chemical magnet to attract sperm cells and this fluid can increase fertility. Female animals can hold dormant sperm within them until they are ready to ovulate. When you know the mysteries, you know what is going on."

The connections were being made in the group's mind as well. Fertility, conception, Jesus, secret societies, myths, and world rulers were swirling among them. The whole picture was like an old television set whose snow once in a while produced a recognizable scene. Still, Marcia wrote as fast as she could. Patty sat up straighter and even Andre's full attention was on the lecture instead of the women beside him. Ken's observations were more on the reaction of the group versus the material itself. Of course he had heard it all before.

"On the Harmonic Convergence a vision or a knowing of the point, spiral, and pattern led people to the dynamic of creation. They grasped how they became. We are being a catalyst for the planet. I could make spiritual people. When one becomes two, you have a universe.

When two becomes three, you have cosmic beings like galaxies, when three goes to four a point of existence emerges for those things of the earth, from four to five is animal life existing in highly specialized reality–we are colonies, we are the guiding consciousness of several levels of lesser beings. When five moves to six, the formation of conscious life is. Set becoming Osiris while six becomes seven is spiritual life. When seven becomes eight, a master is born. From eight to nine, there is a hierarchy of life and the creator of realities. Finally when nine goes to one, there is a reunion with the creator of the universe."

The amount of knowledge was staggering. Though they wanted the revelations to continue endlessly, they needed breaks to digest what was forming in their awareness. Will led them into tai chi for some exercise before the next teaching session.

"The story of the Egyptian pantheon involves one male, Osiris, who was too bright and could not breed with a human. He had no penis. His ancestors on his father's side had no penis. Yet he lost his penis. It is a confusion. Now you might understand the cigar box with a reed in it from the Knights Templar postcards that were passed around earlier." Gayle shrugged at Marcia who looked at her questioning if she had gotten the connection.

"Osiris without a penis could not impregnate a woman. Set could. Nepthys could not give birth to anyone who was human. Isis could. Isis never mated with a human male. No man may lift the veil of Isis. In the tradition, the beings who created Isis were either born as twins or quadruplets. A double twinning? There were a minimum of four beings mated to produce offspring. In the animalistic view, it only requires two. How about both supplying seed and eggs?"

Gayle's memory whirled. The story of Guinevere the barren queen who she so identified with, the UFO abduction dream, the time she thought she was miraculously pregnant but the child disappeared from her womb, the vision of the golden child who was her daughter all were forming a new truth that she wasn't sure that she wanted to know. The inexplicable sudden spike in human consciousness and intelligence now seemed an anomaly. The acceptance of divine intervention of some alien beings was difficult, but seemed logical.

Still Gayle knew that genetic manipulation was being done these days. A test tube baby had been born. In-vitro fertilization was almost routine. Animals were being cloned. Back-breeding had been done to create miniature horses much like their ancient ancestors. Marriage among royalty was not only a political alliance, but a way to insert new genes into the royal pool.

"Despite arguments about whether it was right to create conscious beings, Sumeria was against it and Atlantis was for it, from the genetic makeup of the gods these four were born: Set, Isis, Osiris, and Nepthys. They are S+I+O+N=SION, the name of the secret organization of The Priory of SION. All conscious life descends from Isis, a single female for all of humanity. Isis mated both with a sun god and a dark hairy god of the underworld. All women want both. All women need two men-the man who shines and the one who stinks. This strange dichotomy–why do women crave the biker bad-boy Lancelot? Some shine in the dark. Find the clear upright man and get him to darken. Get the dark male and shine him up. It is easier for women than men. Men suffer with the mother and whore syndrome when they are looking for partners."

The implications of these revelations were profound. No one moved and some had not blinked for minutes. The room was charged with energy that filled their minds and in some ways the group felt like a fertile egg anticipating impregnation.

"Isis had both as lovers and required two: one to inseminate her energetically and one to inseminate her body. The woman wants someone to stir her spirit and her groin–it is rare to find both abilities in one man. All women need two men. As for the cigar box, before Jesus went to crucifixion he turned to Mary Magdalene, to say that he could not love her in the same way. Mary Magdalene is the woman with the alabaster jar in the shape of a womb, small white one. Mary was dark on the outside and white on the inside. Her jar was filled with spikenard. She washed Jesus' feet and dried them with her hair."

Gayle knew from her work with a Native American herbalist that spikenard was used to ease the transition from life to death. The ancient medicine also dealt with emotional distresses. It was extremely expensive oil.

"Consider that Mary was anointing Jesus in an intimate place. When Jesus was taken down off the cross, Mary was the only one to be alone with him. It is said she was tending his wounds. Jesus' circumcision was the removal of the penis. He weakened so rapidly on the cross because he was bleeding from the procedure before he was put on the cross. Of course he could never love Mary again in the same way."

Looks of horror crossed the faces of the men in the group. The sacrifice of their manhood was inconceivable to them. Gayle felt a cringe in her belly as well did most of the other women. A sacrifice such as this seemed worse than death. The trials of Job had new meaning and she could see how in her own life she had been pushed to the limit before being able to move on. However, to sacrifice a part of her body seemed inconceivable. She smiled at her own pun in that thought. Men undergoing this procedure would never be able to help a woman conceive.

"The priests of the temples of the goddesses willingly castrated themselves in order to serve there. Salome asked for the head of John the Baptist. The Knights Templar when they reached the high levels were castrated by having the head of the penis removed. In some of the exotic esoteric paintings, the right hand is shown broken off or the subject is decapitated. Double emphasis: I have lost my good right hand; I have lost my sword or my spear. Arthur lost his penis and was given permission by the Lady of the Lake to have a sword. Arthur was given a replacement or power. Mordred was born long before the Lady of the Lake and never again did Arthur produce a child. Guinevere preferred Lancelot who never lost his lance. Loss of a penis by a man who wished to serve the goddess was required to achieve a certain kind of power.

All reports of the gods bear within them an unusual kind of sexuality. The Egyptians told that the gods were unbelievably sexual. Zeus seduced women by assuming the form of an animal. Quite possibly, he either delegated his role to an animal or assuming an artificial shape such as a swan, drake, or a bull. Some of his rounds of exploration weren't done with a penis at all, but implanting his seed with a retractable penis like a dolphin. Fertile women can get pregnant by having semen drop anywhere near the vagina. The man's penis never entered the body. In a public bath, small amounts of semen escape from men and it is possible a woman could become pregnant. The egg releases chemicals that attract sperm to them. This seems impossible to the woman who cannot get pregnant."

Gayle wanted to put her head down and cry. There was a new picture of reality. Overall, it seemed too much at one time. What seemed impossible was making sense in an entirely new perspective of reality. The revelations went on for many hours. Ron never recorded the mysteries. He assured them that the information was retained in their awareness and would be available to them for lifetimes.

"Ultimately women have some element of consciousness. The woman contains the fluid charge, why not the man? There is a higher source throughout the universe; it is the fluid nature of the elements that cause creation–the great sea, a form of chaos and potential. The woman's energy is the potential energy. Consciousness coming into contact with the sea forms life. Aphrodite rose from the sea and is carried ashore on a shell. The feminine principle carries something more readily than men. They yield to something higher. Men are the conscious observers. They imprint the pattern on the creative potential that causes life. There is something on this plane that only women have and men only have access to it through women. They may pass it on as well."

"Temple dancers and prostitutes," thought Gayle. When she glanced up at Ron, she was surprised to see the ghosts of two men sitting on the couch beside him. When she described them, Ron replied that one was a close friend who had worked in the laboratory with him and the other one was a professional comedian. The rest of the afternoon was used to set the stage for the final ritual of the third wave of the Bonclarken experiment.

"This is the last session–a paradox. The use of paradox is the important thing in this intensive that you learn along with the morning meditations. Why I don't teach only meditation is that you can't handle it. The intellect is the crowning glory of the human being. You must unite the spiritual and animal aspects."

Ron was a talker teacher. He reminded them it took eight times as much energy to balance estrogen with testosterone. The number of Isis was eight and eight was the number of oxygen. The secret of water was HOH, Isis with two men.

"The group must search for clarity. It can think, feel, and know and take part in an aware universe. Yet it needs to maintain physical, intellectual and spiritual to merge into the mystic."

The Final Bonclarken Ritual

When the group gathered in the final circle of their training, Ron put away his tape recorder. He was not recording the event. The Third Wave stood arms around waists in a tight circle waiting for him. It had been a journey that was impossible to explain to anyone who had not been there. Ron was in the kitchen preparing the dough for his ritual pizza. After leaving it on the counter to rise, he joined them.

"Alice Bailey prophesied that a group was the destiny of humanity I don't want a group formed around a doctrine or a personality. Find the essence."

The energy built in the circle in the way that they had been trained to create it. They were no longer a group of individuals, but a complete and whole circle. Ron added his own essence to bring them to the highest awareness.

"Before I tell you the final mystery, are you willing to give up life as you know it?" No one answered as the group seemed to be in a trance like state. "Assuming that your silence means that you agree, we will continue."

The group swayed back and forth building the energy with the rocking motion. Gayle could feel Ron add his essence to shift it to a higher state. The waiting seemed to go on forever. Her arms ached and she wanted to just move on with it.

"Now, here is the last requirement. Will you vow to keep silent about the mysteries?" Most of them nodded or gave some silent indication of assurance. Gayle was conflicted. She made few promises,

because she kept them. She didn't like being asked to keep a secret
before she knew what it entailed. If it was harmful to another, it would
be a hard promise to keep. Could the secret be taught to her own
beginning group? Gayle decided not to answer.

The long pause was getting awkward. The group was feeling
pain by being made to stand there with arms raised to waist level.
Pondering the problem, Gayle opened her eyes. Ron was looking
directly at her waiting. Gayle looked unblinking back. Their eyes met in
a contest of wills. Gayle knew that he would not continue. He waited.

Gayle flashed back to her own dramatic resistance to attendance.
Her ego had put up a valiant fight. Ultimately she had given in and
returned to working with Ron. She had endured cutting criticism, hours
of meditation, and lectures that she could not understand. Now at the
payoff point had arrived and she was holding things up.

There was no doubt that Ron could hear her thought process and
feel her struggle. Gayle realized that the fight was not worth it. With a
deep breath, she agreed silently in the astral. With her acquiescence,
Ron immediately told them the secret they had waited two years to
learn.

As he finished, Gayle could hear his voice in her head. 'Since I
have awakened you, will you awaken me in the next lifetime?' Gayle
nodded slightly.

Ron asked them to maintain the circle while he put the pizza in
the oven. The group crossed hands and let him out of the circle without
breaking its continuity. Marcia turned to Gayle and grinned. The entire
circle seemed to glow with newly acquired knowledge. Things made
sense in a totally new way. Though they may never all stand in the
circle together again, at this moment they knew they were greater than
the sum of the parts.

Ron rejoined the circle and they silently swayed back and forth
accompanied by the most incredible smell of homemade pizza baking.
Though they had not done any hard physical work, the energy work they
had done had depleted their blood sugar levels. When the buzzer rang
signifying the pizza was ready, Ron again asked them to remain in ritual
mood as he went to cut the pizza.

When he returned with a tray of small samples of pizza and a large glass of wine, the circle let him into the center. Now, the concluding part of the ritual was to be done. Ron approached each one of them with the following words.

"This is my body which will be given up for you. Take, eat, all of you."

He followed this by offering each one of them a sip of wine from the communal glass.

"Take this, all of you, and drink from it: for this is the chalice of my blood, the blood of the new and eternal covenant."

He reached heavenward and then unexpectedly collapsed on the floor. Suddenly Gayle felt extreme nausea. A few minutes later she awoke on the floor with Patty beside her.

"You fainted," said Patty. Gayle did not argue. She was not prone to be light-headed or to faint. Ron had died; she knew that at a level that touched her soul. She had no known connection, but something had caused her to react so strongly. She was relieved to see Ron moving toward the kitchen. He wasn't dead after all. He had been resurrected. Gayle laughed it all off. The ritual was complete.

Graduation

Gayle was pleased when Ron had come over to her after the final initiation ceremony. He embraced her in a huge bear hug. The tantric energy they exchanged sent a white flash of light through her head.

"You passed," was all he said.

###

December 21, 2012

To the readers ---

The key mystery is revealed in this book for those with the "eyes to see." The material of the mystery school is holographic and as you ponder on the teachings and insight, a holistic answer eventually emerges.

Some find the non-linearity of the mystery school to be frustrating, but the mysteries may never be spoken. They exist in a plane of consciousness above intellect. Allow yourself to grok the awesome nature of all creation. To thine own self be true.

Gayle Clayton

For further reading ---
- *Transformative Meditation*
- *Seeking Higher Power*
- *Event Horizon 2012*
- *Myths of the Mystery Schools*
- *Amarjah.com*

ARTS & SCIENCE
COUNCIL

This project was made possible through the support of the North Carolina Arts & Science Council, a state agency, the Blumenthal Endowment, and the arts councils in Cabarrus, Cleveland, Gaston, Iredell, Mecklenburg, Rowan, Rutherford, and York (SC) counties.

www.ingramcontent.com/pod-product-compliance
Lightning Source LLC
Chambersburg PA
CBHW070953040426

42443CB00007B/483